Also by Jeff Shaara

GODS AND GENERALS

THE LAST FULL MEASURE

GONE FOR SOLDIERS

RISE TO REBELLION

THE GLORIOUS CAUSE

TO THE LAST MAN

Jeff Shaara's

CIVIL WAR BATTLEFIELDS

Jeff Shaara's
CIVIL WAR BATTLEFIELDS

DISCOVERING AMERICA'S HALLOWED GROUND

BALLANTINE BOOKS | NEW YORK

Published in the United States by Ballantine Books, an imprint of
The Random House Publishing Group, a division of Random House, Inc., New York.

BALLANTINE and colophon are registered trademarks of Random House, Inc.

Maps by Mapping Specialists Ltd.

ISBN 0-7394-6877-4
978-0-7394-6877-7

Printed in the United States of America
Book design by Barbara M. Bachman

Contents

Introduction

In the summer of 1964, a twelve-year-old boy followed his father across a mile of open grassy fields that separated the Union and Confederate lines at Gettysburg. They walked in the footsteps of the men who crossed this same ground on July 3, 1863, Confederate soldiers who made one of the most tragic attacks in our history. Today, we know that event as "Pickett's Charge." As they stepped through the tall grass, the father told the boy the story of what had happened there, who those men were, why they made this extraordinary attack. The father often told stories to the boy, usually about things the boy knew something about: science fiction, sports. But this was different; this was about history.

When the father led his son up and over the low stone wall that marked the position of the Union front line, the father told more of the story. He told the boy about two men, best friends, Lewis Armistead and Winfield Hancock, who had chosen to part ways before the war, each one fighting for something very different, yet each one fighting for what he believed in. But on this day in 1863, the two men would come together again, Armistead leading his men across this field straight into Hancock's guns. The story captured the boy, because the father told it as though he were *there,* could *see* it, could *hear* the guns, and he told the story with the passion the father brought to all his stories. But then the father was silent. The boy saw now that the father's attention had been captured by a low squat stone marker, against which lay a single miniature Confederate flag. In the silence, the boy read the inscription on the marker, which noted the place where Confederate general Lewis Armistead had fallen on that July day in 1863. Then the boy realized that his father was crying.

That boy was me. My father, Michael Shaara, was so inspired by the experience of walking the ground at Gettysburg that he spent the next seven years writing a novel about what happened there. That novel, published in 1974, was titled *The Killer Angels.*

In my father's lifetime, *The Killer Angels* was never a particularly successful book.

That may sound odd, considering that in 1975 the book was awarded the Pulitzer Prize for Fiction. But the book made very little impact, except on those who studied the American Civil War or those in some branches of the military, who had begun to use the book as a guide to understanding the tactics and leadership abilities of the men who were so pivotal to the story. My father went on to write more books, more short stories, none of them having anything to do with history or the American Civil War. Until the end of his life, he never saw any of his books become best sellers and never saw the creation of a motion picture based on his work. *The Killer Angels* had become something of a sad footnote for him, a truly marvelous award-winning book that had failed to find the audience even he felt it deserved.

Michael Shaara died in 1988, believing he had failed to do the one thing that meant more to him than anything else in his forty-year career as a writer. He believed he had failed to leave something behind, something for which he would be remembered. He had failed to leave a legacy.

He was wrong.

What followed over the next several years was an amazing series of circumstances that changed my life and cemented my father's reputation and legacy for all time. It began with Ken Burns's PBS series *The Civil War,* which seemed to wake the American people to renewed interest in that era of our history. Two years later, Ted Turner took an enormous chance and in 1992 financed the production of a major motion picture that was based on my father's book. It was called *Gettysburg.* In October 1993, the release of the film helped propel *The Killer Angels* to number one on the *New York Times* Best Seller List, the first time any of my father's books had received such significant recognition. Five years after his death, his legacy was alive and well.

My father had proven that an audience for this kind of story did in fact exist. And so, the son has followed the father. As a result, *The Killer Angels* is now the centerpiece of a trilogy of novels, something that still amazes me and would have absolutely floored my father.

With every book I've done, the research is the energy behind the story, and the energy behind the research has come from walking in the footsteps of the characters. Often those footsteps are difficult to find. A great many sites from the American Revolution and the Civil War have simply disappeared, swallowed up by time and by the need for Americans to expand and modernize their world. But special places remain, and over the past century, movements have begun to protect that ground from obliteration, to preserve at least some tangible part of our past. Museums are well and good, and safekeeping the artifacts of an earlier time may teach us much about the people who gave us our world. But museums are not the *ground,* just as a zoo is not the jungle.

"Hallowed ground" is a phrase that is often tossed off as something of a cliché, but those who would lightly regard Abraham Lincoln's description of Gettysburg are missing the point. Diaries, letters, memoirs, and even photographs have little resonance if we cannot see *where* an event occurred. If we erase the ground, the hillsides and valleys, the creek beds and rivers, the trench lines and earthworks, then we lose the spirit of our history. We lose the ability to walk in the footsteps, to see what the world looked like to those people who changed our history. No writer can give that to us with as much poignancy as we will find when we walk that ground and see it for ourselves.

This book may not resemble any battlefield guidebook you have ever seen before. That's the point. My attempt here is to paint a portrait of ten specific sites that offer the best interpretation and experience to the visitor, who may not already know every tidbit of historical detail of what happened there. In other words, this book is intended not for the academic historian, but for the curious, those who might have time to stop along the road and visit a battlefield they otherwise might have passed by. The chapters are arranged chronologically, so as to offer some flow to the history of the entire war. If you have some knowledge of the events, if you are something of a Civil War "buff," then perhaps this book will encourage you to visit a site you may not have seen before. It may also inspire you to argue with some of my conclusions. Unlike the historian, who has to abide by certain restrictive rules as to his commentary, I offer a few interpretations that some of you may not agree with. As it should be.

I could have included several more chapters, gone over several more valuable fields, but I wanted to keep this somewhat compact. If you wonder why certain battlefields were left out (and some of you will most certainly wonder), it is not my intention to dismiss or ignore any park where history is well preserved. Examples not included in this book will surprise (and annoy) some: Manassas, Stone's River, Pea Ridge, Fort Donelson, Andersonville, Fort Sumter, among many others. My choices are meant to carry you through some of the most poignant events of our history, by taking you to magnificent places where, if you visit, you will take away something enormously valuable from the experience.

When this book is published, I am making a significant financial contribution to a good many of the battlefield preservation groups whose responsibility it is to preserve and protect these invaluable sites. Those contributions will continue to be made, from a percentage of the sales of this book, for as long as anyone buys it. I respect passion and dedication to a cause, and the people who give so much of themselves to the preservation of these critical historical sites must be supported. "Causes" stare us in the face from every direction, and most of us are bombarded by requests for money: in the mail, in our offices, on television, in our e-mail. If you agree with me about the value of preserving the shrinking and threatened historical sites in this country, then I hope you will respond appropriately. Regardless, the purpose of this book is to show you what happened there, why it was important, and how you can experience some part of that yourself. In the end, I'm simply hoping that this book may inspire more parents to lead their children across some extraordinary piece of ground. Perhaps *their* lives will be changed as well.

Jeff Shaara
April 2006

Jeff Shaara's

CIVIL WAR BATTLEFIELDS

CHAPTER ONE

SHILOH

Shiloh Church, Tennessee

APRIL 6–7, 1862

WHAT HAPPENED HERE

*T*he Battle of Shiloh is the first truly horrifying large-scale battle of the western theater of the Civil War. But to best understand the importance of Shiloh, it is important first to understand what had preceded it. It had been nearly a year since the war had begun with the shelling of Fort Sumter, at Charleston, South Carolina, and in the North the concept of a full-scale rebellion (and what to do about it) was difficult to digest. In the South, the drive for secession had been driven first by politicians, but politicians don't carry a musket, and as the energy for rebellion spread throughout the southern states, the first priority was the creation of some kind of effective army. Predictions came from both sides that this entire affair would be concluded in short order. But as each army added men and training, while the leadership sorted through their various commanders, the noisy bluster from the politicians was replaced by the hard rumble of battle. It was the awful consequence of secession and rebellion that neither side had ever truly expected.

The first significant battle of the war had taken place in July 1861 in northern Virginia, only a few miles from the nation's capital. The social elite of Washington had gathered in celebratory anticipation, picnicking on the sunny hillsides near Bull Run Creek to watch the spectacle as though it were some grand carnival. While most of the northern observers had assumed that their gallant boys in blue would sweep aside the ragtag army of rebels and put an immediate end to this absurd notion of rebellion, the reality instead spread a hard shock through the entire country. Confederate troops under Generals Joe Johnston and Pierre G. T. Beauregard had sent the panicked and thoroughly whipped Union forces scrambling back to the safety of Washington (along with the hundreds of terrified onlookers). In the North the battle was called Bull Run, while in the South it was known as Manassas, after the small railroad junction nearby. (This kind of distinction was to be repeated throughout the war: the North referring to waterways, the South to towns.) For the Union leadership, absorbing the reality of what happened that day caused a somewhat stunned reappraisal of how they were going to deal with this rebellion by the southern states, which had now become a bloody and clearly dangerous affair. While Abraham Lincoln and his generals fumbled with their vague strategies, they began to realize that if this war was in fact to become a drawn-out military confrontation, they had to rely much more on a sound overall plan to defeat the rebels. They had to contend with another reality as well. The southern army was being led by men who had once been some of the highest-ranking and most experienced commanders in the United States military.

Both sides of the conflict regarded the Appalachian Mountains as the dividing line between east and west, and the keys to travel across that country lay along the vital pathways of the rivers and railroads. At the beginning of the war, Union general in chief Winfield Scott had formulated his Anaconda Plan, designed to quickly subdue the rebellion by strangling the economies of the southern states. Scott's plan called for the navy to blockade southern seaports and, as well, clamp a tight hold on the Mississippi River. But Scott was an old man, past his time, and his plan was generally ridiculed, since no one believed that the rebellion would ever become so serious as to require such a widespread and expensive strategy. Scott was forced into retirement, replaced by George McClellan, an extremely capable administrator and organizer, something the Union army desperately required. But as events of that first July would prove, the Union also required generals who could effectively lead their troops into combat. Bull Run had shocked much of the Union leadership into a fever pitch of planning, something McClellan excelled at. But for the next several months, there was very little activity on the eastern battlefields, certainly nothing to compare with what had happened at Bull Run Creek. As the Union soldiers around Washington drilled and waited for McClellan to tell them what to do, in the west, where the Mississippi River served as the great lifeline for both North and South, a great game of chess was being played. Union command there was held by General Henry Halleck, and though Halleck had not proven himself in the field any more than George McClellan, Halleck's department was far more active. Whether or not Halleck and his generals gave any credit to Winfield Scott, the commanders in the west understood that the Mississippi River and its major tributaries might hold the key to winning the war, for either side. In the field, Halleck's unheralded commanders, such as Samuel Curtis and Don Carlos Buell, had begun to show some competence in leading their men to victories. But it was a relatively unknown commander, Ulysses S. Grant, who suddenly caught the attention of both Halleck and the anxious planners in Washington. Grant was a veteran of the Mexican War, but during the chaotic days of Gold Rush San Francisco, he had succumbed to the effects of alcohol and, in the early 1850s, he had been forced to resign from the army in disgrace. Having spent several years as a civilian, Grant was virtually ignored when he joined the Union effort, especially since his elevation to command had come through connections, friendships with prominent politicians in Illinois. Halleck had few expectations of Grant until February 1862, when Grant stunned his superiors by accomplishing the most significant Union victories of the war thus far. Confederate troop positions throughout western Kentucky and Tennessee had been protected by strong bases at two key points, Forts Henry and Donelson, on the Tennessee and Cumberland Rivers in northwestern Tennessee. With the cooperation of navy gunboats commanded by Admiral Andrew Foote, Grant succeeded in capturing both strongholds, capturing nearly half the Confederate troops he faced. The loss had so weakened the Confederate forces in the area that they were forced to vacate Kentucky altogether. A jubilant Abraham Lincoln ordered that Grant be sent a shipment of ten thousand cigars. (Ever after, the pipe-smoking Grant would become, logically enough, a cigar smoker.)

The Confederates west of the Appalachian Mountains were commanded by General Albert Sidney Johnston, who had been a highly respected officer in the Mexican War and in the 1850s had led a major expedition of the U.S. Army to California. Johnston had greatly dismayed Washington when he chose to remain loyal to his home state of Texas and join the Confederate cause. Now he was confronting many of the same commanders he had once served with. Johnston recognized how precarious his position in Tennessee had become, and with the key Confederate forts now in Grant's hands, Johnston ordered his troops southward, to consolidate their position. The southern military had little naval force sufficient to prevent the Union navy from controlling the rivers, and Union gunboats continued to push their way deeper into Confederate territory. With the Union navy now threatening to surround much of Johnston's army, Johnston made the only reasonable decision open to him. He ordered the Confederate forces to move south again, and to the horror of the Confederate politicians in Richmond, he abandoned Nashville.

Though he had sacrificed a major rail and supply center, the move was strategically sound, if not politically popular, and might have saved his army from early destruction.

With Nashville falling into Federal control, and a strong foothold now established in central Tennessee, Union troops were massed for a surge southward again. The waterways provided the easiest routes, and Halleck made great use of his transport boats to shift a large concentration of Federal troops up the Tennessee River, toward the Mississippi state line. Their goal would now be to cut the Memphis & Charleston Railroad, the crucial railway line that connected Memphis to Chattanooga, the most prominent artery for Confederate supplies and troop movements and the lifeline that ultimately connected Tennessee to Virginia. Halleck ordered his generals to concentrate their forces near Savannah, Tennessee, less than twenty miles from the Mississippi state line. Halleck was not an especially bold strategist and insisted that his generals assemble overwhelming strength before making any aggressive move against Johnston's rebels. Once the huge force was in place, the Union troops would march southward to capture the town of Corinth, Mississippi, the closest of the critical railway depots. In late March 1862, as five Union divisions established their camps, the cramped logistics of the landing area at Savannah caused them to seek better ground, and a force of nearly forty thousand men moved a few miles farther south, upriver to Pittsburg Landing. But Halleck ordered Grant's army to wait so that they could be reinforced by Don Carlos Buell's army of twenty-five thousand men, who were marching southward from Nashville. Halleck would not give the final order to advance on Corinth until Buell's added strength had given the Union forces overwhelming superiority over anything that Johnston's rebels might put in front of them.

The ground inland from Pittsburg Landing was high and dry, though cut by several low creek bottoms. The land was a mix of trees and open farm fields, remote, and the various Union generals, including William T. Sherman, found the countryside ideal for drilling many of the untested and inexperienced Union army units. There was barely any real settlement in the area at all, and the local farmers and traders gathered at a single church that served as a meeting place. It was called Shiloh.

In early April, 1862 the Union troops went about their routine, awaiting Buell's men and the order that would send them toward Corinth. But the Confederates had something the Union did not: effective cavalry, commanded by a man whose reputation had already spread beyond Tennessee. Colonel Nathan Bedford Forrest was a tall, muscular man whose look and personality easily inspired stories of his leadership that had already begun to fuel what would become his legendary status as a consummate warrior. Forrest's motto was "Get there first with the most," and that simple homily translated to a tactical wisdom on the battlefield that no one could argue with and few Union commanders wanted to confront. Forrest and other independent cavalry units had soon become the extremely effective eyes and ears for Johnston's army.

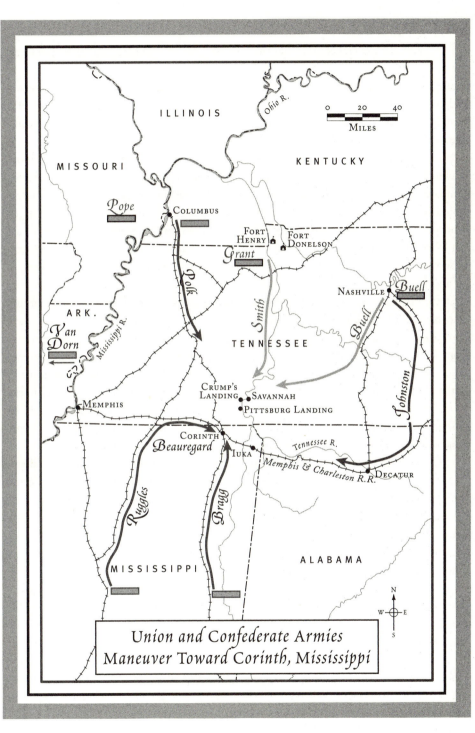

Union and Confederate Armies
Maneuver Toward Corinth, Mississippi

Though the Federal commanders had no real idea where Johnston's troops might be, their assumption was that the rebels were digging in at Corinth, twenty-two miles to the south, waiting for the inevitable attack. But thanks to the Confederate cavalry, Johnston had exact knowledge of the Union position and knew as well that Buell's reinforcements were still on the march and had not yet added to Grant's strength. The Confederate commander saw his opportunity.

Albert Sidney Johnston had assembled forty-four thousand men of his own, troops drawn from the various armies brought out of Tennessee, as well as troops gathered from camps around Mississippi. Johnston understood that the obvious goal of the Union forces would be the rail center at Corinth, and Confederate president Jefferson Davis had urged Johnston to assemble as much strength as he could muster to protect the rail line. To assist Johnston, Davis had sent General P. G. T. Beauregard, one of the heroes of Manassas, to serve as Johnston's second in command. But Johnston believed that simply waiting to be attacked at Corinth by overwhelming numbers of the enemy was not terribly wise strategy. His plan was to march straight at Grant's position at Pittsburg Landing and launch a surprise attack on the Union camps. Once engaged, Johnston hoped to make a hard thrust toward the Union left, toward the landing itself, cutting off Grant's troops from their embarkation point at the river. If successful, the Federal troops would have no avenue of escape except northward, through the rough country along the western banks of the Tennessee River. Unlike the good ground at Pittsburg Landing, the country to the north was at best vast stretches of swamp and undergrowth. If Grant's army could be pushed into retreating into the muddy bogs, Johnston knew he could not only capture most of the Union forces, but he might destroy Grant's army altogether.

On April 4, 1862, Union colonel Ralph Buckland, commanding a brigade of William T. Sherman's infantry, responded to sounds of a skirmish out beyond his section of the camp, a few miles inland from Pittsburg Landing. Buckland discovered that a number of his pickets had simply vanished and accurately presumed that they had been captured. By whom, Buckland had no idea. He quickly led two companies of infantry to scout the area and was suddenly confronted by a regiment of Alabama cavalry. Though the Union infantry chased the rebel horsemen away, Buckland's men were now bombarded with a volley of Confederate artillery fire. Buckland wisely withdrew his infantry, and when he reported the incident to Sherman himself, he was angrily told by his commander that his men had overreacted to a minor rebel reconnaissance force. Though Buckland believed he knew better, Sherman's strong response ended the matter.

The following day, rebel infantry was observed in various locations by more of the Union patrols, and in every case, the reports were hotly dismissed by Sherman, who insisted that no rebels were in the area. Though Sherman reported the incidents to Grant, there was nothing in Sherman's words to hint to Grant just who or what might be marching toward the peaceful camps at Pittsburg Landing.

The Union patrols continued, the field officers far more confident than Sherman that something was brewing. On Sunday, April 6, just before five a.m., another Union patrol was suddenly faced with cavalry and skirmishers, but this time Confederates did not scamper away. The Union soldiers could now see that the skirmishers were backed by an entire battle line of Confederate troops. It was the first wave of Johnston's attack.

As the sun rose, the battle spread out across two open fields, and by full daylight, the entire Union camp was alerted to what was coming. But Johnston's surprise had been nearly complete. The cavalry's intelligence reports had been entirely accurate. The Federals had made no allowance for defense, had constructed no earthworks, and had little but their own tents in which to hide. Though the Confederate assault was somewhat disorganized, the unexpected sight of so many massed rebel troops sent many of the Federal troops into panic. While some of the untested troops simply abandoned their camps and made a mad dash toward the safety of the river, the capable officers rallied as many men as they could, and gradually, many of the Federal troops found the courage to form their battle lines. The confrontation soon engulfed unit after unit of the Union forces, most still in their camps, many fighting through the smoke of their own campfires.

The fight became a general engagement, and Johnston still held to his plan to cut off the Union troops from Pittsburg Landing. But the reality of the battle prevented such a decisive move. As his men pressed forward on their left and center, Sherman and the other Federal commanders struggled to hold their units together. But gaps were punched in the Union line, and the rebels, now caught up completely in the heat of battle, pursued where the openings appeared. The fighting continued to escalate, and despite the loss of cohesion in the Confederate commands, the rebel troops made steady progress, pushing back the Union forces.

Grant's headquarters was a few miles downriver, but the sounds of the battle reached him, and by nine o'clock in the morning, he had arrived by boat at Pittsburg Landing. What Grant saw shocked him. Hundreds of dazed and panicked Union soldiers had crowded the riverbank, troops desperate to escape the terrifying hell that had swirled so suddenly around them. Many of the soldiers had never seen the enemy before, and the surprise of the assault had accomplished what surprise attacks always accomplish: A vast number of Grant's troops were utterly demoralized and had simply quit.

Grant ordered whatever officers he could find to make some effort to reorganize the panic-stricken men, and he rode forward to locate his division commanders. What he discovered was that the camps of his army were in the hands of the enemy, and his own lines, under the skilled direction of men like Sherman, William Wallace, and John McCler-

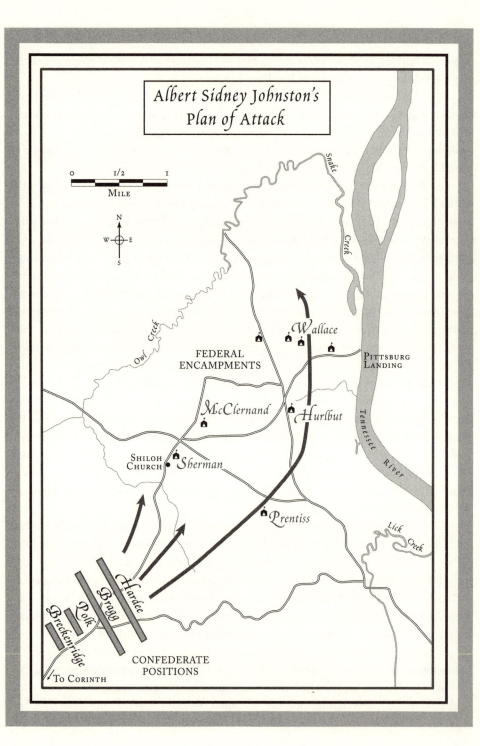

Albert Sidney Johnston's
Plan of Attack

0   1/2   1
MILE

N
W — E
S

Snake Creek

FEDERAL
ENCAMPMENTS

Owl Creek

Wallace

PITTSBURG
LANDING

McClernand

Hurlbut

SHILOH
CHURCH *Sherman*

Tennessee River

Prentiss

Lick Creek

Hardee
Bragg
Polk
Breckenridge

To CORINTH

CONFEDERATE
POSITIONS

nand, had been pulled back into a considerably more compact position. Instead of cutting off Grant's men from Pittsburg Landing, the rebel assault was driving them in an arcing line straight back toward it. In addition, the camps of the Union troops, now held by exhausted rebel infantry, were too tempting to ignore. Many of Johnston's men began to loot the tents, some gorging themselves on food that was to have been the Federals' breakfasts. It was the delay that the Federal commanders needed, allowing them to pull back into stronger defensive lines.

Throughout the assault, Johnston had ridden among his men and so witnessed first-hand the breakdown in his army's discipline. In one camp, he lost his temper at the expense of one of his junior officers. The tirade had caught the attention of a number of his men, and Johnston realized that he could best lead his men back into their pursuit by inspiring, not punishing. Instead of screaming nonsensically to men who would have probably ignored him, he picked up a tin cup and shouted to his men that the simple cup would be his only share of the spoils. The gesture worked (for the most part), and his men began once more to move forward.

Though Johnston still insisted the hardest thrust be made against the Union left flank, the troops in that part of the field had bogged down in savage fighting. In the vicinity of a peach orchard, vicious fighting broke out as the rebels made a massive frontal attack on an outnumbered Union brigade that held the Union far left flank. The brigade was commanded by Colonel David Stuart, who held out heroically against rebel artillery and overwhelming infantry assaults, until his line finally gave way. With the Union left flank shortened, a potential gap had opened that might allow Johnston's troops to push through. His goal of cutting off the Federal troops from the landing seemed suddenly attainable. Johnston rode to that part of the line, intending to lead the final push himself. Though tacticians argue that the commanding general's place should never be at the front lines, Johnston felt that rallying his men was far more important than staring at maps, and judging from the positive results of his appearance at various crisis spots, his behavior could probably be justified. To manage the larger scope of the fight, Johnston had left Beauregard back at his headquarters, believing that his second in command was fully capable of managing the overall battle.

With the Confederate thrust all along the line beginning to slow, as much out of exhaustion as by the defense of the Federals, Johnston renewed his ardor for pushing his right flank toward Pittsburg Landing. But despite the collapse of that end of the Union flank, the Federal troops there continued to hold the rebels away. As he tried to reorganize his exhausted men for a renewed attack, Johnston learned that one of his Tennessee brigades had simply given up the fight, refusing the order to charge into the fray. Furious, Johnston rode to their position and rallied them to join the attack by leading the way himself. The men responded, and the attack resumed. In the midst of the furious storm of fire, musket balls tore at his clothing, but Johnston continued to rally his troops. As the battle moved away from him, Johnston seemed to realize he had been hit. The wound was in his right lower leg and was hidden by his boots. Unknown to Johnston, the musket ball had sliced an artery, and though he continued to lead the fight, the loss of blood finally drained away his strength. Soon he was too weak to remain in the saddle, and Johnston's staff realized what was happening. As his concerned officers gathered around, Johnston was assisted to the ground by, among others, Tennessee governor Isham Harris, who was serving as a volunteer aide. Johnston was placed first at the base of a white oak tree, then moved to safety down into a nearby shallow ravine. Had the wound been found sooner, Johnston could certainly have survived, possibly with the loss of the leg, but by the time anyone could take adequate steps to stop the bleeding, at around two-thirty in the afternoon, Albert Sidney Johnston was dead.

Though Johnston's death was kept as quiet as possible, the effect on his field commanders was immediate, and in the absence of his leadership the rebel attacks lost momentum. Though the rebels were close to realizing Johnston's goal of cutting off the enemy from their base at the river, exhaustion, thirst, and tenacious Federal defense drained away the energy required to complete the task.

While the tragedy of Johnston's death was impacting the Confederate right flank, in

General Johnston Monument, near the site where General Albert Sidney Johnston was mortally wounded, Shiloh, Tennessee PHOTO PATRICK FALCI

The Hornet's Nest, Shiloh, Tennessee PHOTO PATRICK FALCI

the center of the Union position, a different kind of tragedy was playing itself out. Since midmorning, Federal troops had endured a relentless assault there, and by shifting their positions and taking advantage of the uneven ground and thickets of dense woods, they had been able to hold their ground for several hours. The troops in this area were part of two Union divisions, one commanded by Brigadier General William Wallace, who, during the heat of the assault, was mortally wounded. Unfortunately for the beleaguered Federals, by late afternoon, the troops alongside both their flanks had gradually been pushed back, unable to withstand the pressure from the continuing Confederate assaults. Along a half mile front, the isolated Federals continued to hold out, but the fight had reduced their strength to fewer than six thousand men, now under the command of Brigadier General Benjamin Prentiss. As the afternoon wore on, Prentiss, with his shrinking forces and what remained of Wallace's men, fought off eleven separate attacks from numerous rebel units, most under the command of Confederate general Braxton Bragg. The Union troops had sought a defensive position in a sunken road, little more than a narrow farm lane that ran through a patch of dense woods. As they fought throughout the afternoon, the men of Prentiss's command were subjected to such a volume of musket fire that the leaves and branches above their heads were clipped and shredded with a sound that resembled the

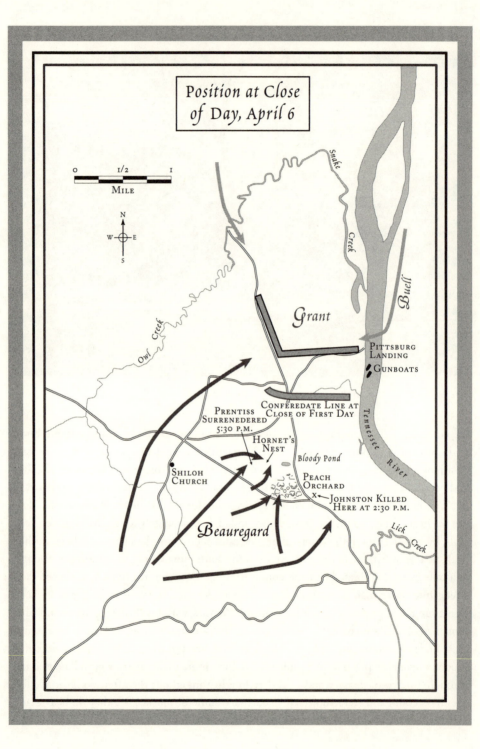

Position at Close of Day, April 6

0   1/2   1
MILE

N
W · E
S

Snake Creek

Owl Creek

Grant

Buell

Pittsburg Landing
Gunboats

Conferedate Line at Close of First Day

Prentiss Surrenedered 5:30 P.M.

Hornet's Nest

Bloody Pond

Shiloh Church

Peach Orchard
X — Johnston Killed Here at 2:30 P.M.

Beauregard

Tennessee River

Lick Creek

buzzing of so many insects. Thus did this part of the field become known as the Hornet's Nest.

Frustrated by mounting losses and the stubbornness of the Federals at the Hornet's Nest, the Confederates assembled every available artillery piece, eleven batteries, a total of sixty-two cannon, all trained on that half-mile stretch of Union ground. At approximately four-thirty in the afternoon, the artillery barrage began and lasted for roughly half an hour. It was, up to that time, the largest concentration of artillery fire ever witnessed in North America. The viciousness of the barrage further decimated the Union survivors in the woods and destroyed much of their own supporting artillery. With his losses mounting at a horrifying rate, Prentiss realized that his men were virtually alone, isolated far out in front of the Union line, and would soon be completely surrounded. Understanding the hopelessness of his situation, Prentiss ordered his men to retreat. Though some of his troops managed to slip through the tightening noose, Prentiss himself and over two thousand of his men were captured.

Grant's army continued to pull itself back toward Pittsburg Landing and frantically constructed a strong defense, including a powerful line of artillery pieces. The line was anchored on the river just south of the landing, its flank protected at the river by two Union gunboats, the *Lexington* and the *Tyler*. As Federal troops streamed back through the woods and fields to take their place in Grant's last line of defense, Grant and his commanders clearly understood that if the line did not hold, Grant's army would be crushed. But, as so often happens at pivotal moments on the battlefield, darkness and utter exhaustion intervened. With Beauregard now in command of the Confederate troops, the fire and inspiration that Albert Sidney Johnston had carried directly to his men was lacking. Though several smaller fights broke out on the rebel right flank, the darkness brought silence to the battlefield.

Throughout the night, the two Union gunboats poured heavy cannon fire into the Confederate position. There was little tactical advantage in doing this, except that it disrupted the sleep for men on both sides. But Beauregard's situation was far more confused than Grant's. Grant had pulled his army into a compact position, directly around his base of supply. The rebels meanwhile were spread out in a snaking line that spread all through the bloody fields and clusters of woods. Beauregard ordered his men to pull back out of contact with Grant's line, and those who could actually receive the order spent the night in captured tents, in the former camps of their enemy. Well after dark, a driving rainstorm swept over the battlefield, adding to the misery of the exhausted soldiers. But the rain offered the men one blessing. It muffled the cries of the thousands of wounded, those who could not be reached by the stretcher bearers, some hidden in the dense thickets or lying helplessly in the open between the two lines.

While officers debated whether or not Beauregard should have called off the battle,

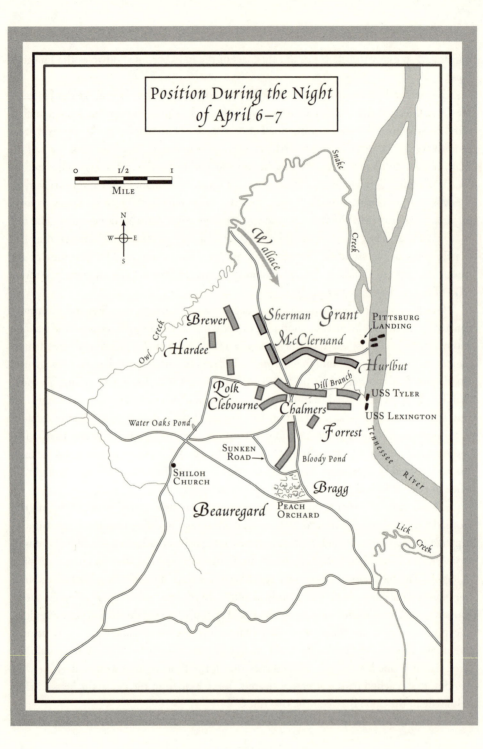

Position During the Night of April 6–7

0   1/2   1
MILE

N
W—E
S

Wallace

Snake Creek

Brewer

Sherman Grant PITTSBURG LANDING

Hardee McClernand

Owl Creek

Polk Dill Branch Hurlbut
Clebourne Chalmers USS TYLER

Water Oaks Pond Forrest USS LEXINGTON

SUNKEN ROAD →

Bloody Pond Tennessee River

SHILOH CHURCH

Beauregard PEACH ORCHARD Bragg

Lick Creek

Beauregard himself believed he had won a great victory, and that night he sent a telegram to that effect to Richmond. But throughout the rebel positions, confusion reigned. In the darkness and soaking rain, no order could be brought to the jumbled commands, and with the cascade of artillery shells coming toward them from the river, the rebels were inclined to stay put, to seek whatever shelter they could find and wait for the dawn.

Grant meanwhile had received two magnificent gifts. As darkness fell, the division of Major General Lew Wallace, which had been camped farther to the north near Crump's Landing, suddenly arrived on Grant's flank. Wallace added nearly eight thousand road-weary men to Grant's line. But far more significant for Grant, to the east, across the wide Tennessee River, some twenty thousand men of Don Carlos Buell's command had finally concluded their long march. As Buell's men ferried the river in darkness, they were observed by Nathan Bedford Forrest, who had stealthily occupied a prominent rise on the riverbank near the Union position. Forrest reported the arrival of the reinforcements to Beauregard, but the rebel commander seemed to ignore the new threat, continuing to tell his officers that with the dawn would come the final crushing blow to Grant's army.

Before first light on April 7, 1862, with Grant's troops on the right and Buell's on the left, the Union commanders ordered their combined forces to launch a counterattack. As the Federals surged up out of Grant's defensive line, the Confederates were immediately at a disadvantage. While the Union troops had full cartridge boxes, many of the rebels were nearly out of ammunition. While the Federal units were led by their own officers, the rebels were stumbling blindly without any coherent command. Gradually, Beauregard organized his men into a solid line of combat, but exhausted and hungry, the rebels could not withstand the pressure from so many fresh troops.

April 7 was simply a replay of the day before, but in reverse. The Union troops now held the momentum, and despite hard fighting all across the field, including several effective rebel counterattacks, the outcome was never truly in doubt. By midday, the Federal troops had retaken the Hornet's Nest, and by midafternoon, they had recaptured many of their camps. As his "complete victory" collapsed in front of him, Beauregard responded to the despair of his men by doing exactly as Johnston had done: He rode out among his troops in an attempt to rally them. But the men would not rise to their commander's call, and after one last-gasp counterattack, Beauregard succumbed to the counsel of his senior officers. Near three o'clock in the afternoon, Beauregard placed approximately five thousand men into position as a rear guard and ordered what remained of his army to withdraw.

Though criticized for failing to force an immediate pursuit of the rebels, Grant understood that too many of his men had made too hard a fight, and as is so often the case, the victorious army was nearly as bloodied as their vanquished and defeated foe. But the

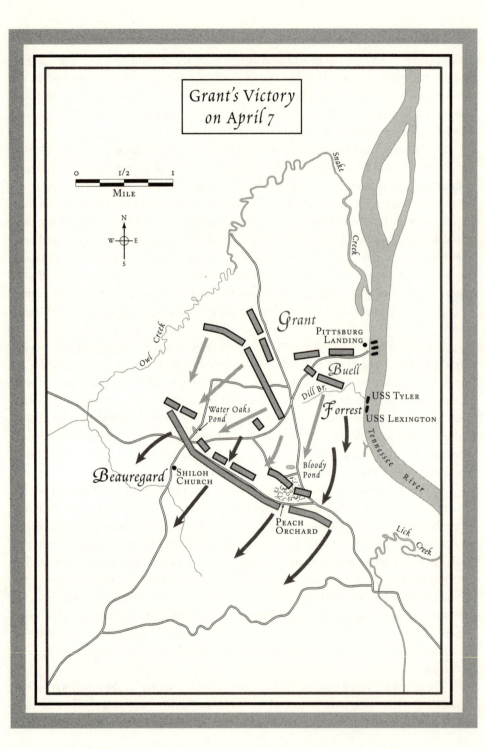

Grant's Victory
on April 7

0   1/2   1
MILE

N
W · E
S

Grant

PITTSBURG
LANDING

Buell

Dill Br.

USS TYLER

Forrest

USS LEXINGTON

Water Oaks
Pond

Beauregard

SHILOH
CHURCH

Bloody
Pond

PEACH
ORCHARD

Tennessee   River

Owl   Creek

Snake

Creek

Lick

Creek

pursuit was ordered as quickly as Grant felt was practical, and the next day, April 8, two brigades of Federal troops, under Sherman, started after Beauregard's retreat. But there would be no continuation of the fight. After a march of six miles, at an intersection called Fallen Timbers, the Union troops were suddenly confronted by Nathan Bedford Forrest's cavalry. Forrest surprised the Federals with a sharp attack, but the Federal strength was too formidable for Forrest to accomplish any sort of significant victory. The rebel cavalry withdrew, leaving the Union troops content to return to Pittsburg Landing. For his part, Forrest was severely wounded in the action but would return after a month of recuperation to fight again.

Beauregard had no choice but to retreat toward Corinth and wait for the Federals to resume their march southward. The attack would come some three weeks later, after Halleck took command of the field himself and after reinforcing Grant's army. He reached the valuable rail center with a force of more than one hundred thousand men. Halleck was finally comfortable that his overwhelming superiority in troop strength had given him the upper hand, and he gave the order for the Federal troops to move against Corinth. But Halleck dawdled near the city for nearly a month, and Beauregard saw no point in turning the city into a battleground. Finally, in late May, with Halleck preparing to subdue the city with artillery, Beauregard wisely withdrew. Within two months Halleck would be called to Washington, to assume the role of overall administrator of the army, serving alongside Secretary of War Edwin Stanton. Overall Union command in the western theater of the war would eventually fall to Ulysses Grant. Beauregard would go east, assuming control of the Confederate forces in the Carolinas. He would be replaced in Mississippi by Braxton Bragg.

WHY IS THIS BATTLE IMPORTANT?

*W*hile Bull Run (Manassas) shocks the civilian population with the spectacle of large-scale combat, Shiloh shocks them far more by the extraordinary carnage. A combined total of nearly twenty-four thousand men are killed, wounded, or missing in a battle in which nothing of significance is gained by the victor. The war does not end, no great cities are captured, no treasured landmarks change hands. For two days, two armies stand face-to-face and massacre each other across a stretch of rural Tennessee countryside. For the optimists in Washington and Richmond, who believe that their causes should prevail by strength of will alone, Shiloh is the first bit of graphic evidence that the cost of this war will in fact be much higher and much more horrible than anyone could have previously imagined.

In the field, the swagger of the Confederate soldier takes a severe pounding. It has been widely preached that "a southern soldier is worth ten Yankees." Shiloh proves that the "Yankee" can handle himself under fire with as much grit, tenacity, and determination as his counterparts from Dixie. Though Albert Sidney Johnston's attack is the surprise he hopes for, after their initial panic, the vast majority of Union troops stand toe-to-toe with their opponent and prevent Johnston's plan from succeeding.

In the East, where the newspapers fill the public eye with the increasingly grim stories of war, names and reputations begin to ascend. The man most lauded after Shiloh is Ulysses Grant, of course ("To the victor belong the spoils"). But Grant is condemned as well, particularly by the armchair generals in Washington (and their friends in the media) who have no understanding of what actually happens on a battlefield. The same is true for Sherman, who is attacked for being too easily panicked or too blind to the movement of the enemy. Though Sherman can certainly be faulted, it is the Union army's lack of effective cavalry that can be blamed as well for the blind arrogance of the commanders. Both men will survive the criticism, and both will prove themselves in future events.

On the southern side is poised one of the most notable what ifs of the Civil War. Had Albert Sidney Johnston survived his leg wound, would he have been able to inspire his men to continue their fight in the darkness on April 6? And would he have succeeded in punching through Grant's last line of defense? More important, Johnston is the highest-ranking Confederate general in the field anywhere in the war (Samuel Cooper outranks Johnston, but Cooper serves only as Jefferson Davis's adjutant and inspector general and never leads troops into battle). Would Johnston have eventually been called east, to take overall command of the entire Confederacy, the position that is eventually assigned to Robert E. Lee? If so, it is entirely likely that the name of Robert E. Lee might simply have faded into historical obscurity.

On both sides, Shiloh establishes that professional officers can turn untested troops into an effective fighting force. That alone will ensure that some of these same soldiers will meet again, on fields that range from the Gulf coast to Missouri, through Mississippi, Tennessee, and Georgia. But those who continue to fight will carry the hard images with them of the men who had been left behind, the men buried in mass graves in what had once been a stretch of peaceful forest and farmland, perched beside the silent flow of a river in southern Tennessee.

WHAT YOU SHOULD SEE

One challenge in writing about the Shiloh battlefield is the sheer number of emotionally charged sites. Of all the battlefield sites west of the Appalachian Mountains, none is as well preserved. I suspect that the primary reason is its remote location, some ninety miles east of Memphis (the closest major city). Fortunately, it is not located in an area that has received extreme pressure from real estate developers, though of course, with its proximity to the Tennessee River, that could change. Besides the pristine state of preservation, Shiloh has another marvelous advantage over so many other sites. The lay of the land, the position of open fields to woods, is virtually identical to the ground as it was in April 1862.

The park, established in 1894 by the efforts of many of the men who fought there, now encompasses over four thousand acres. As is true of most major Civil War sites, I strongly suggest hiring a guide. Though Shiloh is far too large for a walking tour, there are several spots where a short walk is called for.

One site not featured on official National Park Service maps is the actual location where the battle began, the place that inspired historian Wiley Sword to describe Shiloh as the "Pearl Harbor of the Civil War." No more than a hundred yards north of the intersection of State Roads 22 and 142, immediately behind Ed Shaw's Restaurant near the large Park Service sign (ENTERING SHILOH NATIONAL MILITARY PARK), you can walk in a northeasterly direction off Highway 142 into a large open field (Wood's Field), following the exact march of the Confederate advance. At the far end of the first field, you can see a second field (Fraley's Field), the two open areas adjoined at their corners. It is at this wooded junction of the two fields that the Union soldiers faced the enormous onslaught of Johnston's first wave.

Farther north on Highway 142, you will turn in to the main entrance to the park (the Hamburg-Purdy Road). I recommend a right turn onto Corinth Road, to begin your tour. This contradicts the Park Service tour route, but as long as you visit the sites mentioned here, you will have passed by the most significant Park Service stops as well.

Your first stop is Shiloh Church, which is, as is plainly evident, a modern building. However, just to the left of the (new) church is a carefully reconstructed church, built from timbers that date back 150 years, nearly an exact representation of the original church structure. The reconstruction was undertaken by the Sons of Confederate Veterans, in order to show how primitive (and small) the primary meeting place in this area actually was. Though the church is behind Union lines at the start of the battle, as the rebel troops make their advance, the church becomes the headquarters for General Beauregard. It is also the place where the body of Albert Sidney Johnston is first brought after his death.

I won't attempt to describe a step-by-step driving route. That is much better left to a battlefield guide. However, a few sites are of special significance.

On a field that is brimming with monuments and plaques, probably the most poignant is the Confederate Monument. (You don't have to be a Confederate yourself to appreciate the emotion of the extraordinary sculpture.) The granite and bronze monument was sculpted by Frederick C. Hibbard and was placed there in 1917, after considerable effort by the United Daughters of the Confederacy. Notice the profile of Albert Sidney Johnston carved in the granite at the center of the monument (Johnston was the highest-ranking Confederate officer killed in battle throughout the entire war). But the poignancy comes from the three bronze figures at the center of the monument. The primary (female) figure is the Confederacy, flanked by the figures of Death and Night. Together, they symbolize "defeated victory," which is the briefest explanation imaginable of what took place here. On either end of the monument stand Confederate soldiers, representing the differing emotions of the battle, from frustration to tearful submission. In stone, to the right of the central figures are the profiles of eleven Confederate soldiers, heads high, anticipating victory. To the left, the heads, now only ten, are bowed.

While this field is strewn with monuments, many of which deserve attention, there are two of which I would make special mention. Within the National Cemetery itself, at a point closest to the river, is the monument to the 16th Wisconsin Regiment. This monument is dedicated to the regiment's six color bearers, all of whom died while carrying their flag. Close by are two naval cannon, placed so as to face the river. One of these, the

Shiloh Church (reconstructed) PHOTO PATRICK FALCI

twenty-four-pound Dahlgren boat howitzer, is, interestingly, still loaded. (Long-armed adults can reach inside and feel the rounded shape of the cannonball.)

The second monument I would point out is the brand-new Tennessee Monument, placed near the Water Oaks Pond on June 3, 2005. This is the final such structure to be allowed on this field, and it seems fitting that Tennessee should finally have its own monument on its own soil.

An open field that extends east of the Eastern Corinth Road is marked by a sign indicating the location of the Hornet's Nest. Walk this ground. In the woods just north of the main trail, you can clearly see the "sunken road," though it does not appear sunken at all. Unfortunately, this was a somewhat misguided move by the Park Service several years ago to restore what they believed to be the original conditions here. Though officials claimed the road did not lie in a depression, many diaries of soldiers who fought there clearly describe the roadway as having been sufficiently sunken to allow for defense. As you walk midway along the marked trail that leads through the Hornet's Nest, you walk down into a creek bottom. Every time I have experienced the walk through the low ground, I have noticed a marked coolness in the air. While this can logically be explained by the lay of the land and the water itself, it is not hard to accept what some have said, that this small stretch of ground saw so much horror, and so many men died in such a small space, that their spirits inhabit the ground to this day. Draw your own conclusions.

From the Hornet's Nest, look out across the open field to the south. You can see the row of artillery pieces that poured such a vicious fire into the Union position. The rebel guns there represent Ruggles's Battery, the sixty-two cannon assembled for the barrage that finally caused the Union collapse at the Hornet's Nest. Some of these guns are original to the battle, and for anyone who has familiarity with artillery pieces, most of the guns have some markings indicating where they were manufactured. Some of these cannon are in fact British, and many were of a make that clearly indicated they had been captured from the Federals.

At the eastern end of the Hornet's Nest sits the remains of the George cabin and, nearby, the peach orchard. While other "peach orchard" sites are more famous (particularly the one at Gettysburg), this one holds significance for the brutal fight that took place here. The peach trees there today are maintained in the original location of the orchard, though keeping the trees healthy is a constant headache, since the park's enormous deer population delights in devouring the leaves and blossoms of the trees. But there are no more poetic descriptions of battle than those written by soldiers who fought here, several of which describe how the fully blossoming trees were so cut by the storm of musket fire that the white petals swirled around the men "like a snowstorm."

Immediately north of the peach orchard is a short walk to the Bloody Pond. The pond is remarkable for one reason that has nothing to do with the battle. It sits upon the highest geographical point in this county (Hardin County) yet is supplied by an underground spring. While this seems to dispute the laws of gravity, the pond is nonetheless always filled. The water in the pond is roughly three feet deep, and as you stand along the water's edge, you can plainly see among its numerous inhabitants a number of mud catfish, some of which are nearly twenty-four inches in length. At the beginning of the battle, the pond lies behind Union lines and is a natural gathering place and a source of drinking water. But as the battle progresses and the fighting intensifies at the Hornet's Nest and peach orchard, the pond serves a different purpose. An enormous number of wounded soldiers are brought here, and the water in the pond becomes mixed with the blood of the wounded men and, as well, the many dead and dying horses that lie scattered about. As a result, the pond is said to have taken on the color of blood, thus the name Bloody Pond.

South of the pond and orchard, along the Hamburg-Savannah Road, is possibly the most significant historical site on the field. The large stone monument and other markers indicate the place where General Albert Sidney Johnston was removed from his horse after suffering his fatal wound. Notice the white oak tree that stands roughly ten feet to the left of the plaque there. It is a reasonable assumption that this tree is a direct descendant of the tree against which Johnston lay before he was moved down into the ravine. The ravine itself is to your right, and the gravel footpath will take you to the site of his death. Though historians have debated whether this spot is precisely accurate, the placement of the marker there was determined originally by Tennessee governor Isham Harris, who was there at the time. Given the enormous historical significance of the event and the dedication to the cause to which Governor Harris was devoted, I'll take his word for it.

Farther south on the Hamburg Road is the site of a field tent hospital. While this kind of facility would seem reasonably common on battlefields, in fact, this hospital is the first of its kind, the first that does not make use of an existing structure, such as a house or barn. Throughout the battle, surgeons from both sides tend to their wounded, often working side by side, with little thought to what color uniform the man beside him, or on the table in front of him, is wearing. Present here as well are members of the United States Sanitary Commission, most notably a thirty-one-year-old woman named Clara Barton. Barton, who serves here as a nurse, will eventually found the American Red Cross and, beginning in 1881, serve as its first president.

There are special monuments throughout the battlefield to mark the specific spot where significant commanders were killed, and the one honoring Union general William Wallace has a painfully memorable story to go with it. As his troops are being driven back, Wallace's body is left on the field, his men believing that the head wound he suffered is fatal. That afternoon, Wallace's wife arrives at Pittsburg Landing, only to be told that her husband had been killed. Yet on the second day of the battle, as the Union troops retake

The Bloody Pond, Shiloh, Tennessee PHOTO PATRICK FALCI

the same ground, Wallace's body is found, and, amazingly, he is still alive. Unfortunately, though his wife is able to see her husband for their final good-byes, Wallace dies three days later.

Near the Park Service Visitor Center (which is open every day of the year except Christmas), the Pittsburg Landing Road shows signs indicating the location of "Grant's Last Line" of defense. Note the artillery pieces, including some of the largest cannon used on the field, guns that would certainly have been effective had the Confederates attempted a major assault on Grant's position. Notice as well that the ground falls away sharply to the south, the direction from which the rebels would have had to come. It was Grant's good fortune that his position nearest the landing was also some of the highest and most defensible ground on the entire field.

I always pay special attention to the cemeteries that are usually located on these sites. As is the case on many other battlefields controlled by the National Park Service, the cemetery at Shiloh is a National Cemetery. It was established immediately after the war and contains the remains of more than three thousand Union soldiers, some two-thirds of whom remain unknown. There are also graves for soldiers killed up through the Vietnam war. While it was (and is) illegal to bury Confederate soldiers in a National Cemetery (talk to your congressman), two rebel soldiers are buried here. Both were wounded pris-

Grave site of the six flag bearers of the 16th Wisconsin, Shiloh National Cemetery, Shiloh, Tennessee PHOTO PATRICK FALCI

oners of war who died shortly after the battle. They can be located by number: grave sites #2783 and #2784.

There are other grave sites on the battlefield as well, and here is a shameful reminder of the legacy of animosity that exists between North and South immediately after the war. The National Cemeteries are populated in the late 1860s by enormous numbers of Union dead, mostly reinterred from mass graves that are first dug right on the battlefield. It is no different at Shiloh, except that the mass graves of the Confederate dead are still there, and still filled with bodies, estimated to be stacked seven deep. One of these mass graves in particular, located on a small loop of a road just north of the Water Oaks Pond, contains seven hundred bodies. After the war, the families of the dead are not allowed to remove the remains, and thus, in an extraordinary gesture, the park allows the Confederate flag, the Stars and Bars, to fly over that one site. Shiloh is the only battlefield park controlled by the National Park Service where this is allowed. Though five such burial trenches are marked here, it is certain that at least two others remain undetected, their locations still a complete mystery.

By the way, in a final stroke of irony, "Shiloh" comes from the Hebrew word meaning "Place of Peace."

CHAPTER TWO

ANTIETAM

Sharpsburg, Maryland

SEPTEMBER 17, 1862

WHAT HAPPENED HERE

With the Battle of Shiloh awakening the North to the potentially brutal task that lay ahead of them, their army's commander, George McClellan, finally began to move forward on a campaign in the east to subdue the rebellion. The catastrophe of First Bull Run (Manassas) was still fresh in his memory, so to eliminate the chance of another such disaster, McClellan chose to attack the Confederacy from another direction. His plan called for a circuitous route, transporting the bulk of his forces down the Potomac River, making a landing at the tip of the Virginia peninsula. He could then drive up the peninsula and capture Richmond by striking from the east, rather than simply driving straight down from Washington. But McClellan was never one to strike anywhere with haste, and though he eventually placed his army on the peninsula, McClellan so completely overestimated the number of rebel forces he might confront that he took far too much time to advance his men toward their goal. By May 1862, the Confederates, commanded by Joe Johnston (no relation to Albert Sidney Johnston), had adequate time to prepare for McClellan's assault. When McClellan finally moved, the result was a series of difficult fights that inflicted casualties on both sides and accomplished little else. The two sides collided first at Yorktown and then at Williamsburg, and by late June, as Johnston slowly and strategically withdrew his Confederates closer to Richmond, the rebel commander used the countryside to his advantage. With McClellan pursuing cautiously, Johnston led the rebels into a series of sharp engagements known as the Peninsula Campaign. Neither side was completely victorious, and the various fights took the Federal troops close to Richmond, but not close enough. Though neither side could claim any sort of major victory, one monumental event occurred that could not have been recognized at the time. During one of the fights, the Battle of Seven Pines, Joe Johnston was wounded and was unable to remain in command. Within twenty-four hours, President Jefferson Davis, who happened to be close by, made perhaps his most brilliant decision. The ailing Joe Johnston was replaced as commander of the Army of Northern Virginia by Davis's most trusted adviser, the man who had designed the Confederate defenses at Manassas—the man who was so respected in Washington that at the start of the war in April 1861 he had been offered command of the *Union* army. His name was Robert E. Lee.

Lee took charge immediately, and in a bloody campaign known as the Seven Days' Battles, he succeeded in clearing the peninsula of McClellan's army. The Union withdrawal came about as much from McClellan's own defeatism as from any great victory on Lee's part. Smarting from his failure to capture Richmond, McClellan and his army limped back up the Potomac. A deeply frustrated Abraham Lincoln responded by removing George McClellan from primary command of the Union army in the field.

While the Federal strategists fumbled for both a new leader and a new plan, Lee began to reorganize his forces, removing the incompetent political generals that Jefferson Davis had often coddled. Lee then divided the Army of Northern Virginia into two wings and elevated two men to the new commands, officers who had demonstrated considerable skill in leading troops in the field. They were James Longstreet and Thomas Jonathan Jackson (who, at Manassas, had been given the descriptive name of "Stonewall").

Lincoln was beginning to feel desperate for anyone who could actually lead with some effectiveness against the rebels in Virginia, and he took the advice of his two primary decision makers, Secretary of War Stanton and General Halleck. They decided to place their faith in Major General John Pope, who was summoned eastward from the campaigns along the Mississippi. Pope had shown moderate ability to lead troops into action, but he accepted the new command with bombast and arrogance, threatening harsh measures against prisoners and southern sympathizers. Pope's boasts made Union veterans uneasy but played well in the southern ranks. Lee grew to despise Pope but realized that Pope's foolish bravado had done much to energize the spirit of the Confederate soldiers who would soon confront him in the field. The meeting came in late August 1862, on virtually the same ground where the Battle of Bull Run (Manassas) had been fought. Logically, the battle was called Second Bull Run, or Second Manassas. Though George McClellan still had command of nearly ninety thousand troops in and around Washington, Lee's cavalry observed that McClellan was staying put. Thus, Pope's army confronted Lee with nearly equal numbers, close to fifty thousand men on each side. As the battle unfolded, Pope faced Jackson first, and then Longstreet, and after a brutal two-day fight, Pope was overmatched both by ability and by the fighting spirit of the men he faced. As had happened the year before, the battle (most commonly known as Second Manassas) was a Union disaster. Pope's army escaped northward, and Lincoln made the inevitable decision and quickly removed Pope from command. Lincoln had no choice but to turn once more to the most senior commander available to him. Once more, McClellan was put in charge.

Enormous numbers of new Union recruits had been pouring into the capital, and true to form, McClellan focused his attention on their training and organization. Lee, meanwhile, had been energized by his success at Second Manassas. Flush with victory, the Confederate troops were anxious to continue their campaign, believing, as did Jefferson Davis, that their success in the east could soon decide the war in their favor. Shortly after Second Manassas, Lee and Davis devised a complete change in southern strategy, to take full advantage of the momentum their victories had given their army. But the new plan was a contradiction to the sense of "cause" that had inspired many southerners (and quite a few northerners) to join in the rebellion. Instead of the morally respectful position of defending southern homes from the evil of northern invasion, the plan called for the Army of Northern Virginia to make an invasion of their own. Lee and Davis believed that the time had come to take the war into the North. Virginia in particular had been so bloodied that much of her essential farmland had been laid to waste. Thus, the southern people and Lee's army had desperate need of an uninterrupted harvest season. The Confederacy also needed help from beyond its own borders. The British in particular had kept a sharp eye on Confederate fortunes. Britain relied heavily on trade with the South, particularly for cotton, and the northern blockade of southern seaports was a serious and costly annoyance. In Richmond, it was believed that the British simply needed some positive jolt to give them confidence in the southern cause, so that they might actively join the war on the southern side. At the very least, the British navy might break the blockade that was having a devastating effect on the southern economy. But the British would not enter the war without feeling confident of a southern victory. It would be up to Lee to show them that the South could win.

Lee proposed a march through the neutral state of Maryland, moving up to the west

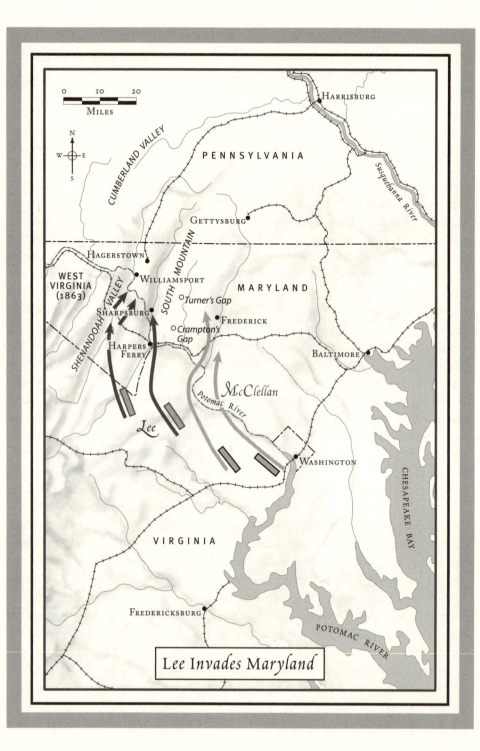

Lee Invades Maryland

of South Mountain in the center of the state, so as to hide his army's movements. Lee anticipated one immediate benefit of such a strategy. As his army marched through Maryland, Lee predicted that they would be seen not as conquerors, but as friends, encouraging huge numbers of Marylanders to join Lee's increasingly ragged army. Bolstered by this new strength, Lee would have the option of marching north and east, to threaten an attack on Harrisburg, Pennsylvania, or possibly Baltimore. For Lee's plan to work, the attacks did not necessarily have to be carried out. It was reasonable for Lee to believe that the presence of his army on northern soil might be sufficient in itself. It was entirely likely that the citizenry of the North would realize with horror that the bloody battlefields of the South could now become bloody battlefields closer to home and that such a threat might cause so much alarm and panic that the U.S. Congress would be pressured to end the war.

Militarily, there was a thorn in the side of Lee's plan. On September 4, 1862, as Lee moved his army across the Potomac, the Federal garrison downriver at Harpers Ferry was now in his rear. Harpers Ferry was occupied by twelve thousand men, who, if they ventured out to fight, could cause Lee's army serious trouble. The town was a key rail and river junction, a gateway to both the Shenandoah and the Ohio Valleys, of enormous value to whoever controlled it. But both sides knew that Harpers Ferry was completely indefensible. The town itself was positioned in a low bowl, surrounded by tall mountains. No matter what kinds of defenses were built in the town itself, any artillery placed on the mountains could easily drop shells directly on the town and anyone who occupied it.

To deal with the potential threat from Harpers Ferry, Lee divided his army, sending Stonewall Jackson to subdue or possibly capture the garrison there, while the rest of his forces, under Longstreet, would watch the South Mountain passes, in the event McClellan decided to make some move toward them from Washington. Lee's instructions to his commanders were spelled out in detail on paper, Special Order #191. In one of the most decisive strokes of misfortune to befall the Confederacy, a copy of Lee's orders was lost and picked up by Federal soldiers near Frederick, Maryland. Despite all Lee's emphasis on secrecy, McClellan now knew the exact disposition of Lee's army. Inspired by the huge strategic advantage he had been handed, McClellan ordered his army to march out of Washington, intent on crushing Lee before the rebels could bring their army back together.

On September 15, 1862, after launching a masterly artillery attack, Jackson accomplished his mission at Harpers Ferry. The town was secured by Confederate troops, who forced the surrender of nearly twelve thousand Federal prisoners. As ordered, Jackson moved quickly to rejoin Lee's army. At Harpers Ferry, he left one division behind, some six thousand men, both as security for the rear of Lee's army and to administer the logistics of patroling the captured Union soldiers. The division was under the command of one of Jackson's least favorite generals, A. P. (Ambrose Powell) Hill. It is entirely likely that Jackson chose Hill to remain behind simply because the two men despised each other.

Though Lee knew McClellan would not be quick to move, McClellan nonetheless prodded his sluggish army westward. At the primary mountain passes, Lee's men were pushed hard by the advancing Federals, and Lee realized that he could not hold the passes. Once McClellan was on Lee's side of the mountain, Lee could not resume his northward advance. Strung out on the roads, the Confederates would be far too vulnerable to attack. In addition, Lee had been dismayed to find that the Marylanders were not so welcoming after all, and very few young men had flocked to join his army. With McClellan clearly moving toward him, Lee decided to stand and fight and ordered his men into a strong defensive position near the small town of Sharpsburg, Maryland. Jackson and Longstreet anchored their men on high ground to the west of a deep and muddy tributary of the Potomac called Antietam Creek.

Lee's force totaled roughly forty thousand men, but as McClellan laboriously pushed his army through the mountain passes, Lee realized he was facing a Federal army twice the size of his own. Potentially worse for Lee was the Potomac River, which was now in his rear. If Lee's army was forced into a hasty retreat, the wide river could prevent his army from escaping at all. Though Lee had the stronger defensive position, his decision to wait and confront McClellan at Sharpsburg was a major risk. Though McClellan seemed to have the advantage, the Federal commander delayed his attack, a habit that had become completely predictable both to Lee and to McClellan's frustrated subordinates. When the Federal troops were finally ordered into action, the rebel defenses were prepared as well as Lee could have hoped.

McClellan intended to strike Lee's army on both flanks at the same time and then make a hard push into the center. The plan was simple and logical. But in battle, what is drawn on paper rarely holds true. At five-thirty a.m. on September 17, 1862, Union general Joe Hooker sent units of his 1st Corps down the Hagerstown Pike, which eventually ran past a plain whitewashed building, the Dunker Church. Hooker's men advanced southward into the head-high thickets of a ripening cornfield, intending to slam into the rebel left flank. The Confederates were situated closer to the church itself (the meeting place, ironically, of a pacifist sect of German Baptists). Behind the church, to the west, the rebels had formed defensive lines in a thick stand of forest, called (now) the West Woods, which provided excellent cover. As the Federal troops moved through the cornfield, they had no way of seeing what waited for them on the far side of the field. But the rebels, part of Jackson's command, could see the tops of the battle flags of the Union regiments as they advanced, and when the Federal troops emerged into the open at the far edge of the field, they were met with a storm of musket fire. As the Union troops melted back into the cornfield, the Confederates pursued, driving into the cornfield themselves. But Hooker ordered in additional troops, and the fight seesawed in the cornfield, close-range fire that mowed the field to stubble, with both sides absorbing horrific losses. As the Union troops seemed to regain their momentum, a fresh line of Confederate troops suddenly appeared near the Dunker Church, and once again the Union forces were devastated by rebel musket fire. As the fight spread, the precise order of the battle lines dissolved, men making a fight wherever they could find the enemy. Along the Hagerstown Pike, men faced each other only a few yards apart, firing at one another from either side of the road. After losing an astonishing number of men, many of the Union troops had seen enough, and their lines broke, the men fleeing to the north, up the Pike.

Instead of crushing the rebel's left flank, Hooker realized he was looking at a potential disaster, so he urgently called for help from the next Union corps in line, the 12th, led by Joseph Mansfield. At almost the same time that Mansfield's troops began to reach the field, Hooker was wounded in the foot, which he considered serious enough that he left the field (something for which Hooker was roundly criticized later). As he was being carried to the rear, Hooker sent word to Mansfield, urging him to take command of the situation. Unfortunately for the Union, and for McClellan's overall plan, at about that same moment, Mansfield was killed.

With McClellan's attack on the Confederate left flank now leaderless, the troops there were bogged down in a muddled mess. McClellan ordered the Union 2nd Corps, under Edwin "Bull" Sumner, to relieve the beleaguered Federal troops and thus continue the attack on Lee's left flank. It was during this time that McClellan's army began to suffer the consequences of a catastrophic mistake that was to affect the entire outcome of the battle.

According to McClellan's original plan, while Hooker pushed against Lee's left, on the far end of the line, General Ambrose Burnside's 9th Corps was to attack Lee's right flank, which was Longstreet's position along Antietam Creek. But Burnside delayed, and in so doing, he allowed Lee to shift troops from one end of his line to the other, wherever they were needed at the moment, to meet McClellan's piecemeal assaults. Thus Lee completely negated McClellan's vast numerical superiority.

As Sumner moved one Union division, under John Sedgwick, toward the Dunker Church, the troops were surprised by the sudden arrival of two fresh divisions of Lee's men, who emerged from the thick woods right into Sumner's flank. Once more, the Federal troops were sent reeling back. Sumner recognized that the Union troops had seen enough of the fighting around the now battered church, so he shifted his assault, and instead of pressing Lee's flank, he sent two divisions of fresh troops toward the center of Lee's lines. But on the far end of the field, Burnside had still not attacked Lee's right flank, and thus Lee could continue to shift troops to whatever part of the field faced the immediate threat. It was in Lee's center, along a half mile of farm road, that the greatest horror of this horrible day would come to pass. The rebel troops there were Alabamans

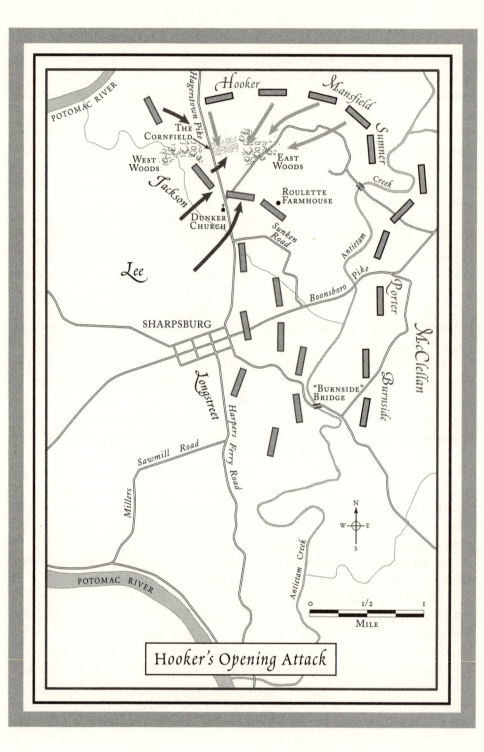

POTOMAC RIVER

Hooker

Mansfield

Hagerstown Pike

THE
CORNFIELD

WEST
WOODS

EAST
WOODS

Jackson

Sumner

Creek

ROULETTE
FARMHOUSE

DUNKER
CHURCH

*Sunken
Road*

Lee

Antietam

Boonsboro

Pike

Porter

SHARPSBURG

McClellan

Longstreet

Burnside

"BURNSIDE"
BRIDGE

Harpers Ferry Road

Sawmill   Road

Millers

Antietam Creek

POTOMAC   RIVER

N
W · E
S

0   1/2   1
MILE

Hooker's Opening Attack

and North Carolinians commanded by Daniel Harvey Hill, who had placed his men along the road, which was a natural defensive position. The road had been worn low into the ground by years of horse and wagon traffic and was lined on both sides by a split-rail fence. As the Federal troops made their attack, the sharply undulating countryside hid the road from their view, neither side knowing exactly when their enemy might suddenly appear in front of them. As the Federals continued their advance, they eventually crested a wide hill that was no more than two hundred yards directly in front of the sunken road. The Confederates had a perfect massed target right in front of them. Sumner's two divisions, including the Federal Irish Brigade, made a gallant effort to reach the road but were cut down in wholesale slaughter, entire rows of men simply obliterated by musket fire. The fight lasted for nearly four hours, the Alabamans continuing to fire as quickly and as often as their muskets could be reloaded. No veteran on either side of this already horrifying war could imagine the slaughter he would witness along the sunken road, which almost immediately became known as the "Bloody Lane."

Dunker Church, September 1862, Antietam, Maryland PHOTO COURTESY OF THE LIBRARY OF CONGRESS

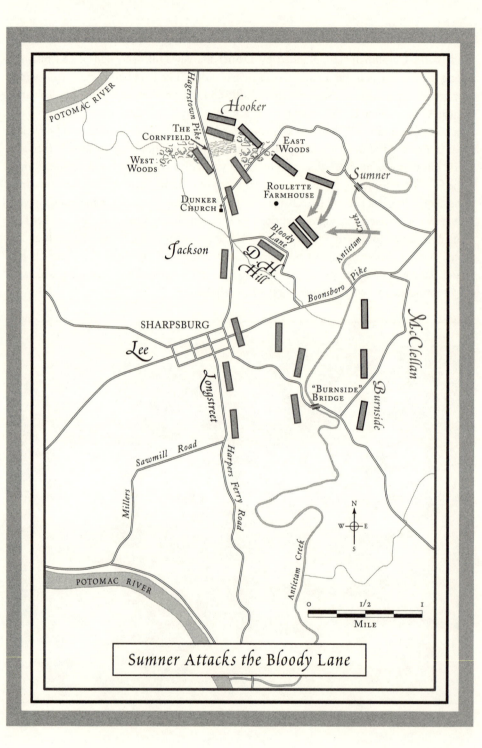

POTOMAC RIVER

Hagerstown Pike

Hooker

THE
CORNFIELD

EAST
WOODS

WEST
WOODS

Sumner

ROULETTE
FARMHOUSE

DUNKER
CHURCH

Antietam Creek

Bloody
Lane

Jackson

D
H
Hill

Boonsboro Pike

McClellan

SHARPSBURG

Lee

Longstreet

"BURNSIDE"
BRIDGE

Burnside

Sawmill Road

Harpers Ferry Road

Millers

POTOMAC RIVER

Antietam Creek

N
W — E
S

0   1/2   1
MILE

Sumner Attacks the Bloody Lane

The Bloody Lane, September 1862, Antietam, Maryland

Fearing that he might be overrun, D. H. Hill finally withdrew his Confederates out of the road, and the remnants of Sumner's corps occupied the road themselves. By now, the fight along that part of the line had completely exhausted both sides. As the fights along the Union right and center grew less active, on McClellan's left, Burnside finally began his attack. What had begun as a piecemeal Union assault across the entire front was to end that way as well. Burnside's mission was to push his corps across Antietam Creek, in the vicinity of a stout stone bridge known as the Rohrbach Bridge. Though he attempted some minor reconnaissance to locate shallow river crossings—and in fact there were shallow fords his men could have used downstream—Burnside fixated on the bridge itself. Across the creek, only five hundred Georgians were dug into the steep embankments that rose high above the creek. When Burnside ordered his men forward, one un-

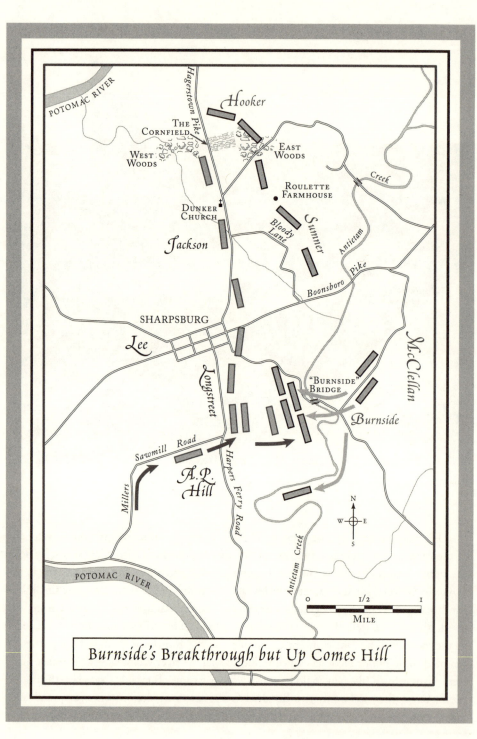

POTOMAC RIVER

Hagerstown Pike

Hooker

THE CORNFIELD

WEST WOODS

EAST WOODS

Creek

DUNKER CHURCH

Roulette Farmhouse

Jackson

Bloody Lane

Sumner

Antietam

Boonsboro Pike

SHARPSBURG

Lee

Longstreet

McClellan

"Burnside" Bridge

Burnside

Sawmill Road

A.P. Hill

Harper's Ferry Road

Millers

N
W — E
S

POTOMAC RIVER

Antietam Creek

0   1/2   1
MILE

Burnside's Breakthrough but Up Comes Hill

fortunate Federal column marched directly along a farm road that actually paralleled the creek for some two hundred yards. For the Georgians on the far side, the Federal column marching slowly past became a shooting gallery. That attack dissolved before any Federal soldier could even get close to the bridge. Burnside continued to send men forward, more men in column, some emerging from a wooded hill situated back from the creek, directly across from the Georgians. The results were the same, the Georgians astounded at the idiocy of the tactic, more than one man among them sickened by the slaughter they were inflicting on Burnside's men. After two hours of fruitless attempts, a column of Federal troops approached to the right of the bridge, where they were somewhat protected by a low stone wall. Here, many of the Union marksmen began to fight back, using the wall as protection, finally inflicting some damage. Then several dozen Union soldiers, men from Pennsylvania and New York, suddenly rushed the bridge itself and succeeded in making it across. The Georgians finally gave way, and Burnside's men began to pour across the creek.

The attack was successful, and Lee realized that his right flank was now in serious trouble. Burnside's men seem energized by their success, and they pushed forward far beyond the creek, right into the town of Sharpsburg. But there was one more surprise.

Early that morning, in Harpers Ferry, A. P. Hill had received an urgent message from Lee to bring his division toward Sharpsburg. Hill responded by force-marching his men along the seventeen-mile route in just seven hours, a route that was mostly uphill. Nearly half of Hill's six thousand men fell out along the way, but the rest continued to push forward till they reached the field, where they suddenly appeared as a massive force on Burnside's left flank. The rebels reaped the fruits of yet another mistake. On the far left of his advancing force, Burnside had positioned a regiment of Connecticut troops who had never experienced fire from the enemy. A. P. Hill's men slammed right into the Connecticut line. The result was a complete collapse of Burnside's advance and, thus, a complete turnaround of momentum. As darkness began to settle over the field, Burnside's panicked men made their escape by scampering back across what would become known as "Burnside Bridge."

With the daylight gone, the battered armies faced each other in more or less the same positions in which they had begun the day. Between them, across the rolling hills, cornfields, creek beds, and patches of woods, more than twenty-three thousand men lay dead or wounded. It was the bloodiest single day of the Civil War and the bloodiest single day in American history.

The next day, September 18, with both sides stunned by what had occurred, there was little action along the lines. Lee braced himself for another attack, but, as could be predicted, McClellan did nothing. Later, the criticism of McClellan was loud and harsh, primarily because he still had two full corps of fresh troops who had not seen action. Lee had

used nearly every unit in his exhausted army.

As a hard mist settled over the bloody fields, a truce was called so that both sides could collect their wounded. Lee knew his army could not make another ma-

The Burnside Bridge from the Confederate perspective, Antietam, Maryland

PHOTO PATRICK FALCI

The Burnside Bridge from the Union perspective, September 1862, Antietam, Maryland

PHOTO COURTESY
OF THE LIBRARY
OF CONGRESS

jor fight, and that night, using the rainy darkness for cover, he quietly withdrew his army away from Antietam Creek and through Sharpsburg and marched them back across the Potomac River. McClellan made plans to attack Lee once more on September 19, but early that morning, as the Union pickets felt their way forward, they found that Lee's defenses were empty. McClellan had missed his chance to end the war.

Though the battle is judged by strategists and historians to be a draw, McClellan immediately boasted of a great victory. However, despite the tens of thousands of fresh troops at his disposal, he seemed content to rest on his laurels. Pushed by a furious Abraham Lincoln, McClellan began a feeble pursuit of Lee's army and finally moved his army across the Potomac, requiring eight days to accomplish what Lee had accomplished in one night.

Though the Federal army sustained considerably more casualties during the battle than the Army of Northern Virginia, the losses to Lee's army were far more difficult to replace. Lee himself could take no comfort in any claims of a tactical draw. By withdrawing across the Potomac, he understood that he had been forced to take the war back into Virginia.

WHY IS THIS BATTLE IMPORTANT?

"Horror" may seem to be an overused word to describe the Battle of Antietam, but there is no more appropriate description. In both North and South, the newspapers report what occurs here to a public that absorbs the figures with utter disbelief. But accounts of the battle soon arrive in town squares all over the country in a new way. Shortly after the battle concludes, as the Union troops search for anyone who might still be alive, two civilians arrive on the battlefield. They are employees of an increasingly famous photographer named Mathew Brady. The men record the grisly scenes in some of the most famously gruesome photographs of the entire war. Unlike Shiloh, where the horror is confined only to words, here, from the Bloody Lane to Dunker Church, from the cornfield to Burnside Bridge, the images are locked in time. Very soon, the images are viewed by a public that, for the first time, will be able to see for themselves the shocking truth of what this war has become. With the war well into its second year, the public absorbs this truth in differing ways. Some people begin to insist vigorously that the war should simply be stopped, that the South has made its point, that no such astounding loss of life can be justified by a political disagreement. But to others, the northerners who believe wholeheartedly in the sanctity of the Union, it means the war must be fought to a clear victory. Loud voices call out, and renewed pressure is put on the northern politicians. The public will no longer tolerate the costly missteps of martinet generals. In Washington, Stanton and Halleck are aware that despite the public outcry that pours over McClellan's failure to end the war, George McClellan is enormously popular with his troops. The War Department knows that removing him could cause serious morale problems in the Union army, possibly even mass desertions. Thus, his replacement must be a popular man as well, a man with a great many friends, but one who is not as headstrong and independent as McClellan. Unfortunately for Abraham Lincoln and the Union army, their choice is Ambrose Burnside.

As is the case with Shiloh, reputations are made at Antietam. On the Union side, the older, veteran commanders do not fare well, Sumner in particular. The attrition rate is high among the generals and in one case, the death of Israel Richardson, a division commander in Sumner's 2nd Corps, elevates a brigadier to take his place, a man whose star will continue to rise. His name is Winfield Hancock.

On the southern side, both Jackson and Longstreet justify Lee's confidence in their abilities. One other name rises as well: Ambrose Powell Hill, the man who essentially saves the day for Lee's army and spawns a phrase that will live long after the man himself: "Up came Hill."

With Lee's grand plan for ending the war now in shambles, hope dissolves that Great Britain will announce official support for the Confederacy. Lincoln is aware that the British have closely observed what happened at Antietam, and he realizes that the timing might be right for making his own statement, a carefully thought out political move designed to focus the cause of the war more toward the abolition of slavery as well as the preservation of the Union. It is a position that Lincoln believes will unite many of the political factions in the North, whose support he desperately needs. Five days after the battle, Lincoln issues his Emancipation Proclamation, ordering that as of January 1, 1863, all slaves held in the rebellious southern states will be legally granted their freedom. Though the act has no immediate effect on the slaves themselves, it is the final nail in the coffin of British support for the Confederacy. The British had themselves outlawed slavery decades before. Thus, the British know that they cannot now publicly endorse the fortunes of any government that continues to endorse the institution of slavery, which Lincoln has now openly and officially condemned.

The Army of Northern Virginia must again anticipate confronting a Union invasion, defending land that has already seen too much of war. Far from deciding the issue, the Battle of Antietam forces Robert E. Lee to once again find the means to defeat the Union army on yet another bloody field in Virginia.

WHAT YOU SHOULD SEE

*E*xamining the National Park Service map of the Antietam battlefield, one can immediately understand the challenges involved in trying to preserve such a historically important piece of ground. The park now covers approximately 3,300 acres but is intersected by a considerable amount of private land, much of which spreads across ground where much of the action occurred. Fortunately for the modern observer, most of the field remains more or less exactly as it was in 1862. Efforts continue to be made to restore those areas that have undergone changes, including, in one notable effort, the restoration of the West Woods by the planting of hundreds of young trees. All in all, the Antietam battlefield is the best-preserved site of its kind in the eastern theater of the war (though Gettysburg is starting to catch up).

One piece of enormous good fortune is that what was once the Hagerstown Pike, running directly in front of the Dunker Church, is now simply a road included within the park and thus is not subject to the stress of modern traffic. The primary modern thoroughfare is now State Road 65, which runs north from the town of Sharpsburg and eventually resumes the original pathway of the Hagerstown Pike. Though the highway bisects some western edges of the park, it is not nearly the intrusion it could have been.

The battlefield, like so many, is considered a critical historical site immediately after the war (and in fact, in 1864, while the war still rages, Confederate units and their commanders march through this area again, nearly always pausing along the way to reflect upon what had occurred here). The park is established first around the cemetery, built to hold the remains of some 4,800 Union soldiers who had fallen here. (Confederates are buried in several cemeteries in nearby towns and villages, including Hagerstown, Maryland, and Shepherdstown, West Virginia.) Preservation of the battlefield begins in earnest in the 1890s, and as at so many other sites, it is the veterans of the battle itself who spearhead the efforts. And like so many other battlefield sites, Antietam is absorbed into the National Park Service in 1933.

The Visitor Center should be your first stop. It houses an excellent bookstore, where it offers one of the better introductory films of the battle. On the battlefield itself, the Park Service driving tour is essential and follows a route that follows the timeline of the battle. Starting on the north end of the battlefield, where Hooker's Federal troops made their first assault, several stops should be made.

North of the church lies the open farmland that had been the bloody cornfield, the site of the first great slaughter on this ground. The field is (usually) still planted in corn, the ground leased out to local farmers. Along the road (Cornfield Road) on the south side of the field sits a unique marker, consisting of three stacked muskets, dedicated to the 90th Pennsylvania, who fought on this ground. The original monument is held in safe storage by the Park Service. What sits beside the road now is a replica, which is probably a wise precaution against theft.

Northwest of the cornfield, near the Miller Farmhouse, is a marker dedicated to fifteen-year-old Johnny Cook, a bugler for the 4th U.S. Light Artillery. While stories of brave young "bugle boys" abound, it is likely that Cook's story is the inspiration for some of the more mythical tales. Cook received the Medal of Honor for rescuing his wounded captain during the battle as well as assisting to load and fire the artillery pieces, since more than half of the battery's men were shot down. He went on to participate in more than thirty other engagements during the war, including a stint in the U.S. Navy. He eventually became a clerk in the Government Printing Office and died in 1915. (With all due respect to the fine men and women employed by the Government Printing Office, I wonder how a Medal of Honor recipient settled into that sort of civilian job and how many of his co-workers were made aware of his accomplishments.)

The Dunker Church structure sits in its original location, but the building itself is a replica. The building is destroyed by a storm in 1921 and rebuilt in 1962, the effort energized by the centennial commemoration of the battle. Behind the church, you can see the restoration of the West Woods, in progress. Given time, these small trees will grow to resemble more accurately the appearance of those woods at the time of the battle. Note the

The Town of Sharpsburg

IN THE SOUTH, THE BATTLE OF ANTIETAM IS OFTEN REFERRED TO as the battle of Sharpsburg, though the town itself plays only a minor role. However, there are many Civil War–era buildings and homes still to be seen, with some specific sites worth viewing, including a few structures that have pockmarked damage from artillery shells. Some of the homes had basements that housed the local civilian population during the battle, and, of course, a great many of these homes were used as hospitals. Walking tours are available from a variety of local tourist sites, and there are a few small exhibits to be seen.

At the corner of Church and Main Streets, there is a "slave stone," said to have been used as a focal point during the numerous slave auctions conducted here prior to the war. With all respect to the historical interests in the town, it is more likely that the particular stone on display is simply a "stepping-stone" used to assist people as they climbed into a carriage.

If you drive on Main Street westward (State Road 34), heading toward Shepherdstown, you will pass a marker on the right showing the location of Lee's headquarters during the battle. Farther to the right of that spot, in the distance, is a red house. Though private now, this home served as the headquarters for Stonewall Jackson. A little farther out of town on Route 34, on the left side of the road, is an imposing residence, the Grove House. This is the site where Alexander Gardner's famous photograph was taken, showing Abraham Lincoln posing with George McClellan and McClellan's staff officers.

Antietam National Cemetery

THIS IS THE FINAL RESTING PLACE OF 4,800 UNION SOLDIERS, AND I would make mention of two particular monuments. The first official government marker was placed here in 1880 and is hard to miss. It is nicknamed "Old Simon" and is a massive 250-ton monument constructed to memorialize the private unknown soldier, of which there are more than eighteen hundred buried nearby. The second is the grave site for Patrick Roy, one of the seventeen young sailors who lost his life in October 2000 as a crewman on board the USS *Cole*.

Harpers Ferry

IF YOU DRIVE WEST OF SHARPSBURG ON STATE ROAD 34, YOU WILL cross the Potomac River at Shepherdstown. You can then follow the signs for the short drive to Harpers Ferry. The historic waterfront buildings are more or less intact, and though the town offers all the fudge, ice cream, and T-shirts you could want, there is also an excellent bookstore as well as a number of exhibits reflecting what life was like in the town before and during the war.

The town was founded in 1733 and drew its name (logically) from a ferry business operated by Robert Harper. In 1824, the first bridge was built across the Potomac, and the ferry became obsolete. Prior to the Civil War, the town served as a primary "gateway to Ohio," as both a rail center and navigable waterway, but during the war, the town was nearly destroyed by the continuous fighting and the repeated changing of hands from North to South. Immediately prior to the war, Harpers Ferry gained considerable attention as the site of John Brown's famous raid on the Federal arsenal there. The arsenal was destroyed during the war and was never rebuilt.

I strongly suggest you walk out to the small park at the tip of the point of land where the town juts out into the river junction. Notice the mountain peaks around you, and imagine what it must have been like to be a soldier standing helplessly as artillery from those peaks rained shell fire down on you. You too will realize what commanders on both sides of the war understood. This is no place to try to "hold the fort."

RESTRICTED ROAD sign for the path that runs westward behind the church. The road is worth a short walk, to view several monuments to the extraordinary fighting in and around the West Woods. One in particular, the 125th Pennsylvania, is dedicated to the regimental color bearer George Simpson, notable because the monument was commissioned not by his unit, but by the man's sister.

Though not part of the tour within the park boundary, it is worth a brief excursion out onto Highway 65. (Be careful: There is considerable traffic here.) North of the park's main entrance, the highway passes by several monuments, two in particular worth a mention. One is that of a lion, dedicated to the 15th Massachusetts Volunteers. The lion is shown to be wounded and "defiant of death." Just south of that monument is a marker to Colonel Lemuel Stetson, of the 59th New York, a cousin to the founder of the Stetson Hat Company.

Now that you've survived the hazards of Highway 65, return to the safety of the park and, at the Visitor Center, turn right (south). You now begin to enter the region where the battle's second phase occurred. Turning left (east) onto Richardson Avenue, you'll see another RESTRICTED ROAD sign for the path to the left that leads to the Roulette Farm. This is again a walkable road, and if you're inclined to get some exercise, take a stroll down the long hill toward the farm. The farm itself is a very recent acquisition by the park, having been a private residence up until 2003. I cannot imagine what it must have been like for a family, who may or may not have had any interest in history, to have lived on land right smack in the middle of the bloodiest battlefield in American history. The farmhouse and surrounding buildings are now being restored by the Park Service.

If you continue on Richardson Avenue, you will see a brick observation tower that looms high over the far (southern) end of the Bloody Lane. Just to the left of the tower is a large bronze monument dedicated to the Irish Brigade, so many of whom died on this ground. The monument is constructed of granite actually hauled from County Wicklow, Ireland, and was sculpted by Ron Tunison in 1997. I believe that his work, as evidenced by this monument, is some of the best being produced by any of the modern artists now focusing on the Civil War.

I usually despise battlefield towers, which normally take more away from a site than they contribute. This one is an exception. If you're up to it physically, climb the tower. The structure was built originally in the 1890s by the army, to train soldiers on battlefield observation and tactics of movement over terrain. But it is that terrain that is most interesting from this vantage point. One of the causes of so much of the loss at Antietam is that so many troops went into battle having no idea when they would suddenly confront their enemy. Notice the rolling, undulating lay of the land. It is easy to imagine men walking in line down into a depression, blind to what lay beyond, while their enemy moved into position just beyond the next rise. Those sorts of surprises in a battle lead to short-range, face-to-face firefights, a viciousness that can only decimate enormous percentages of the men involved. Such was exactly the case here.

From the tower, you gaze (northward) directly down the Bloody Lane, the site of one of the most famous and most horrific Brady photographs of the Civil War. Now it's time to walk it.

The stroll is fairly tame, and if you're there in the warmer months, the ground is rich with lush green grass and a few flowers, bits of color that could have lined this road at the time of the battle. As you walk the roadway, the ground rises to a gentle peak before falling away again. At this high spot, the roadbed is bare, the grass worn away. Note the hard gravel surface and an outcropping of bedrock. Bedrock isn't something that can be

altered on a spot like this, and I'm certain that the rock there was trodden by the feet of the men who fought, and died, on that spot.

It's quite easy to see how a soldier would seek the shelter of the depressed roadbed and how the split-rail fences offered a perfect place to make a stand against continuing attacks. Again, note the rolling countryside, which would hide the enemy from view until he was too close to escape the awful firepower that a roadbed packed with soldiers could offer. The Bloody Lane is one of those places where it is essential to pause, sit on the sloping banks of the roadbed, and just absorb the silence.

From the tower, continue

*Jeff at the Bloody Lane,
the Sunken Road,
Antietam, Maryland*
PHOTO PATRICK FALCI

on Richardson Road southward until you meet State Road 34. Continue straight across on what is now named Rodman Avenue. To the left you see the Sherrick Farm, which served as a hospital during and after the battle. The original barn, also serving as a hospital, burned in the 1980s.

Turn left just past the Sherrick Farm, and you will reach the Confederate overlook at Burnside Bridge. It's a fairly steep but short walk down to the bridge, and it's an excellent opportunity to see the perspective from both sides of Antietam Creek. On the west (near) side, several rifle pits of the Georgians who held up the crossing are still in evidence, and their vantage point is obvious. As you walk down across the bridge, notice how deep the creek is at that point. There has been considerable argument over the years that Burnside could have sent his men across the creek alongside the bridge and thus crossed without exposing them so severely on the bridge itself. For troops carrying muskets and cartridge boxes (which needed to stay dry), the water is far too deep for anyone to wade across at that point.

The bridge itself is original, though it had to be repaired after the battle, which considering the amount of shell fire the bridge could have absorbed is a testament to the wisdom of building bridges out of stone.

On the Union (east) side of the creek, note the large wooded hill to the rear. This was the staging area for many of the troops who received the order to advance to the bridge. Note the wording on the monument to the 51st New York: "In compliance with orders received from General Burnside on the morning of September 17 . . ." Perhaps I'm reading more into that wording than was intended by the author, but it sounds as though no one was especially excited about advancing straight into the bridge. There are no superlatives, no patriotic rallying cries, nothing about vanquishing the enemy. What the men of the 51st New York did was simply . . . comply.

Though I've read reports of the low stone wall that extends out to the right of the bridge, the stone wall there today is possibly a reconstruction. However, from the Union foot soldier's point of view, I hope the wall was as formidable then as it appears now. Anyone trying to cross that bridge needed all the help he could get.

If you examine the two engraved plaques to the right of the bridge, both show scenes of the fight, and both show a tree perched right alongside the bridge. That tree is still there, one of the few "witness trees" on the battlefield.

There are points of interest not mentioned in the official tour. Driving back toward Rodman Road, if you turn left, you'll come to the park boundary at Harpers Ferry Road. Turn left and then make a quick right onto Millers Sawmill Road. What is not indicated plainly is that this road is the pathway traveled by most of A. P. Hill's men as they drew close to their heroic moment in Confederate history. Note that as you continue the drive (heading more or less in a southwesterly direction), you are going in the opposite direction as Hill's men. Now observe how steep the road is and that for many miles Hill's men marched uphill. It is not difficult to understand why nearly half the men fell out along the way, too worn out to continue. Even more remarkable is how many of them not only completed the forced march, but, upon arriving on the field, immediately launched an attack. When Hill's men thoroughly routed Burnside's flank, they quite probably saved Lee's army, an army that, despite the astonishing cost of the Battle of Antietam, would continue to fight for another two and a half brutal years.

CHAPTER THREE

FREDERICKSBURG *and* CHANCELLORSVILLE

Though the battles of Fredericksburg and Chancellorsville are distinctly separate events, they are linked in several important ways. For purposes of this book, their proximity alone is a strong enough link. The two battlefields are less than ten miles apart, and the National Park Service tours typically encompass both. They are linked as well historically, by the cast of characters and by the fact that the Battle of Chancellorsville would not have occurred at all if the Federal army had not experienced such a disaster at Fredericksburg.

Fredericksburg, Virginia

DECEMBER 11–14, 1862

WHAT HAPPENED HERE

From the beginning of the war, the Union commanders had been blessed with greater manpower and better equipment than their enemy and had succeeded in choking off the South's trade with Europe. Thus, by anyone's measure, the North should have been the inevitable victor in this conflict. In the western theater of the war, events had been reasonably positive for the Union, which by late 1862 had seized control of most of the primary river routes and had bested the Confederate forces in several major fights. But in the east, mainly Virginia, all the material advantages enjoyed by the Federal army had been squandered by the astounding lack of effective leadership. To give credit where it's due, the southern generals had, for the most part, been far more flexible and far more efficient in the field. Despite Jefferson Davis's need to put his finger into the plans of every major campaign (what would today be called micromanaging), Robert E. Lee had proven to be a superior tactician to his opponents. His primary subordinates, Jackson and Longstreet, as well as cavalry commander James Ewell Brown ("Jeb") Stuart, had outdueled their adversaries at nearly every opportunity.

Lincoln's frustration with McClellan had come from McClellan's mistakes in battle, certainly, but also from McClellan's tendency to ignore the president's wishes. By replacing McClellan with Ambrose Burnside, the Union leadership in Washington believed they now had a commander who would at least obey orders. Whether or not Burnside was the right man to lead the Army of the Potomac was a matter to be decided later.

In early November 1862, Lee had divided his army (yet again). Jackson was at Winchester, at the northern end of the Shenandoah Valley, guarding against a sudden assault into Virginia's vulnerable breadbasket. Longstreet stayed closer to the primary rail lines at Culpeper, to meet any advance that might come toward any point east of the Blue Ridge. It was a risky strategy for Lee, and he could only hope that should a major threat suddenly develop, he could unite the two wings of his army in time to confront it. He had one distinct advantage. Until now, the Union commanders had shown little ability or talent for launching any kind of rapid attack.

After Antietam, when McClellan crossed the Potomac River, he seemed to pause, as though hesitant to confront Lee again so quickly. Though he continued to exude a boastful confidence, in Washington it was apparent that McClellan had no real plan for what to do next. As the autumn months passed toward winter, the Federal troops were camped over a broad area that stretched for twenty miles, from the rail lines west of Manassas Junction down through Warrenton. It was entirely possible that McClellan could have launched a major campaign against either wing of Lee's army and would have gone into either fight with overwhelming superiority. But McClellan seemed to know that his days in command were numbered. He was right. The official notice came to his camp on November 7, 1862, notifying McClellan that he had been relieved of his responsibilities with the Army of the Potomac, and to the surprise of many of his senior commanders, his replacement was Ambrose Burnside.

The new commander had been handed the same resources as McClellan, but unlike the bombastic John Pope, Burnside would not make broad pronouncements without first consulting the War Department. He was generally well liked, had a genial personality, and seemed to be a man intent on pleasing everyone. At the moment, the people he most needed to please were in Washington. It was unlikely that his first order of business would be to throw his army right into a full-scale confrontation. Though Abraham Lincoln hoped that the new commander would actually *use* the vast resources available in the Union army, Halleck and Stanton felt as Burnside did, that perhaps the war could be won without another costly battle. His plan took root in the same strategy that had driven the Union commanders since the start of the war: Capture Richmond. It was a philosophy as old as warfare itself, that if the enemy's capital falls, the war simply ends. As rapidly as possible, Burnside would gather his troops, and before Lee could respond effectively, the Federal army would drive directly toward Richmond. The defenses there would be no match for such an overwhelming force, and with Lee's army still in the distance, the Confederacy would likely collapse.

Burnside studied the Virginia waterways and realized that from the position of his army and his routes of supply, sooner or later he would have to cross the Rappahannock River. The river was navigable below Fredericksburg, which meant it was subject to tide changes, a possible disadvantage to moving an entire army across in a timely way. The river could also be patrolled by rebel artillery batteries and cavalry, which could make any crossing considerably dangerous. Fredericksburg stood out for other reasons as well. As the largest city between Washington and Richmond, it was an important rail crossing and the intersection of a network of good roads that spread out into central Virginia. Even though winter was fast wrapping itself around both armies, Burnside was quite sensitive to both Lincoln's and the public's criticism toward McClellan's amazing talent for delay. Burnside could not even consider ordering his army to wait until spring. If Burnside was to have his opportunity, there would be no pause, and his army would push across the river at a place where Lee would certainly not expect—directly into Fredericksburg itself. But there was one detail over which Burnside had no control. The Rappahannock River at Fredericksburg was approximately four hundred feet wide, and the bridges there had been burned, a precaution taken long ago by Lee's army. In order to move his powerful force into position for their final thrust toward Richmond, Burnside would have to supply his own bridges, fashioned out of pontoons. Burnside was told by General Henry Halleck that by the time Burnside's men reached the banks of the Rappahannock opposite the city, they would receive all the pontoons they needed. By mid-November, Burnside's army, nearly 120,000 men, began their march southward. Their commander had every reason to feel a euphoric optimism that finally the Army of the Potomac had a plan that would work.

On November 17, Burnside's troops reached Falmouth, Virginia, a small town just upriver, across from Fredericksburg. As Burnside had hoped, Fredericksburg was virtually undefended by Lee's army. The Federal troops were in position to make their crossing unmolested. So far, his plan was working perfectly. There was just one problem. The pontoon bridges had not yet arrived.

Assured by Halleck that the pontoons would be delivered at any time, Burnside could do nothing but gaze across helplessly at the church steeples in Fredericksburg. His subordinate commanders were as frustrated as he was, and some began to seek the means to cross the river on their own. Though shallow fords existed upriver, Burnside ordered against any smaller excursions, fearing that with the unpredictability of the winter weather, should the river suddenly rise, there was danger that a regiment or possibly an entire division might find itself stranded on the far side. As well, Burnside felt that his plan was cast into stone, that the War Department would be impatient with any sudden changes. For ten days, the Union troops sat idly beside the Rappahannock, until finally, on November 27, the pontoons arrived. Despite the breathless relief in Burnside's headquarters, one key element of his plan had now disappeared: surprise. Though Burnside's move to Fredericksburg had indeed surprised Lee, with the delay, Lee could now respond. Word had gone out to both wings of Lee's army, and as Burnside's delay grew longer, Longstreet's corps had begun to arrive, occupying the hills just to the west of town. Jackson was on his way as well, Lee growing increasingly certain that Burnside had shown his hand, that the Federal army was not simply feigning the move to cross at Fredericksburg. Despite losing the element of surprise, Burnside still had an enormous tactical advantage. Even with the addition of Stonewall Jackson's corps, which was still on the march, Lee had fewer than eighty thousand men to confront a Union army half again as large. But Lee had been given the extraordinary gift of time, the time he needed to choose the ground where he could best make his stand. The hills west of Fredericksburg were a near perfect defensive position, the taller hills closest to the town so steep as to be nearly unassailable by infantry. The hills to the south were more shallow but were mostly covered in thick woods. As Lee placed his troops and artillery into position, he had to believe Burnside would realize that the wiser strategy would be for the Federal troops to bypass Fredericksburg altogether and move farther downriver. To Lee's amazement, the Union forces stayed put, right across the river, and prepared to build their bridges.

But Burnside amended his plan after all, just not the way Lee expected. The presence of Lee's army gave Burnside an opportunity he had not expected. No matter what kind of ground Lee had placed himself on, Burnside's superiority of numbers meant that the Federal army had the chance to atone for McClellan's mistakes at Antietam. If Burnside could crush Lee's army, a march to Richmond might not even be necessary.

Construction of the pontoon bridges was begun in the predawn hours of December

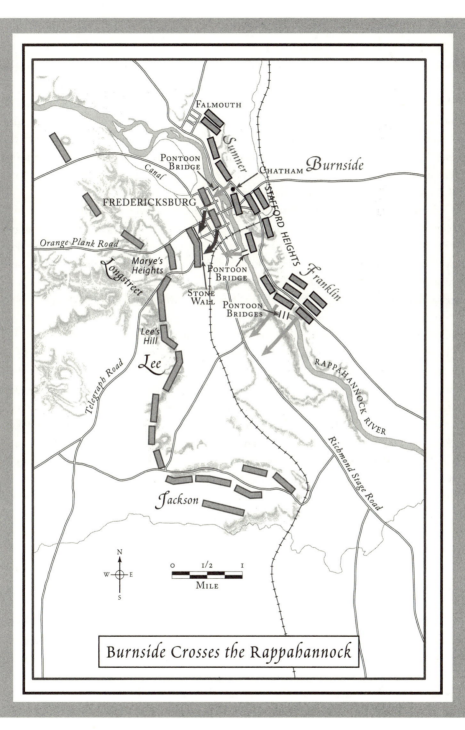

FALMOUTH

Sumner

PONTOON
BRIDGE

Canal

CHATHAM *Burnside*

FREDERICKSBURG

STAFFORD HEIGHTS

Orange Plank Road

Marye's
Heights

Franklin

Longstreet

PONTOON
BRIDGE

STONE
WALL

PONTOON
BRIDGES

Lee's
Hill

Lee

RAPPAHANNOCK RIVER

Telegraph Road

Jackson

Richmond Stage Road

N
W   E
S

0   1/2   1
MILE

Burnside Crosses the Rappahannock

11. The engineers and carpenters of Burnside's army floated and assembled their pontoons, pushing their way slowly across the ice-crusted Rappahannock in a dense fog that masked their movements. But the sounds were unmistakable to the rebels in the town. While Lee had kept the bulk of his army digging in to the heights behind the town, one brigade of Mississippians, under William Barksdale, had positioned itself in the basements of the homes that faced the river. Lee knew that Barksdale could not hold back the Federal efforts for long, but any delay would give the Confederates more time to improve their defense on the heights. In addition, Jackson's corps had not yet fully arrived on the field, and Lee needed more time to put those troops into position.

As the daylight cut through the dense fog, the engineers who were working feverishly to construct their bridges were silhouetted just enough to give Barksdale's riflemen a target. At their commander's signal, the Mississippians fired a volley at the shadowy figures now helplessly exposed. The musket fire took its toll: Many of the men on the pontoons were struck down, some tumbling into the icy river. Immediately, the Federal engineers scrambled back to the safety of the shore. Over the course of the next several hours, they would repeat the same routine nine times. Each time, the engineers and their carpenters would make their way out onto the pontoons, only to be cut down again by the unseen rebels. Finally, an outraged Burnside responded by ordering Federal cannon to shell the houses along the waterfront. Some 150 artillery pieces began a barrage that eventually dropped more than 8,000 shells, and not just on the waterfront. Most of the homes and buildings in Fredericksburg were either damaged or destroyed. But Barksdale's men kept firing, many now protected by the rubble of the very houses whose basements they inhabited. With the losses among his engineers growing, and the men themselves showing no enthusiasm for continuing their work, Burnside approved an alternate plan. Squads of Federal troops began to make their way quickly across the river in pontoon boats. Still peppered by fire from the shore, the Union troops began to land in sufficient numbers to root the Mississippians out of their hiding places. Barksdale ordered his men to fall back, but their mission had been accomplished. Though Lee had not expected the Mississippians to put up any real resistance, they actually caused a full day's delay in Burnside's crossing of the river.

On December 12, with the rebels now safely back on the heights, the Federal army completed its crossing on five pontoon bridges and occupied the town as well as the broad plain downriver. Burnside now put another plan into action. The assault on Lee's army would be made in two prongs. On the left, below the town, the plain west of the river was far enough from the rebel lines that the troops there would have ample space to maneuver. There, some sixty thousand men, under the overall command of Major General William Franklin, were charged with assaulting Lee's right flank, which was thought to spread out along the shallow wooded ridgeline. Burnside's right prong encompassed the town itself. There, the troops were crowded into the streets, a good deal closer to the rebel

View of Fredericksburg from across the Rappahannock River, 1862
PHOTO COURTESY OF THE LIBRARY OF CONGRESS

positions. Even though the Federal troops were within range of rebel cannon, Burnside guessed correctly that Lee would not do as the Federals had done. Lee would not order his artillery to shell a Virginia town.

The logistics of moving so many men into place across the river caused yet another day-long delay. The town had already suffered so much from Burnside's artillery attack that a great many of the homes were wide open, doors and windows shattered. Many of the civilians had gone, a tragic parade of carts and wagons that carried a few precious possessions away from the inevitable hell of the fight. As the Federal troops filled the town, they had little to do but wait, and men began milling about the vacant streets and alleyways. Before long, they lost their discipline and quickly assumed the characteristics of an uncontrollable mob. Despite the best efforts of at least some officers, they began to loot the homes and shops, smashed furniture and glass, either destroying or attempting to steal virtually anything they could find. As the day passed, the mob began to lose its energy, and finally the provost marshals regained some kind of order. But what the artillery shells had not accomplished, the men in blue had. Most of Fredericksburg was simply gutted.

In the early morning fog of December 13, 1862, Burnside ordered his assault to begin.

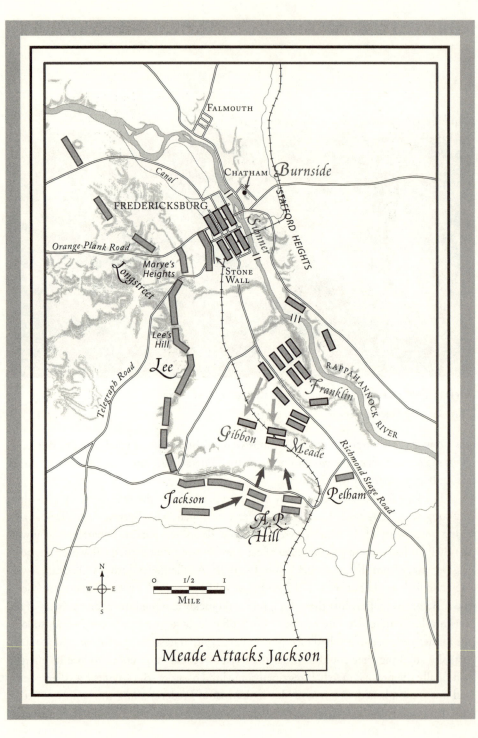

FALMOUTH

CHATHAM *Burnside*

Canal

FREDERICKSBURG

Sumner

STAFFORD HEIGHTS

Orange Plank Road

Marye's Heights

Longstreet

STONE WALL

Lee's Hill

Lee

RAPPAHANNOCK RIVER

Franklin

Telegraph Road

Gibbon

Meade

Jackson

Pelham

Richmond Stage Road

A.P. Hill

N
W — E
S

0   1/2   1
MILE

Meade Attacks Jackson

The first movement was to come from Franklin's men on the left, a hard thrust into Jackson's lines in the low wooded hills. Once Franklin had engaged the enemy, Major General Edwin "Bull" Sumner, in command of the troops in the town, would send his men forward as well. For reasons debated long after the battle, Franklin ordered only one division, commanded by General George Gordon Meade, to begin the attack. Meade's forty-five hundred men were supported on his right by one division, under John Gibbon, and another, commanded by Abner Doubleday, would protect Meade's left and rear. Meade had every reason to assume that the remainder of Franklin's enormous force would join the attack, possibly sweeping around to the left, into Jackson's flank, thus enveloping that entire section of the rebel position. As Meade pushed his men toward the low hills, the last traces of fog lifted, and just as quickly, Meade's lines were suddenly punched by artillery fire. The fire came not from the great mass of Jackson's artillery in the trees, but far to the left. Two twelve-pound field guns, under the command of Confederate cavalryman John Pelham, had moved out into the open and were firing directly into the flank of Meade's advancing troops. The effect caused Meade's line to waver, the men who bore the brunt of the fire stumbling into confusion. Union artillery attempted to respond, and soon one of Pelham's cannon was destroyed. Pelham, under orders from Jeb Stuart to withdraw, wisely did so, but not before causing a significant delay in Meade's advance. The delay had given

Effects of the Union artillery barrage, December 1862, Fredericksburg, Virginia

the last units of Stonewall Jackson's corps the time they needed to move into position, men who had only just arrived on the field.

Meade began his advance again, and as Jackson's artillery and muskets began to open up, Meade's men sought cover by funneling into a patch of woods that jutted out toward them from Jackson's position. The ground there was low and swampy, and the division commander in that section of the line, A. P. Hill, had considered the area impassable for troops. Thus, Hill had left a gap nearly six hundred yards wide in the center of Jackson's position. But the ground proved more solid than Hill had estimated, and Meade's men unknowingly continued their assault at precisely the weakest point along Lee's entire position.

As Meade's men surged into the opening, their confidence grew, and the Federal troops actually reached a road that ran behind Jackson's position. But Meade's lone division did not have the manpower to take advantage of the breach, and Jackson responded quickly to the crisis. Within a short time, Meade's advance was choked off by Jackson's reserves, and in a sharp fight, Meade was forced to retreat. Meanwhile, across the open plain behind him, tens of thousands of Franklin's troops stood idle.

Meade's fight had lasted until early afternoon, and only now did Burnside order Sumner's men to advance out of the town, to attack Lee's positions on the taller hills. The larger hill directly in their line of attack, called Marye's Heights, rose steeply above a roadbed that ran along its base. The road there was well-worn and so was another of the sunken lanes that typified so many well-traveled avenues. Lee had placed one brigade of Confederate riflemen there, under Georgian Thomas Cobb, supported by one regiment of North Carolina infantry. Unlike the sunken road at Antietam, the roadbed along the base of Marye's Heights had an added advantage as a defensive position. It was lined by a stout stone wall. Cobb's men gathered in the road, fully protected by the stone wall, and trained their muskets on the massive lines of Federal infantry that plodded toward them.

The advance of the Federal troops took them first across a half mile of wide-open ground, which was cut by a deep canal. Though the canal had been partially drained of water by Federal engineers, the crossing could be made only at several bridge points. Confederate artillerymen had been given ample time to find the range so that their cannon could pinpoint the bridges as the Union troops made their way across. In addition, rebel artillery had been placed so as to fire directly down the canal, with devastating effect on any Union soldiers who sought shelter there. As Confederate artillery commander Edward Porter Alexander had told Lee, the Confederate artillery had such an effective field of fire that once the assault began, "a chicken could not live on that field."

The first Union division to make the assault against Marye's Heights was commanded by Major General William French. French's men absorbed the punishment of Lee's artillery, and then, as they crested a shallow rise 200 yards in front of the stone wall,

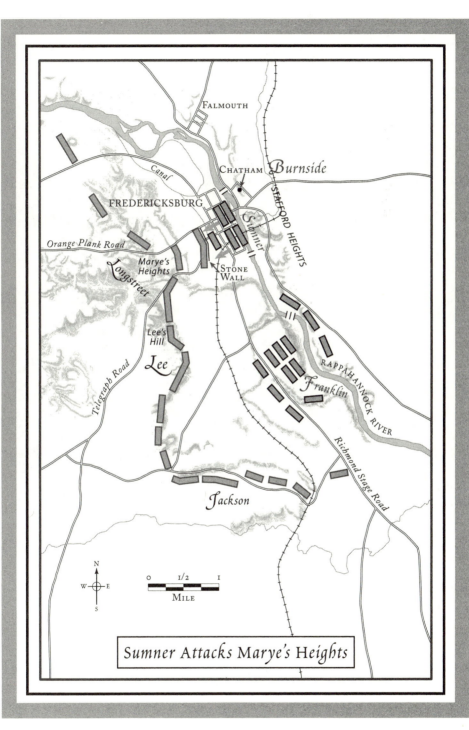

FALMOUTH

Canal

CHATHAM *Burnside*

FREDERICKSBURG

Sumner

STAFFORD HEIGHTS

Orange Plank Road

Marye's
Heights

STONE
WALL

Longstreet

Lee's
Hill

Telegraph Road

Lee

RAPPAHANNOCK RIVER

Franklin

Richmond Stage Road

Jackson

N
W—E
S

0   1/2   1
MILE

Sumner Attacks Marye's Heights

Confederate dead at the stone wall, Marye's Heights, Fredericksburg, Virginia
PHOTO COURTESY OF THE LIBRARY OF CONGRESS

Cobb's muskets opened a blistering fire. The effect was devastating, and though many of French's men held their ground, no Union soldier came within twenty-five yards of the wall. Behind French came the next division, under Winfield Hancock. As they pushed forward, the sheets of musket fire from the wall cost Hancock's division 40 percent of its strength, some two thousand men.

During the fighting, the Georgian Cobb was killed, but his men were reinforced by another of Longstreet's brigades to add to the fierce storm of musket fire the rebels were throwing at the Federal advance. The Confederates had stood four and then six deep behind the wall, the first rows of men firing and then handing their muskets back to be reloaded as a fresh musket was put into their hands. Before the sun went down, the Federals had thrown six separate waves of troops against Marye's Heights. To the stunned disbelief of the rebels, the assaults had continued to come straight at the stone wall, where every attack absorbed the same horrific fate. With darkness finally settling over the field, the slaughter of the Union troops had come blessedly to an end. In the day's fighting, Burnside's army had suffered nearly thirteen thousand casualties, the same number the Federal army had absorbed at Antietam. Two-thirds of those men had gone down in front of the stone wall at the base of Marye's Heights. Overall, Lee's army had suffered less than half that number of dead and wounded.

The chilly night of December 13 passed with Confederate sharpshooters eyeing the darkened ground in front of the wall, where thousands of wounded Federal soldiers called out. Thousands more had been unable to retreat to the safety of the town and had no choice but to endure the night in near freezing temperatures. The next day, December 14, little activity occurred along the lines. Union troops began to make good their withdrawal, exhausted men surviving the rebel muskets as best they could, seeking any kind of shelter along the undulating ground. Across the river, Ambrose Burnside responded to word of the disaster by insisting he would launch yet another attack, would lead his own 9th Corps toward Lee's position. It was a rash and emotional decision, and Burnside was finally talked out of what would certainly have been suicide. (Little was recorded about just how many men of the 9th Corps might actually have followed Burnside toward the wall.) After Burnside sought counsel from his senior commanders, he decided that no benefit could come from holding Fredericksburg. The morale of the Union troops had been so crushed by the fight that Burnside's wisest move was to withdraw the army back across the Rappahannock, where the depleted units could be reorganized and the wounded could be sent away without danger from harassing fire from Lee's troops. It was decided that the withdrawal had to be made during the night, and as the sun set on December 15, Burnside's troops began to march slowly back across their pontoon bridges.

That night, the skies over Fredericksburg were suddenly ablaze with a glorious display that most of the men on either side had never seen. In a phenomenon unusual for Virginia, the aurora borealis, or northern lights, burst across the night sky with a dancing cascade of color. Men on both sides paused from the business of war to wonder if a divine hand was offering some message, a blessing for the fallen or perhaps a condemnation of what had taken place here.

On the morning of December 16, Lee received word that the Federal troops had withdrawn and had destroyed their bridges over the Rappahannock. That morning, an emotional Lee rode into the town and witnessed firsthand the devastation the Federal troops had left behind.

In Burnside's camp, the army reacted to their commander as might be expected, and morale was dangerously low. Burnside was immediately condemned in Washington and by the northern newspapers, and he publicly accepted responsibility for the disaster. This seemed to satisfy Halleck and Stanton, but to the chagrin of some of Burnside's subordinates, he remained in command. The primary condition for his survival was that Burnside continue the push and not simply settle his army into winter quarters. Burnside obliged and devised yet another plan. Lee seemed content to keep his army in place on the heights, so Burnside would march his army upriver, seeking to cross at a point where he could attack Lee from a more favorable direction. On January 20, 1863, Burnside ordered his disgruntled army to march northward, toward the shallow fords he should have used the preceding month. Though his army seemed willing at first to cooperate with Burnside's strategy, the weather did not cooperate at all. For two days, the misery of the Union troops was made far worse by a chilling rain that turned the roads beneath them to thick mud and sent every creek out of its banks. With the roads virtually impassable, no wagon, no artillery piece, could move, and the men themselves settled down into makeshift camps where sleet, snow, and freezing rain drained away every regiment's willingness for a fight. By January 23, Burnside accepted that his plan had become simply another failure, and he ordered his troops into winter quarters.

Burnside's "Mud March" was the last straw for Washington. On January 25, 1863, Burnside was replaced as commander of the Army of the Potomac by Major General Joe Hooker.

WHY IS THIS BATTLE IMPORTANT?

*W*hile the cost in human terms is (yet again) horrifying, the Union clearly bears the brunt of the loss. However, as has always been the case, the northern army draws manpower from a population source that far outweighs the availability of fighting men in the South. Thus, Lee's loss of (only) five thousand men is a price that Lee cannot afford to pay. No matter that Fredericksburg is a decisive victory for Lee and a catastrophic failure for Burnside; should Lee be forced to fight on many more battlefields like Fredericksburg, the losses will eventually defeat his army in ways the Union commanders seem unable to accomplish.

In terms of technology, Burnside makes considerable use of a tool that holds enormous promise for the future. It is the observation balloon, inflated with hydrogen and anchored to the ground by long tethers. The balloons are equipped to carry aloft at least one man, who will have the unique ability to offer reconnaissance as valuable to the army as any mountaintop lookout. The bravery of those few pioneers who man these balloons cannot be underestimated. On the Federal side of the Rappahannock, these balloons are used to great effect to allow northern tacticians to observe Lee's troop movements. On the southern side, the men stare in wonder at these fat sausages floating above the Union artillery positions, very few having any idea how this kind of technology might evolve in the future.

On the Union side, Generals William French, Winfield Hancock, and Andrew Humphreys acquit themselves extremely well in an impossible situation at the stone wall, as do most of their brigade commanders. While George Meade furiously protests the useless sacrifice of his division, there are signs that on the Union left, Generals Reynolds, Doubleday, and Gibbon did all they could to assist him. Though Burnside accepts overall responsibility for the disaster, he lays a great deal of blame at the feet of William Franklin, who, with enormous resources at hand, does virtually nothing. After the war, the Congressional Committee on the Conduct of the War agrees that Franklin and Burnside both deserve a significant share of the blame.

On the southern side, there are no major surprises. Stonewall Jackson faces the greatest crisis and handles it with perfect skill by tossing Meade's division completely out of the gap in the rebel line. Though Jackson (and Lee) presumably knew the gap existed, Jackson loudly blames A. P. Hill, thus fueling their mutual animosity, a clash of personalities that has plagued Lee from the beginning of his command.

Despite Lee's deep concerns that the defenses on Marye's Heights are insufficient to hold the Federal army away, Longstreet's assurances that his defense can stand any assault proves to be accurate. While Jackson remains the most aggressive and effective battlefield commander in either army, James Longstreet has rapidly become a master of defensive tactics.

In terms of commanders lost, Lee suffers the greatest cost. Two very capable southern generals are killed: Thomas Cobb and Maxcy Gregg.

One bright light for the Confederacy is Major John Pelham, whose two field guns did such effective work against Meade's advance. He is ever after referred to as the "Gallant Pelham," and his actions at Fredericksburg make him a hero to the Confederate cause. He continues to lead field artillery under Jeb Stuart but is killed in action barely three months after the battle.

The wanton destruction of the town of Fredericksburg is a stain against the Union soldier that is not easily erased in the South. Though the action is loudly condemned by Union commanders, it deepens the hatred that the war has already fostered. The destruction of the town becomes a rallying symbol for southerners, which strengthens their resolve to continue the war.

Burnside's failure reinforces Abraham Lincoln's frustration that regardless of the spirit and determination of the northern soldier, the Union hierarchy seems woefully inept at finding a competent commander. Many senior officers in the army continue to voice their opinion that Burnside should never have been given command in the first place, some insisting that the most deserving and the most capable had in fact been Joe Hooker. Now they would learn if they were right.

Chancellorsville, Virginia

MAY 1–3, 1863

WHAT HAPPENED HERE

*A*s the winter of 1862–1863 passed, it was "Fighting Joe" Hooker's turn to take the stage. Though generally disliked by many of his subordinates, Hooker at least seemed willing to put an immediate squeeze on the rebel army, and he was not likely to plague Washington with meaningless delays. Abraham Lincoln understood that Hooker was nothing like George McClellan, but Hooker's bursts of bravado made even Lincoln uncomfortable. Hooker is said to have remarked: "May God have mercy on Bobby Lee, for I shall have none." Lincoln had heard this same sort of boastfulness from John Pope. But Lincoln could not fault the man who insisted that his sole mission would be to "destroy the army of General Lee."

Lee's army had spent the winter on or around the hills west and south of Fredericksburg, and the logistics of feeding and clothing his exhausted troops had become as difficult as ever. The very problem Lee had tried to alleviate by marching into Maryland now pressed his army into a weakened gloom. In February, Lee received reports that Federal forces might be mobilizing along their coastal forts in the Carolinas to begin a new thrust toward the Virginia peninsula. It was a threat to Richmond that Lee could not ignore, and prodded by Jefferson Davis, he weakened an already weak army. Two divisions, under George Pickett and John Bell Hood, were sent toward Richmond, along with their commander, James Longstreet. At the very least, Lee hoped that Longstreet would be able to forage considerable supplies for Lee's army that the men desperately needed. As spring approached, and with it the certainty of a renewed campaign, Lee hunkered down on his hills with approximately sixty thousand men. Across the river, Hooker outnumbered him by more than two to one.

Hooker's plan was to take full advantage of his superiority in numbers. To hold Lee close to the river, Hooker made a great show of strength, positioning Major General John Sedgwick opposite Fredericksburg with some forty thousand men, roughly a third of Hooker's command.

In late April, with the roads hardened by the warmer weather, Hooker began to march the remaining two-thirds of his army upriver, following much of the same route that Burnside had used in January to such poor results. But Hooker's army was energized, both by the spring and by their commander's raw enthusiasm. The subordinate commanders were enthusiastic as well, all of them knowing that Hooker's plan was the correct strategy and, if executed properly, could end the war. But in the minds of some of the most capable Federal officers, there was certainly the nagging thought that this was a refrain they had sung before.

At Fredericksburg, Sedgwick put another part of Hooker's plan into motion, and on April 29, he crossed the Rappahannock, spreading out into camps south of the town, the same ground that had been occupied by William Franklin's men in December. But Sedgwick made no threatening move toward Lee's heights, and though Sedgwick was carefully watched by Lee's observers, Lee's attention began to shift to the west.

Approximately ten miles west of Lee's camps, on the main road leading out from Fredericksburg, there sat an intersection occupied by a single residence called the Chancellor House. The mansion gave the immediate area the name of Chancellorsville. The mansion was Hooker's concentration point, and he marched his men without hesitation, sending them across the Rappahannock at several of the fords that dotted the river northwest of Fredericksburg. On April 30, some forty thousand Union troops began to assemble at the Chancellor intersection, with another forty thousand held back across the river. Hooker's plan was simple. Lee's army was now pinned on its hills between two sizable forces, with another massive force waiting to be called into use wherever the advantage might lie. Once Sedgwick began his own movement toward the heights at Fredericksburg, the question was not whether Lee would be attacked, it was which part of Hooker's army would attack him first. In either event, if Lee turned to face one assault, the other would very soon gobble him up from the rear. Hooker and his entire command knew: Lee was in serious trouble.

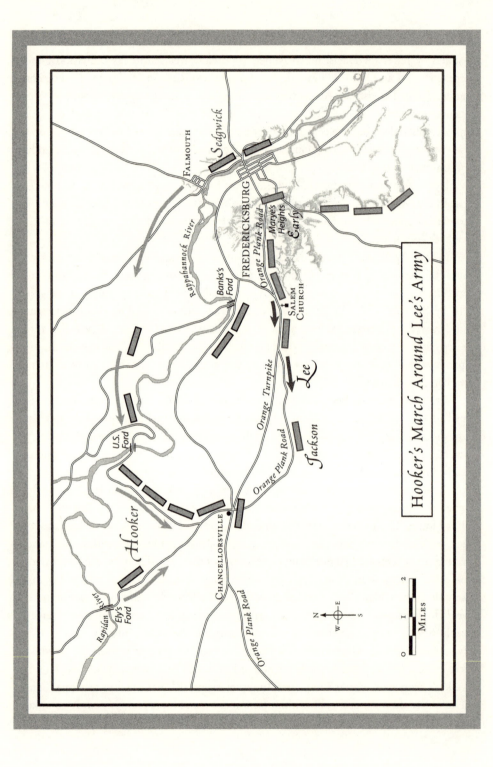

Hooker's March Around Lee's Army

In the vicinity of Chancellorsville, mostly south and farther west, there were several small ironworks, millworks, and charcoal makers. For many of them, wood was the essential fuel, and as a result, much of the big timber had disappeared from the forests. In its place, with few farmers clearing the land for cultivation, dense undergrowth had flourished. As the years had passed, vast stretches of the ground around Chancellorsville had become an impenetrable tangle of brush and heavy thickets. The area was generally referred to as the Wilderness, and other than the primary roads, there were few trails, few stretches of open ground, and virtually no easy way for an army to form battle lines.

With Jeb Stuart's cavalry informing Lee of Hooker's exact whereabouts, Lee observed that Sedgwick was still not moving, so Lee concluded that the greatest danger he faced was to the west. Accordingly, he sent Stonewall Jackson in that direction with as much force as Lee felt he could spare, while Lee kept the remainder on the heights at Fredericksburg.

Hooker knew that he had to push his army out of the Wilderness that engulfed the roads around Chancellorsville, and early on the morning of May 1, 1863, he began to march them east on the main road (the Orange Turnpike) toward Fredericksburg. As the Federal troops began to break free of the dense Wilderness, they made a long climb toward a wide ridge, in the vicinity of a small building, the Zoan Church. Here, the ground was open and high, and Hooker's commanders breathed much more easily, knowing that the Union troops could now form powerful battle lines. Unfortunately for the Federals, Jackson arrived at the Zoan Church the same time they did. The battle was more of a sharp skirmish, but the Federal commanders continued to press forward, bringing more of their strength into play. Jackson was outnumbered, and the Federal commanders seemed poised to break through the rebel position. Then, "Fighting Joe" Hooker lost his nerve. The order went out to the frontline units, to commanders who stared at one another in furious disbelief. Back at the Chancellor House, Hooker had ignored the reports sent by his frontline commanders, and instead of pressing the attack, he ordered his men to retreat.

The fury of his subordinates did not diminish as the blue-coated troops marched back to Chancellorsville. Hooker ordered his troops to dig in, and the men began constructing earthworks and log works, digging trenches, to face what their commander must have believed to be an enormous wave of the enemy. Despite the pleadings of his senior officers, Hooker had decided to change his entire plan. No matter what Sedgwick might do at the river, out here, in the thickets around the Chancellor House, Hooker would wait to be attacked. And to make sure the Federal troops could put up a stiff resistance, Hooker ordered his reserve to march down and join the troops already in place. By nightfall on May 1, Hooker had assembled nearly eighty thousand men and had them digging in to hold off what he could only have believed was some demonic force led by Stonewall Jackson, a force that was in reality half the size of Hooker's army.

Early in the evening of May 1, Lee rode out to meet with Jackson, to discuss just how to deal with Hooker's position. Their meeting took place beside a campfire, the two men sitting on wooden boxes. In the midst of their discussion, cavalryman Jeb Stuart suddenly rode into camp and excitedly explained that he had located the far western flank of the Union line. Stuart had determined that the Federal position resembled a spoon, curving around the mansion, with the "handle" extending far out to the west along the Plank Road. On the far end, the Federals had done little to protect themselves, had not dug trenches, prepared no earthworks, and their artillery was not in position to ward off any assault. It was quite obvious that Hooker expected that any attack would come in the vicinity of the mansion. The troops that stretched out along the Plank Road were there only because, surrounded by the dense Wilderness, they had nowhere else to make their camps.

After hearing Stuart's report, Jackson proposed to Lee that the army be divided, that Jackson lead some twenty-eight thousand men on a discreet march to the Union west flank and launch a surprise attack. Jackson insisted that a successful attack there would cause the Federal flank to collapse and could drive Hooker's entire force toward the river in disorder. It was possible that Hooker might even be compelled to surrender his army. But the risk was extraordinary. Should Hooker discover Jackson's movement and suddenly attack the men while they were on the march, Jackson's plan and much of Lee's army would simply dissolve. And Lee himself would be left facing the bulk of Hooker's force with only fourteen thousand men. Should Hooker regain his nerve and once more march eastward, Lee's small force would be swallowed up.

In the early morning of May 2, 1863, Jackson's men began their march. Their route covered roughly thirteen miles, a route designed to take them far enough below the Plank Road that Hooker's troops would not detect the movement. But some of the Federal commanders had indeed detected the march, and despite a brief thrust into Jackson's line of march by units of Dan Sickles's 3rd Corps, no one at Hooker's headquarters seemed concerned. Word began to circulate by overconfident Union officers that the rebel troops seen marching westward were no doubt retreating.

The far flank of the Union position was manned by the 11th Corps, commanded by Oliver Otis Howard. Howard was a capable commander who had lost his right arm during the Seven Days' Battles, the final chapter in McClellan's Peninsula Campaign. The 11th was composed mainly of German immigrant troops, many of whom could not speak English. Howard had been in command of the corps for less than a month and was still learning the names of his senior officers and dealing with the language barrier. The position of the 11th Corps on the far end of the line was no accident, since even Hooker seemed to recognize that this might not be the most efficient fighting force in the Army of the Potomac. By sending Howard's men far to the west, Hooker had simply put them out of harm's way.

Jackson continued to drive his men toward their goal, but the march did not move as quickly as Jackson had planned. Instead of reaching their jumping-off point by four in the afternoon, the men did not gather on the far end of the Union line until after five. Jackson was aware that if the attack was to work as he had hoped, his men would have to accomplish a great deal in roughly two hours of daylight.

Jackson spread his troops into a battle line a mile wide, three heavy lines deep. With as much stealth as possible, the Confederates filed out into the thickets, and when the order was given, they began to push straight through the dense undergrowth, right toward Oliver Howard's camps.

The men of the 11th Corps were preparing their supper, the muskets stacked, the men stopping occasionally to gaze toward a far-off rumble of activity on the far eastern end of Hooker's lines. The only sounds of a fight they had heard all day was a diversionary attack Lee had launched to hold the bulk of Hooker's army in place. Despite the reports from various lookouts that a large column of Confederates had been seen on roads to the south of them, Howard's troops were simply going about their business.

As Jackson's rebels pushed toward them, wildlife of all variety suddenly burst out of the dense undergrowth, followed by the high-pitched cheer that some of the men in blue had come to know well. It was the rebel yell. The surprise was complete and overwhelming. Jackson's men burst into the Federal camps in a massive wave, pouring over every obstacle. Howard's troops made virtually no effort to hold them back, and the entire Union flank collapsed into a mob of panicked, fleeing men. The panic was so complete that some of Howard's men ran as far as the river or in some cases stayed near the Plank Road and ran right through the Union defenses at the Chancellor House, which faced the other direction. In a futile gesture, Union officers attempted to rally their troops. Finally, Jackson's men were slowed by exhaustion and by opposition from more disciplined units from other Union corps. But Jackson's momentum continued to push the Federals back, and quite likely, if there had been another hour of daylight, most of Hooker's army, and Hooker himself, might have been inspired to withdraw to the safety of the river.

As daylight faded, a furious Jackson continued to push his men. Even as his men began to halt themselves in the growing darkness, Jackson rode forward, trying to seek a route by which his troops could cut off any Federal retreat. Accompanied by his staff, Jackson rode out through dense woods along a narrow trail, and as his nervous aides began to insist that Jackson was in a place he shouldn't be, shots rang out. But the musket fire did not come from the enemy, whose lines Jackson had nearly crossed. They came from a regiment of North Carolinians, exhausted and nervous men who fired at what they

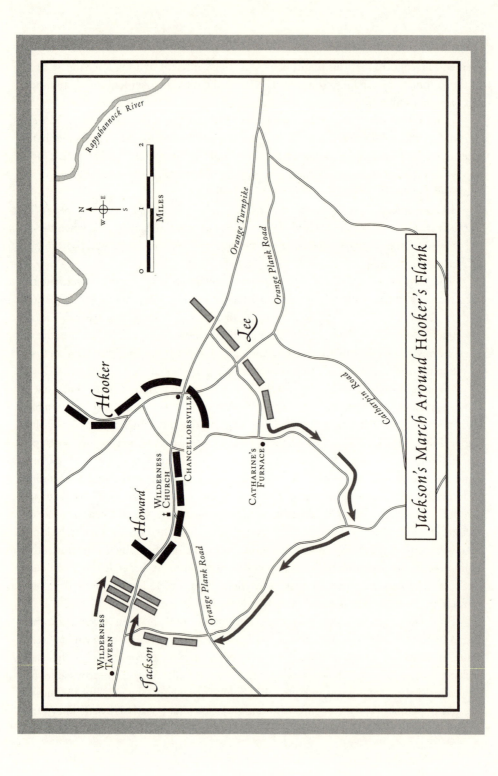

Jackson's March Around Hooker's Flank

believed to be Union cavalry. Jackson was severely wounded and was taken from the field on a stretcher.

During the night, Hooker and Lee both scrambled to put their troops into some kind of order. Not all the Federal troops had been so affected by Jackson's surprise attack, and around the Chancellor House, men like George Meade and Winfield Hancock, knowing that Hooker would not even consider an attack of his own, prepared formidable defensive positions to deal with whatever Lee would bring.

To replace Jackson on the western flank of the hopelessly confused field, Lee first sought out A. P. Hill. But Hill had also been wounded, so Lee ordered Jeb Stuart to take command. On the morning of May 3, Stuart continued the same assault that Jackson had started and pressed hard into the Union right. The fight lasted all day, a vicious affair with heavy casualties on both sides. On a high plateau called Hazel Grove, barely a mile from the Chancellor House, Stuart's artillery gathered and began to shell the mansion itself and the Federal troops positioned there. The mansion was quickly destroyed, but there was a much greater impact on the Union army. During the assault on what had been his headquarters, Hooker was struck by a piece of debris and was dazed sufficiently that the flow of orders from commander to subordinate virtually stopped. Though the Federal soldiers had plenty of fight in them, their commander did not. To the enormous despair of his senior officers, Hooker did little else but pull his troops into an ever tightening defense around the ruins of the mansion.

Site of the mortal wounding of Stonewall Jackson, Chancellorsville, Virginia

PHOTO PATRICK FALCI

At Fredericksburg, meanwhile, John Sedgwick had finally launched an assault of his own and was making significant headway toward breaking Lee's defenses on Marye's Heights. But with Hooker now content to order troops to sit defensively around the Chancellorsville ruins, Lee took another risk and sent a sizable force away from Chancellorsville to hold Sedgwick back. The normally capable Sedgwick was suddenly confronted by far more strength than he had expected, and as a result, his entire force was withdrawn back across the Rappahannock. On May 6, after two more days of inconclusive action, Hooker withdrew as well. Though pressed hard by Stuart's Confederates, the Federal troops were protected by a perfect rearguard action by Hancock's division. Led by their commander, the Army of the Potomac pulled back across the Rappahannock and limped out of harm's way.

"Fighting Joe" Hooker's days in command were numbered.

WHY IS THIS BATTLE IMPORTANT?

*T*hirty thousand casualties. Once again, though Lee has sustained far fewer losses than his adversary, the men erased from his army cannot be easily replaced. But one casualty outshines all others.

Stonewall Jackson survives the wounds he receives, though he suffers the loss of his left arm. But soon after the surgery, Jackson begins to develop symptoms of pneumonia. On May 10, 1863, with his wife by his side, Thomas Jonathan Jackson dies.

Though Jackson's absence will prove to be a crushing blow for the fortunes of both the Confederacy and Lee himself, one small light emerges: Jeb Stuart shows himself to be a fine commander in the field, both on and off a horse.

With yet another crushing loss, morale in the North suffers again, resulting in pressure on Lincoln to end the war any way possible and energizing ambitious men who believe Lincoln's presidency is an utter failure. With the election of 1864 barely eighteen months away, Lincoln realizes that unless the fortunes of war can be changed to favor the North, his opportunity to reunite the country will simply vanish. Others are certain that the war will not even continue that long, and many in the capital call for peace on any terms the South offers. The failures in the east get far greater newspaper coverage, but in the west, Lincoln has good reason for optimism. Despite the parade of ineptness that has plagued the Army of the Potomac, if Lee's forces can just be held in check, Federal successes in the west might finally take their own toll on Confederate fortunes. Lincoln has to believe that regardless of the gloom of the newspapers, and regardless of the failures in the eastern theater, the war can still be won.

Though the Confederacy rejoices in Lee's victories at Fredericksburg and Chancellorsville, Lee knows that these kinds of victories cannot continue. The victory celebrations are tempered by the death of Jackson, and the southern people deeply mourn their fallen hero. But Lee understands that the loss is not merely symbolic, that Jackson was no mythical figure. The Army of Northern Virginia is suffering from a lack of good commanders, a lack of reinforcements, and a lack of supply for the men in the field. Half a dozen more "victories" like the ones just past, and Lee knows he will have no army left at all. With Jackson gone, Lee must look again for some spark, some way to give his army not only victories in the field, but the means to bring the war to a close. Conferring with Jefferson Davis, Lee begins to look northward again. He reads the same newspapers as Lincoln and begins to understand that the South's best hopes for ending the war lie with the growing civilian pressure on the U.S. Congress. Despite the bloody results of Antietam, Lee is convinced that the strategy of moving northward is still sound. The Confederacy cannot feed its army, and Virginia cannot be made a desolate wasteland. Davis agrees. Lee will make another attempt at carrying the war into the North, another invasion, another sharp thrust into Pennsylvania.

WHAT YOU SHOULD SEE

Fredericksburg

In terms of acreage, Fredericksburg pales in comparison with parks such as Shiloh or Antietam. Indeed, much of the original battlefield now rests beneath the streets of a greatly enlarged city. However, great significance can still be found in the details of what remains.

The park isn't officially founded until 1927, far later than most other battlefield parks, which certainly contributes to the park's lack of vast tracts of green space. Politics certainly plays a role, since of course, Fredericksburg is a Confederate victory, not something that generates much enthusiasm in the North, where most of the votes in Congress lie. In 1933, Fredericksburg opens its Visitor Center, which at the time is one of the finest such facilities at any battlefield park in the country. Besides the usual bookstore (housed separately), the main building contains a surprisingly comprehensive museum. If there is one advantage to a smaller battlefield park, you find it immediately when you enter the Visitor Center parking lot. Immediately adjacent to the Visitor Center is the actual sunken road, which runs along the base of Marye's Heights. The sunken road has recently been closed to traffic, and both the road and the accompanying stone wall have been restored to their 1862 condition. Two of the houses closest to the wall (Brompton House and the

The original section of the stone wall, Fredericksburg, Virginia PHOTO PATRICK FALCI

Innis) are original to the time of the battle. Walking away from the Visitor Center, toward the far end of the road you come to the intersection of Mercer Street. Just beyond is a section of the stone wall that is completely original. My hat goes off to the particular landowners who could easily have removed this wall anytime in the past. The design of the refurbished wall is based on this existing section and is patterned as well after the period photographs taken at the wall. In addition, below the road, the modern wooden fence line to the east now rests on National Park Service property, and eventually the open space in front of Marye's Heights will be enlarged.

The original section of the old stone wall is adjacent to the statue of the "Angel of Marye's Heights" (which is pronounced, by the way, exactly like "Marie" and not "Mary"). This story could have come straight from the pen of a Hollywood scriptwriter but is entirely true. On December 14, with the ground in front of Marye's Heights littered with wounded Federal soldiers, a nineteen-year-old Confederate infantryman named Richard Kirkland loads himself with canteens and moves out in the midst of sporadic musket fire to give aid to the wounded enemy. Men on both sides cease their fire, marveling at the young man whose compassion seems, on that ground, to be so severely out of place. The monument to Kirkland is sculpted by Felix deWeldon, whose more famous work includes the Iwo Jima Memorial near Washington, D.C.

Marye's Heights is now the home of the Fredericksburg National Cemetery. First authorized in 1866, the cemetery holds the remains of more than fifteen thousand Union soldiers, nearly thirteen thousand of whom are unknown. Note the smaller gravestones.

They are numbered twice. The top number represents the grave number, the bottom tells how many men are buried in that particular grave. Even in a National Cemetery, there are mass graves.

The cemetery is the final resting place of two Medal of Honor recipients: First Sergeant William O. Jones, Company A, 73rd New York Infantry, and Lieutenant Colonel Edward Hill, 16th Michigan Infantry. In 1901, Colonel Hill gives the speech at the groundbreaking ceremony for the large monument to the 5th Corps and asks that upon his death his remains be buried near that spot. His wish is granted.

Lafayette Boulevard, which runs in front of the Visitor Center, follows the route of the original Telegraph Road, which divided Marye's Heights from the hill immediately to the south, known then as Telegraph Hill, now called Lee's Hill. The Park Service has a road (Lee Drive) that extends just below the crest of the hill. Take the road all the way to the end, and you will pass through the area where Jackson's men held off the assault from Meade's division. There are noticeable remains of Jackson's trenches. The land out to the left (east) is now a private farm. At the far end of Lee Drive is a stone monument called the Meade Pyramid, indicating the "high-water mark" of Meade's attack.

Following Lee Drive back up to Lee's Hill, you'll note signs leading you up to the crest. If you're in reasonably good physical condition, you can walk the well-groomed trail to the spot where Lee observed the battle. Note the large thirty-pound Parrott cannon. During the attack, as Lee's artillery was shelling the Federal troops below, a duplicate of this gun suddenly exploded near that spot. The bursting gun could easily have killed Lee and some of his senior commanders. Lee and Longstreet, among several others, escaped injury. It's interesting to wonder how history might have been changed on *that* day.

Restored stone wall at Marye's Heights, Fredericksburg, Virginia PHOTO DON PFANZ

One sad note: Avoid looking *behind* you. You'll simply be staring into some private citizen's backyard. During and after the battle, Lee's headquarters was located somewhere behind the crest of the hill, a spot lost to development. As valuable as the Fredericksburg National Battlefield is, Lee's Hill is an outstanding advertisement for the urgent necessity of battlefield preservation.

Ignoring the house to your rear, gaze out toward the town of Fredericksburg. Though the trees immediately in front of you are a constant maintenance issue for the Park Service, you will have a splendid view of the lay of the land, the town itself, and you can see clearly across the Rappahannock River. The distant ridge on the far side of the river is Stafford Heights. This is the position of the extensive Union artillery batteries during the battle (the guns that destroyed much of the town) and is the location as well of Chatham, also known as the Lacy House. Chatham is Burnside's headquarters and well worth the short drive across the river. The house itself is completed in 1771, and the estate originally encompasses nearly thirteen hundred acres of land. Over the course of the war, it serves as headquarters for a number of Union commanders, as a picket post and communications center, as a stable, and as a hospital after the Battle of Fredericksburg. The interior of the house is more or less wrecked by Union soldiers, but the house today is a valued museum and historical site. A number of exhibits offer a view of civilian life at Chatham from the era of the Revolutionary War to the present, and other exhibits examine the Union army's use of the estate. Shortly after the battle, more than 130 soldiers are buried on the grounds near the house, three of whom remain. Today, the property includes eighty-five acres and houses the headquarters of the National Park.

To me, the most valuable aspect of Chatham is the perspective you get by standing outside, on the grounds that face the river. (There are numerous scenes in the book *Gods and Generals* that take place on this ground, and coming here was invaluable to me as a point of research.) Put yourself in the shoes of Burnside and his frustrated commanders in December 1862 as they stare across helplessly at the town they could not reach, knowing that in those hills behind the town, Lee's army is moving into place.

Chancellorsville

The area that can be rightfully described as the battlefield is so large that it spreads today over several square miles of open fields, dense woods, and developed subdivisions. While the Park Service has done an admirable job in securing certain key spots, a great deal of imagination is also required. As you drive westward out of Fredericksburg on what is today Route 3, you are following the route of the Plank Road. Two sites are readily accessible along the way: Salem Church was the site of a stiff fight between Confederate forces and John Sedgwick's Federals. Farther out, Zoan Church marks the high ridgeline that was contested by both sides the morning of May 1, at the time Hooker ordered his men to retreat.

Approximately three miles west of Salem Church lies the site of the first day's battle, which took place on May 1, 1863. On the north side of the highway is a significant piece of land, encompassing 140 acres, that was recently saved from development. The battle was a contentious one and pitted the interests of historical preservation against the interests of private enterprise. In this case history prevailed, but only because of the un-

Jeff at the burial site of Jackson's arm, Ellwood, Virginia
PHOTO PATRICK FALCI

Remains of the Chancellor House, Chancellorsville, Virginia PHOTO PATRICK FALCI

Original photo of what is today the Jackson Shrine
PHOTO COURTESY OF THE LIBRARY OF CONGRESS

precedented cooperation of the public, the preservation community, a proactive county board of supervisors, and an enlightened developer. This story had a happy ending, but this is the sort of battle that will continue on historically valuable land all over the country.

Roughly ten miles west of Fredericksburg is the clearly marked intersection at the site of the Chancellor House, destroyed during the battle. After the war, another structure was built on this spot, but it burned in the 1920s. Since then, the land has been left vacant. Thanks to efforts by local preservation groups, the original footprint of the house has been excavated and is plainly visible now.

If you look across the highway toward the south, you will see a cleared hilltop, roughly a mile in the distance. This is Hazel Grove, where Stuart's cannon played havoc with the mansion; the site is accessible by car.

Roughly a mile west of the site of the Chancellor House is the Chancellorsville Visitor Center. There is a significant monument between the center and the highway showing the spot where Stonewall Jackson fell. Though the monument indicates otherwise, there is no way to know the precise spot. More meaningful to me is a subtle depression that leads eastward away from the center itself. If you go to the Park Service plaque that explains Jackson's accidental wounding, look straight ahead, into the woods. There is a faint trail, and if you walk out that way, look carefully for the remains of an old roadbed. This is the road on which Jackson was riding when the shots from the men of the 18th North Carolina cut him down.

About four miles farther west on Route 3, turn left onto Route 20. You will soon come to Ellwood, also known as the Lacy House. This property is conspicuous for two reasons. Built in the 1790s, this house was visited, coincidentally, by some of the most famous people in American history. Two primary figures from the American Revolution visited here, including the Marquis de Lafayette (during his grand tour of the country in 1824–1825), and Henry "Light Horse Harry" Lee (Robert E.'s father), who lived here for a while. It is said that Light Horse Harry penned his memoirs here after his release from debtor's prison. As was the case with so many similar homes at the time of the Civil War, Ellwood was a hospital and holds particular significance for what is buried in a small cemetery on the property: Stonewall Jackson's amputated arm. Though there has been considerable argument over whether or not the arm should be reunited with its owner (Jackson is buried in Lexington, Virginia), thus far the arm remains undisturbed.

Whether or not Robert E. Lee knew that his father had once made use of the house at Ellwood, what is known is that Lee stopped here himself: on his way to Gettysburg.

The Stonewall Jackson Shrine

FORGIVE ME IF I SEEM UNDULY ATTACHED TO THE VARIOUS ASPECTS of Thomas Jackson's demise, but my first visit to the Jackson Shrine, in 1994, was a powerful source of inspiration for my first book (*Gods and Generals*). Whether you are an admirer of Jackson or not, this place holds an enormously emotional significance to anyone with an interest in the Civil War.

Drive some fifteen miles south of Fredericksburg on Interstate 95, and you'll come to a large brown sign that will direct you to the Jackson Shrine. Follow the signs a few miles along a country road eastward, and you cross railroad tracks at what was once a major rail depot, called Guinea's (or Guiney's) Station. Located a short way past what remains of a rail yard, the Jackson Shrine is a simple wood-frame whitewashed building. The structure was originally an outbuilding to what was once the Chandler Plantation. The plantation house is long gone, but its corners are marked by four short posts in the ground. Walk into the small structure, and you will be met by the graciousness of a park ranger. His or her office serves also as a small bookshop, and the ranger will offer you a tour that will explain exactly what happened here. There are other exhibits in the structure, including a display of medical instruments in a room that was used by Dr. Hunter McGuire as he administered care to his ailing patient. But the ranger will then guide you to the most notable place, and if he or she is as sensitive as the guide who first accompanied me, you will be directed to a small room whose open doorway is guarded by a metal railing, where you may stand for a long moment and simply

Jeff at the Thomas "Stonewall" Jackson Shrine, Guinea Station, Virginia
PHOTO PATRICK FALCI

absorb what you see. Note the bed frame, the blanket on the bed, and the clock on the mantelpiece. All are original and were in this room on May 10, 1863. To anyone with a sensitivity to key moments in history, especially in the American Civil War, this place is unsurpassed. This is the room in which Thomas "Stonewall" Jackson died. His final words fill the silence, the empty space:

"Let us cross over the river, and rest under the shade of the trees."

CHAPTER FOUR

GETTYSBURG

Gettysburg, Pennsylvania

JULY 1–3, 1863

WHAT HAPPENED HERE

*W*ith the Federal army remaining close to Fredericksburg, Lee knew that he could not repeat the kind of quick, spearhead advance into Maryland he had attempted the year before (which had resulted in the Battle of Antietam). Lee knew that the Union command was in shambles and the Union army completely demoralized after Chancellorsville. It was logical that Washington would insist that any new Federal strategy include what had been the main focus of Burnside's original plan. Thus, it was entirely likely that the Army of the Potomac would aim once again for Richmond. Once Lee finalized his strategy for another invasion of the North, he knew he could not simply march away and ignore the Federal threat.

After the death of Jackson, Lee reorganized his army into three corps, under Generals James Longstreet, Richard Ewell, and A. P. Hill, a total of about eighty thousand men. As his troops began to mobilize for the march once more across the Potomac, he left A. P. Hill's Corps on Marye's Heights to keep an eye on the Federals, who were still camped near the Rappahannock River. Hill's presence might convince the Union commanders that the rebels were just sitting still, which could give the rest of Lee's army a considerable head start on his march northward. But such secrecy was not to be.

For most of the war, Confederate cavalry had far outclassed its opponents, the Union commanders seemingly uninterested in using their horsemen for much more than guarding supply trains. Thus, it was an unexpected tactic from the Federal command when a large force of cavalry probed Lee's positions north and west of Fredericksburg, to verify the rumors that Lee was marching northward yet again. The order came from Joe Hooker, one of his final and most effective decisions made as commander of the Army of the Potomac. (The irony, of course, is that if Hooker had used a significant cavalry screen to probe for Lee's position before and during the Battle of Chancellorsville, it is unlikely that Jackson's surprise flank attack would have been a surprise at all.) On June 9, 1863, the Federal cavalry, under Alfred Pleasanton, surprised his nemesis Jeb Stuart at what became known as the Battle of Brandy Station, the largest cavalry engagement of the entire war. The result was essentially a draw, but the Confederate horsemen absorbed twice as many losses. The fact that his cavalry had been caught so completely unaware was a serious embarrassment to Stuart, who had made much of his reputation as the most celebrated horseman in either army. Though the battle seriously wounded Stuart's pride, the fight gave Joe Hooker something much more valuable: concrete information that the bulk of Lee's army was well away from Fredericksburg and was moving north.

Though Hooker still favored a quick march southward toward Richmond, he couldn't simply ignore Lee's army. In Washington, it was obvious that the sudden change in Confederate strategy meant that Lee's forces could pose a significant threat to the capital. Hooker conceded that Richmond would have to wait. Throughout mid-June, as Lee marched his army toward Maryland, Hooker gave his final orders as commander and began to shift his army so as to protect a nervous Washington, D.C.

The vanguard of Lee's army crossed the Potomac River on June 15, and soon the rest of the Army of Northern Virginia gathered near Hagerstown, Maryland. Once again their movements were screened by South Mountain, and once again they had their eyes focused on a march into Pennsylvania.

The end came for Hooker on June 27. With Lee renewing his threat to northern cities, Washington would not rely on a man who had shown no backbone for a serious confrontation. Among ranking Union officers, the consensus favored Major General John Reynolds to be Hooker's successor. Despite Reynolds's clear-cut qualifications for the job, he was viewed by official Washington as a man with political ambition who might use the position to speak out against Lincoln's policies, a charge that few in the army took seri-

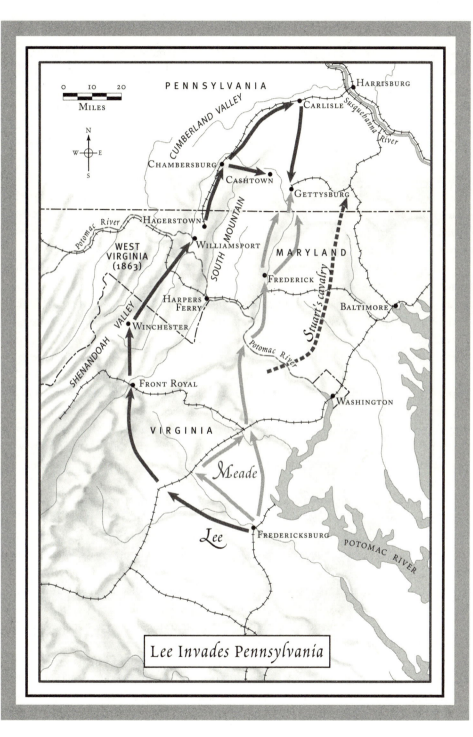

Lee Invades Pennsylvania

ously. Despite the army's support of Reynolds, the choice more amenable to Washington was the distinctly apolitical George Meade. Meade was a chronically short-tempered man, quick with a sharp tongue, and though he was respected by his troops, he was not especially well liked by many of his (new) subordinates. Meade himself was surprised by the appointment and was not overly eager to accept the new assignment. He agreed with some of the men around him that there were others better qualified for the job. But Meade also knew his duty, so with a possible crisis looming, he quickly accepted the responsibility.

Unlike Burnside, who sought out less challenging options, Meade could not afford the luxury of time. He had no choice but to protect the capital, while at the same time he had to make every effort to figure out just what Lee was up to. With uncharacteristic speed, the Federal army matched Lee's northward march, Meade keeping the Federal forces between South Mountain and Washington.

Lee had every reason for optimism. Jefferson Davis shared his belief that another hard push into Pennsylvania would accomplish a great deal toward ending the war. Once again, Lee could feed his army from the unspoiled farmlands of the Cumberland Valley, and if he could push his men to the Susquehanna River, that valley would lie open to him as well. His options would increase every mile he marched into Pennsylvania and he could create panic in the minds of the U.S. Congress, the fear that even if Lee bypassed the capital, he might lay waste to Harrisburg, Baltimore, or even Philadelphia. If there was to be a great last-ditch battle to save the Union, there could be bloody devastation not only in the fields, but in towns and cities that had, until now, been spared the graphic horrors of war. Another option for Lee was that by cutting the major rail lines north of Washington, he could isolate the capital, ensuring outright chaos in the city. Lee might end the war without firing a shot. To both Lee and Jefferson Davis, this time, the advantages were all on their side. Except one.

Jeb Stuart had been ordered to keep a close eye on Meade's army and to report any significant movements to Lee. Stuart knew that he was Lee's "eyes and ears" and that if a major battle was to take place, the added power and mobility of Stuart's eight thousand cavalrymen could make all the difference. On June 24, Stuart led three brigades of his men eastward, where they quickly located the rear of Meade's army. But instead of keeping himself between the two armies, as Lee had hoped, Stuart pushed his men farther, until he was on the far eastern side of Meade's line of march. From this point on, there is considerable debate and speculation about what Stuart was trying to do. On two previous occasions, Stuart had led his cavalry completely around the Union army, great glorious escapades that had embarrassed Union commanders and put Stuart's name prominently into newspapers in both the North and South. It is entirely likely that by making such a triumphant ride now, he would embarrass the enemy once again and redeem himself for his humiliating failures at Brandy Station.

Stuart put his men to good work, cutting Meade's supply train, capturing a considerable haul of wagons and several hundred Union prisoners. In addition, he rattled the Federal flanks by making potshot skirmishes along their routes of march. But the spoils captured from these "victories" gave Stuart encumbrances that slowed him down. Meade was marching northward far more efficiently than the Confederates had reason to expect. Thus, when Stuart knew he should be reporting Meade's movements to Lee, his horsemen were trapped on the far side of Meade's army. There was simply no way Stuart could get word to his commander without passing a courier straight through the Army of the Potomac. Stuart had no choice but to leave Lee in the dark, while the Confederate cavalryman figured out how his men could best get back to where Lee needed them to be.

Though Lee was uncertain just where Meade's army was, he ordered Ewell's troops to push onward to the banks of the Susquehanna River, putting Confederate forces just downriver from Harrisburg. If possible, Ewell was to cross the river and make every effort to seize the city. Lee would follow with Longstreet and Hill, supporting Ewell's movements. What Lee did not know was that, on the opposite side of South Mountain, Meade was aiming for Harrisburg as well.

Lee's blindness was cleared up for a brief moment by an unlikely source. On June 28, a civilian spy employed by Longstreet reported that Meade's army was moving exactly parallel to the Confederates and had gathered close to the town of Frederick, Maryland. The report surprised Lee, who hoped that the Union forces might still be south of the Potomac River. Lee realized that if Meade continued to move northward, Ewell's corps, now close to Harrisburg, could be cut off and crushed by the Federal army. Lee began to gather his forces, and he ordered his army to shift eastward, through the South Mountain passes. Ewell's plan to capture Harrisburg was called off, and a frustrated Ewell pulled his men away from the banks of the Susquehanna and began to move south, to unite his forces with the rest of Lee's army. Now in unfamiliar country, and still without the eyes of Stuart, Lee had to rely on maps, which showed an extensive network of good roads converging on one small town, which sat like the hub of a wagon wheel, a natural location for pulling his army together from its scattered position. The town was Gettysburg.

On June 30, 1863, Cashtown Pass, just west of Gettysburg, was occupied by a division of A. P. Hill's corps, under the command of Major General Henry Heth. Heth's patrols into Gettysburg had indicated the presence of supplies, including a warehouse, which supposedly contained shoes. But Heth's scouts had also sighted Union cavalry. Heth's commander, A. P. Hill, approved a plan for Heth to lead a much stronger reconnaissance force into the town the next morning.

The Union cavalry was commanded by Brigadier General John Buford, who arrived in Gettysburg and immediately realized its value as a concentration point. Buford realized as well that there was a great wave of Confederate troops moving in his direction. With barely two brigades of cavalry at his disposal, Buford made a quick assessment of the lay of the land and moved his men out to the north and west of Gettysburg, to hold back whatever Confederate force might attempt to occupy the town. Buford knew what Lee did not: Several miles behind Buford, on the roads that approached from the south, was the entire Army of the Potomac.

Meade, who was nearly fifteen miles south of Gettysburg, had not expected his army to reach the town in time to prepare for a major engagement. Knowing that Lee was so close, Meade felt that the Federal troops should make a stand well south, a good defensive position around a place called Pipe Creek. But Buford saw the opportunity that Gettysburg offered, a strong ridge of high ground that spread from north to south along the eastern edge of the town itself. Buford's challenge would be to hold off Heth's Confederates long enough for the Federal infantry to occupy the good ground.

The Union 1st Corps, under John Reynolds, was only a short distance below the town when Buford's fight began. Buford's cavalry had an advantage of confronting the rebels with breech-loading carbines, and though greatly outnumbered by Heth's infantry, they held up the rebels just long enough for Reynolds's infantry to reinforce them.

Lee had been quite adamant that he was not yet ready for a general engagement at Gettysburg and had been reassured that Heth's foray into the town would brush aside whatever small force of cavalry they would find there. By late morning, Lee could hear much more than a skirmish coming from the town, and when reports reached Lee that Union infantry was reinforcing the Federal cavalry, Lee knew that, like it or not, a general engagement was just what he was getting. Lee ordered Ewell, who was approaching Gettysburg from the north, to hasten his march and confront the Union forces, troops who were already in a sharp fight around the northwest corner of the town.

As Reynolds moved his infantry into position, the fight grew hotter. Despite the extraordinary effort by both Buford and Reynolds, the fresh Union infantry was confronting an enemy on two sides, an enemy whose numbers continued to grow. With men falling around him, Reynolds continued to shift troops into position, attempting to stem the rebel tide. Reynolds knew that directly behind his 1st Corps, Oliver Howard's 11th Corps was fast approaching. Despite the dismal reputation the 11th had earned for their collapse at Chancellorsville, here, the 11th might save the day. The Union right flank was feeling severe pressure from the north, and if the 11th could be put into position to the right of the 1st Corps's bloody fight, they might prevent Reynolds's men from being annihilated. As Reynolds rode along his lines, encouraging his men, he was suddenly struck in the back of the head by a musket ball and tumbled out of his saddle. On the eve of the greatest confrontation of the war, the Union army's finest field commander had been killed.

Though the death of Reynolds sent a hard shock wave through the Union lines, they continued the fight, the 1st and newly arrived 11th holding off an ever growing wave of

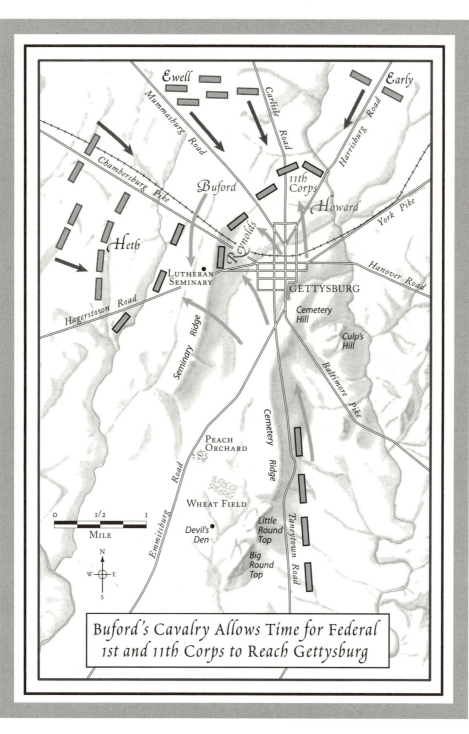

Ewell

Early

Carlisle Road

Mummasburg Road

Harrisburg Road

Chambersburg Pike

Buford

11th Corps

York Pike

Howard

Heth

Reynolds

Hagerstown Road

Lutheran Seminary

Hanover Road

GETTYSBURG

Cemetery Hill

Culp's Hill

Seminary Ridge

Baltimore Pike

Peach Orchard

Cemetery Ridge

0   1/2   1
MILE

N
W—E
S

Emmitsburg Road

Wheat Field

Devil's Den

Little Round Top

Big Round Top

Taneytown Road

**Buford's Cavalry Allows Time for Federal
1st and 11th Corps to Reach Gettysburg**

rebel troops. The fight ebbed and flowed all across the undulating ridges and patches of woodlands, tearing great gaps in the lines of both sides. But greater numbers of Confederates continued to push down from the north, and finally, by late afternoon, the Federal troops gave way. Faced with no alternative, Oliver Howard ordered his 11th to pull back, which exposed the flank of the 1st Corps, now under the command of Abner Doubleday. Doubleday had no choice but to follow Howard's retreat. As the blue-coated troops pulled back through the town itself, they brought the rebels with them, both sides pressing toward the imposing high ground that lay east of the town. The exhausted rebels could not prevent the Federal troops from withdrawing up the high hills and ridgelines that John Buford had done so much to preserve. As the beaten Federals made their way up the slopes, they were startled to see fresh troops meeting them at the crests, earthworks already under construction, Slocum's 12th Corps quickly filling the new defensive position. Behind Slocum came the 2nd Corps, Hancock's men, Hancock himself instructing his troops on how to prepare their position. As darkness came, the fight ended.

The fight on July 1 had been a distinct southern victory, and once again the 11th Corps had been the weak link in the Federal army's chain. Though Lee had insisted that Ewell continue his forward movement, with daylight fading, Ewell decided against an attack directly on the Union high ground, a decision his subordinates immediately condemned. With the guns growing silent, Lee didn't need the eyes of Jeb Stuart to tell him what he was facing. In the deepening dusk of July 1, he could see for himself that the entire Army of the Potomac was gathering on the high ridge east of Gettysburg.

Meade did not arrive until very late that night, but in a farmhouse that would become his new headquarters, he was assured by Hancock that the best place to make a fight was exactly where it had been made and where the Union troops now held the high ground.

Before dawn on July 2, Lee had a difficult decision put before him. As his army spread along a ridgeline just west of Gettysburg called Seminary Ridge, a mile away, the Army of the Potomac was digging in, and it was apparent that Meade had no intention of going anywhere else. Longstreet strongly advised Lee that the Confederate forces should make a decisive move to the south of Gettysburg and place themselves directly between the Union position and Washington. In Longstreet's eyes, the impact of such a move might accomplish exactly what Lee had intended from the start: to put so much fear into the capital that both the Congress and possibly Abraham Lincoln would feel the pressure to sue for peace. Whether or not Lee seriously considered Longstreet's strategy is a subject of considerable speculation, but one definite problem with moving his army away from Gettysburg was that Lee was still without the eyes of Stuart's cavalry and would be plodding headlong through unknown countryside. No matter how sound Longstreet's strategy might be, Lee would be unable to keep close tabs on Meade or on any other forces that might gather in their path. Lee made his decision. Meade's army seemed to be digging in for a fight, so Lee would give him one. If the Confederate forces prevailed, there would no longer be any argument about what to do next. In all likelihood, the war would be over.

The Union position now resembled a fishhook, the northern end curved around two large hills close to the town, straightening out into a line that trailed away to the south. Lee's strategy on July 2 consisted of two primary attacks, one on either end of the Union position. Longstreet was ordered to make a large-scale attack on the right, the Union left flank, which was thought to be in the vicinity of a large wheat field. Longstreet's scouts were unsure exactly where the attack should fall, and in an attempt to keep his troop movements hidden from Union observers, Longstreet consumed most of the day in preparation. When he finally put his men into action, the actual point of Longstreet's attack was determined for him, the result of an extraordinary blunder made by Union general Dan Sickles.

In the early morning hours of July 2, Sickles's 3rd Corps was at the extreme end of the Union left flank. Sickles was awaiting additional troops to extend his lines southward (mainly the 5th Corps, which was just now coming onto the field) when he suddenly decided to take matters into his own hands. Ignoring Meade's instructions on the placement of his corps, Sickles advanced his men nearly three-quarters of a mile forward and occupied what he saw as a crest of slightly higher ground that ran just west of the same wheat field Lee had seen and continued into an adjacent peach orchard. Sickles anchored his left flank in an area known as Devil's Den, a low patch of ground strewn with gargantuan boulders. The new position created a fat bulge on that end of the Union position, which lay directly in the path Longstreet would attack.

Longstreet has been blamed for petulance and a purposeful delay in getting his troops into position, debates that rage to this day. Regardless of his motives or his attitude, his attacks did not begin until four o'clock in the afternoon. A vicious fight soon swirled around Sickles's position, the men of the 3rd Corps engulfed in some of the most violent and costly fighting of the war. Both sides attacked and counterattacked, the lines wavering, then recovering, sections of the orchard, the wheat field, and the rocks of Devil's Den changing hands more than once. Eventually, Longstreet succeeded in pushing Sickles back, opening up a breach to the right of the peach orchard that threatened to cut the entire Union position in two. In response, Winfield Hancock put in troops from his 2nd Corps, preventing Longstreet's men from pouring through the gaps. By sealing the gap, Hancock prevented Sickles from being cut off from the rest of Meade's army, which likely prevented the 3rd Corps from being destroyed.

Immediately behind Sickles's position were two prominent hills, the hills that Meade had ordered Sickles to occupy in the first place. To the south, the larger, thickly

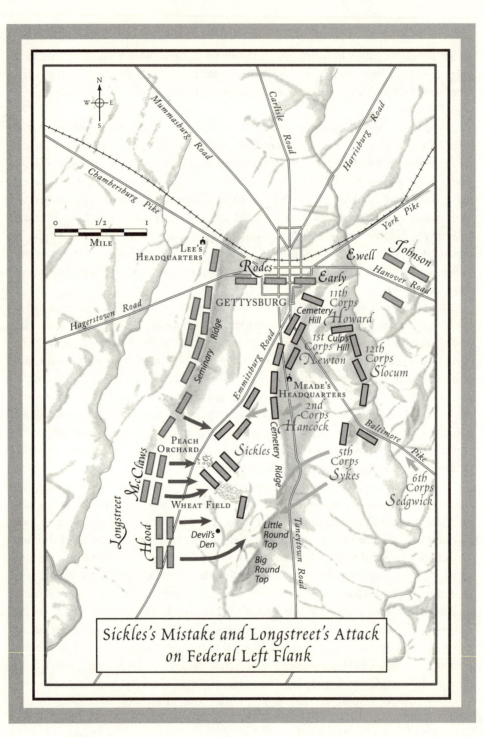

N
W   E
S

Mummasburg Road

Carlisle Road

Harrisburg Road

Chambersburg Pike

York Pike

0   1/2   1
MILE

LEE'S
HEADQUARTERS

Rodes

Early

Ewell

Johnson

Hanover Road

Hagerstown Road

GETTYSBURG

11th
Corps

Cemetery
Hill

Howard

Seminary Ridge

Emmitsburg Road

1st
Corps

Culp's
Hill

Newton

12th
Corps
Slocum

MEADE'S
HEADQUARTERS

2nd
Corps
Hancock

Cemetery Ridge

Baltimore Pike

McClaws

PEACH
ORCHARD

Sickles

5th
Corps
Sykes

6th
Corps
Sedgwick

Longstreet

WHEAT FIELD

Hood

Devil's
Den

Little
Round
Top

Big
Round
Top

Taneytown Road

Sickles's Mistake and Longstreet's Attack on Federal Left Flank

wooded hill was called Round Top, and the smaller, bare hill blanketed with large rocks was known as the Rocky Hill, or Little Round Top. To the enormous credit of Longstreet's subordinates, including most notably John Bell Hood, it was observed that Sickles's salient had left the two hills vacant. Hood could see that control of that high ground meant that the Union position might be encircled from the south, threatening Meade's entire line. As the fight continued in Devil's Den, some of Hood's men shifted just far enough to the right to press their advance directly toward the two unoccupied hills.

The importance of the two Round Tops was noticed as well by Union general Gouverneur K. Warren, who was Meade's chief engineer. Standing on Little Round Top, Warren was observing the fight below him in Devil's Den when he saw Hood's men making their way toward the hills. Warren responded immediately by ordering a brigade of the 5th Corps, under Colonel Strong Vincent, to occupy Little Round Top. As Vincent's men

Devil's Den, 1863, Gettysburg, Pennsylvania PHOTO COURTESY OF THE LIBRARY OF CONGRESS

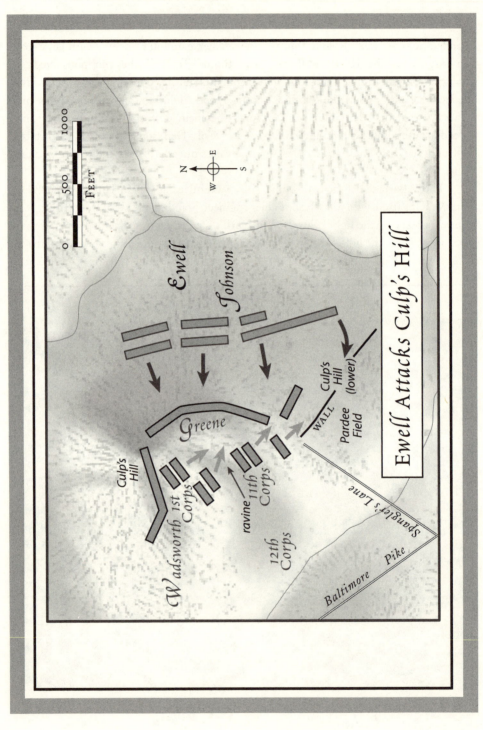

Ewell Attacks Culp's Hill

hurried into position, the last unit in line was the 20th Maine Regiment, under the command of a former college professor, Colonel Joshua Lawrence Chamberlain. As Chamberlain's men filed into position on the end of the line, they were told to hold that position "at all costs." The Maine troops were barely in place when they were attacked by determined Alabamans under the command of Colonel William Oates. Oates pushed his men up the hill in five separate attacks, each time threatening to break Chamberlain's tenuous hold on the flank. The fighting all along the crest of Little Round Top quickly took an enormous toll, including Strong Vincent himself. Despite the rough ground and the July heat, Hood's men seemed destined to turn the Union flank and sweep the Federal soldiers off the critical high ground.

As the 20th Maine struggled to hold back the Alabamans, both sides were taking heavy casualties. Chamberlain's men, their line stretched thin, seemed on the verge of collapse. Chamberlain anticipated that the Alabamans were just as exhausted as his own men, and with the Maine soldiers nearly out of ammunition, Chamberlain ordered his men to fix bayonets and charge down the hill. The unexpected tactic so stunned the weary

View of Little Round Top, July 1863, Gettysburg, Pennsylvania
PHOTO COURTESY OF THE LIBRARY OF CONGRESS

Confederates, and so energized the Union regiments to Chamberlain's right, that the rebels were swept completely off the face of Little Round Top.

Though Sickles's maneuver had nearly caused the destruction of the Federal left flank, the fight now wound down, and the 3rd Corps was finally withdrawn to a safer position, strengthened by the 5th and 2nd on either side. Hood's attack on the Confederate right had exhausted itself in the heat and amazingly rugged terrain, and Hood himself had been severely wounded. Because of the work of men like Warren, Vincent, Hancock, and Chamberlain and the extraordinary efforts of a great many more Union heroes, what had nearly been a Federal disaster had instead become a stunning success.

But the fight on July 2 was nowhere near concluded.

On the opposite end of the line, Lee had ordered a reluctant Dick Ewell to assault the right flank of the Union position on Culp's Hill, with the qualification that Ewell attack only if he felt he could succeed in capturing the hill. Even if the hill was too strongly defended, at the very least Ewell was to offer assistance to Longstreet's efforts by making a sizable demonstration against Culp's Hill, to prevent Union troops from that end of the line from being sent to their far flank to reinforce against Longstreet's assault. Nearly two hours after Longstreet's attack began, Ewell launched his own attack on Culp's Hill. But

Little Round Top, position of the 20th Maine, Gettysburg, Pennsylvania   PHOTO PATRICK FALCI

Battered trees on Culp's Hill, 1863, Gettysburg, Pennsylvania
PHOTO COURTESY OF THE LIBRARY OF CONGRESS

because Ewell had delayed, Union troops from Henry Slocum's 12th Corps had already been pulled off the hill and sent toward the far end of the line.

Culp's Hill was in reality two hills, one tall peak and a shorter one, connected by a narrow saddle. Late on July 2, with the full-scale fight raging on the far end of the Union lines, the peaks were defended by only one Union brigade. The brigade was commanded by the oldest general officer in the Army of the Potomac, sixty-two-year-old Brigadier General George Greene. Greene, a descendant of Revolutionary War hero Nathanael Greene, was beloved by his men, and as a holdover from the regular army, he ws a considerable taskmaster. True to form, Greene had ordered his men to construct a stout log wall that most of them considered a waste of time and effort. As Ewell's men began their assault, Greene's forces were considerably outnumbered and, after a vicious fight, were pushed off the lower peak. Greene then withdrew his small force up to the safety of their log works on the higher peak. With the Union right flank engulfed by a far larger number of rebel troops, darkness began to fall. But Ewell's attack did not stop. Unwisely, the rebels continued their assault, relying on the lay of the land to guide their advances. But Greene's log wall was now the best friend the Union soldiers had, and in the confusion of the darkness, the rebels did as much damage to one another as they did to Greene's battered brigade. As the fight finally faded away, Greene's men hugged their tall peak, knowing that barely a hundred yards away, the lower peak was in rebel hands.

To Greene's enormous relief, the Federal soldiers on Culp's Hill had not been forgotten, and during the night, they were strongly reinforced. The Confederates close by were reinforced as well, both sides anticipating a renewed attack on July 3.

During the night of July 2, Meade had a council of war with his primary commanders. The cautious Meade was concerned that the proper course might be to withdraw from Gettysburg and meet Lee's army on more desirable ground. Meade was likely reacting to the horrific losses his army had endured, including the deaths of a great many outstanding field officers. But the losses were shared by both sides, and none of the Federal corps commanders believed that the Federal army should leave. If there was to be another day's fighting, it would come on this same ground.

To the west, Lee's army licked their wounds as well and contemplated all those who had been lost. The dead included William Barksdale, whose men had done such good work at Fredericksburg. And though he survived the day, John Bell Hood lost the use of his left arm. In Lee's camp, there was one reason for muted rejoicing: Jeb Stuart had finally arrived. Though many in Lee's command, including Longstreet, believed Stuart should have been severely reprimanded for his failure to keep Lee informed, Lee welcomed Stuart with only a brief chastisement, knowing that Stuart's cavalry could still make the difference in a hotly contested fight.

Early on July 3, Lee ordered Ewell to resume his attack on Culp's Hill, while at the same time, units from Longstreet's and Hill's corps would assault what Lee assumed to be the weakest point in the Union position: the center. Despite Longstreet's vigorous objections, Lee ordered three divisions, under George Pickett, Isaac Trimble, and James Johnston Pettigrew, to prepare to make a direct attack that Lee believed would cut right through the heart of the enemy's position. The attack would be opened first by an enormous blaze of artillery fire, every available gun aimed at the location where the Confederates would direct their assault. Lee was convinced that the devastating fire would destroy whatever Union artillery could support that portion of the line and might so demoralize the Federal troops there that there would be little resistance remaining. Should Pickett, Trimble, and Pettigrew force a solid breakthrough in the Union center, reinforcements could pour through the breach, thus dividing the Army of the Potomac into two chaotically unorganized mobs. In the same way Stonewall Jackson had routed the Federals at Chancellorsville, Meade's army might be swept away.

On July 3, 1863, at four o'clock in the morning, Ewell's men began to stir expectantly, facing their enemy on Culp's Hill. They did not realize that during the night, the Federal reinforcements included not only men, but a considerable force of artillery from other parts of the Union line, now trained on their position. Before Ewell had time to give the order, the Union commanders beat him to it, and well before daylight, thunderous artillery blasts began to decimate the rebel positions on the lower peak of Culp's Hill. But the artillery alone could not drive the rebels away, and with the dawn, the infantry on both sides began their fight. The battle poured out over the ridges and the saddle of Culp's Hill until eleven in the morning. It was the longest sustained fight of the entire three-day battle. But there were too many Union troops now for the Confederates to push away, and when the guns grew quiet, Ewell's men limped back to their original position below the hill. Both peaks of Culp's Hill were again firmly in Federal hands.

With no activity now on either Union flank, Meade's commanders had time to shift their positions, filling and strengthening gaps along their entire line. The men who occupied the center of the Union position rested along a line of shallow trenches, while behind them, the crews who manned the Union artillery batteries went about the routine maintenance of their guns. Farther back lay Meade's headquarters, and spread out in all directions were the field hospitals, which were seething with the wounded men from the fight the day before. From first light, the men in the Union center had heard only the sounds of the fight at Culp's Hill, most believing that the rest of the day might pass with no other action at all. At approximately one p.m., they were severely shaken out of their complacency. Across the open ground along the rebel positions, puffs of smoke suddenly appeared, and in short seconds, the air above the Federals seemed to tear open, long hollow shrieks followed by bursts of dirt and fire. More blasts followed, all variety of screams, tumbling lead, whistling shells, the ground behind the Union lines rising up in a thunderous fog that destroyed guns and wagons and the men who stood near.

The cannon were under the command of Colonel Edward Porter Alexander, Lee's fine artillery officer, whose guns had performed with such perfect execution at Fredericksburg. Under Alexander's supervision, some 160 cannon directed their fire on Union artillery batteries as well as a piece of ground in the Union center not quite half a mile wide. The order given Alexander was simple: Destroy anything that might put up a defense to the rebel assault. The artillery barrage lasted for nearly two hours, until Alexander felt he had used up too much of his available ammunition. When it ended, with the dense clouds of white smoke drifting off the field, the Union troops across the way began to peer up out of their shelters, wondering what was next. At that moment, along the tree-covered crest of the ridge that protected Lee's troops, nearly thirteen thousand men emerged in battle lines. As the Union troops stared in amazement, flickers of colors dotted the solid gray line, battle flags caught by a gentle breeze. There was more movement now, officers moving out in front of their men, and then a faint ripple of motion, driven by orders the Fed-

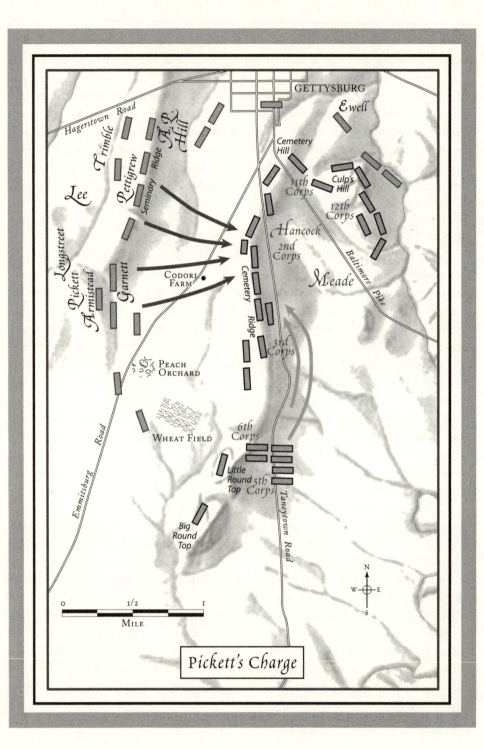

GETTYSBURG

Ewell

Hagerstown Road

Cemetery
Hill

11th
Corps

Culp's
Hill

Seminary Ridge

A. P. Hill

Trimble

12th
Corps

Lee

Pettigrew

Hancock
2nd
Corps

Meade

Baltimore Pike

Longstreet

Garnett

Codori
Farm

Pickett

Armistead

Cemetery Ridge

3rd
Corps

Peach
Orchard

Wheat Field

6th
Corps

Little
Round
Top

5th
Corps

Emmitsburg Road

Taneytown Road

Big
Round
Top

N
W · E
S

0   1/2   1
MILE

Pickett's Charge

eral troops could not hear. As the blue-coated troops scrambled for their muskets, their officers drawing swords and pistols, a mile away, the massive line began to move forward.

Their goal was plainly evident to the Confederates and their commanders: a copse of trees that seemed to anchor the center of the Union position. Though the three divisions would begin their march across a mile front, they would compact as they crossed the open ground, driving a hammer blow into a narrow section of the Union position.

That was Lee's intention. The reality was that Pickett, Trimble, and Pettigrew had to send their men across nearly a mile of wide-open ground, which was bisected by a fence-lined road that would slow the advance even further. There were other realities as well. Though Alexander's artillery had destroyed a good many Federal batteries, Lee did not realize that much of Alexander's fire had overshot their targets in the Union center. Most of the shell fire had come down far behind the troops who manned the front lines, troop positions Lee had expected to be obliterated. Though hospitals had been shattered by the blasts, and Meade's headquarters had to be evacuated, the dense troop concentrations on both sides of the copse of trees were still intact. In addition, Alexander's barrage had not been matched by a Federal response. Lee could have assumed that the enemy's guns had simply been destroyed. But Union artillery commander Henry Hunt had kept his guns silent for a reason. Hunt knew that such a sustained artillery attack from the rebels meant that an infantry assault would follow. In response, the Federal guns would be well stocked with ammunition.

The panorama that opened up across the field from the Federal side was spectacular, a perfect parade ground display. As the Confederates stepped forward, they began to shift their brigade positions, textbook maneuvers to draw their forces into a tighter, more condensed formation. The Federal troops who stared in utter amazement did not have long to reflect on what they were seeing. It was time for the Federal cannon to begin a barrage of their own. Hunt's guns began to take aim at the mass of men rolling slowly toward them, and the effect was immediate and devastating. Great gaps were blown in the rebel lines, the men pushing forward through a fog of fire and smoke. After several minutes, Lee's troops reached the Emmitsburg Road, where the fences had to be pulled down, causing the entire assault to pause, while they still absorbed the Union artillery fire. As the Confederate troops made their way across the road, the ground began to rise, so they had to climb. They fought through a new storm now, canister fire, bursts of shrapnel, splinters of hot metal that ripped great holes in the rebel lines. Still they pushed on, up the gentle sloping hill, the final four hundred yards to the low stone wall that protected the Union riflemen. Now those muskets added their fire to the artillery, a perfect storm of destruction that ripped the heart out of the rebel advance, men tumbling down in vast waves across the entire length of the assault. On either end of the rebel lines, men began to see movement out in the open fields on their flanks, columns of Federal troops marching at the double quick, forming lines of their own. Those who could hear anything at all might have heard quick shouted orders from blue-coated officers, followed by sheets of musket fire. The enfilade fire withered the flanks of the Confederate formations that were growing smaller by the second.

As they continued the slow climb toward the Union positions, the rebels could see that on the low stone wall, in the shallow trenches, the Union muskets were packed thick. No great opening had been blasted by Alexander's cannon, no weak point waited for them at all. Instead, the Union officers had pushed reinforcements into line, musket fire now pouring down the hill from rows of Union troops two and three deep. But the rebels kept moving forward, guided through the smoke by the slope of the hillside, led by men whose unimaginable bravery would cost them their lives, men like Lewis Armistead and Richard Brooke Garnett. Armistead would lead them as far as any senior officer would go, the Confederate general stepping up and over the low stone wall. He put his hand on a cannon, caught his breath, perhaps, and turned, calling for his men to use their bayonets; then he was shot down, like so many of the men behind him. Though few officers remained to lead them, the men made breakthroughs in several places along the line, small bubbles of Confederate gray bursting through. But there was no breach, each small victory swallowed up, engulfed by a new wave of blue, more reserves, and too many muskets. The attack simply died out, the rebels who reached the wall dissolving away, some, amazingly, surviving only to be captured. As the guns and muskets grew silent, the smoke drifted away, and the fury drained out of exhausted men on both sides, who stared into one another's faces with the shock and stunned disbelief of what they had just endured. And it had taken barely half an hour.

Lee observed the assault from a perch at the edge of the open ground, and as the smoke drifted away, he could see his men retreating, barely half as many as had begun the attack. In a moment of supreme despair, Lee rode out and met them as they stumbled and dragged themselves and their wounded comrades back to safety. He made some attempt to rally them, told them in a plaintive cry that it was all his fault. But Lee was still the commander, and no matter what his tactics had done to these men, he forced himself to focus on the Union lines, the copse of trees, the place where he believed they would find victory. He had to believe that Meade would do what any good commander would do, that the Federal troops would counterattack, make perfect use of their victory. But few who moved toward him heard Lee's words. Many of those same men had been witness to the horrors of Fredericksburg, a horror they had inflicted on the men in blue. Now the tide had turned, some of them having just heard the cry up along the Union lines, men in blue screaming at them with vengeance in their voices:

"Fredericksburg!"

There had been no joy in the cry, no pleasure. It was simply a reminder to the men on both sides that yesterday's slaughter is today's victory. No matter the senselessness of what they had been ordered to do, and no matter that they had done this all before. Every man knew that it was in their hearts to do it all again.

By nightfall, Lee understood that there was no more fight to be made on this ground, that his valiant effort to end the war by driving a hard spear into the North had ended in failure. As a torrential rain opened up on the devastation of the battlefield, the Confederates sent their astonishing number of wounded away on every wagon they could find. It was a wagon train nearly seventeen miles long. Lee ordered his army to follow, to make their way back through Maryland yet again, back to the crossings along the Potomac.

While the three Confederate divisions were being virtually destroyed against the Union defenses, Stuart's cavalry had fought a major engagement with Federal horsemen far out to the east of Gettysburg. The fight had no great significance, no effect on the outcome of the battle. As Lee withdrew his forces, Stuart had a new responsibility, far more important than some duel for the honor of his cavalry. He was to serve as the rear guard, protecting Lee's men from what Lee still believed to be the inevitable Federal pursuit. To add to Lee's despair, when he reached the banks of the Potomac, he could see that the continuing rains had swelled the river so that Lee's army could not cross. Every day they expected a mass of Federal forces to appear, pressing them back against the banks of the river. They remembered the retreat from Sharpsburg, when McClellan had them desperately vulnerable and could have destroyed them as they struggled to cross the Potomac. For ten agonizing days, Lee waited for the Potomac to grow calmer, until finally his men could make their escape. And like McClellan, Meade did not come.

WHY IS THIS BATTLE IMPORTANT?

*A*s Lee returns to Virginia, the cost of what happened at Gettysburg reverberates throughout the entire nation. Almost immediately there are those who understand that what was once a virtually unknown crossroads in southern Pennsylvania is now the site of the Civil War's greatest catastrophe. In three days, more than fifty thousand men are killed, wounded, or missing, nearly 60 percent of them Confederates.

Meade finally pushes forward a toothless pursuit of Lee's army, but he is soundly criticized for not cutting Lee off from the Potomac and taking advantage of the Confederate vulnerability on the muddy roads. What the armchair generals cannot realize is that the Federal army is nearly as shattered as the men they vanquished from the field. Besides the extraordinary loss in men, equipment, and horses, Meade's entire command structure has suffered and is weakened nearly as badly as Lee's. In Meade's army, one corps commander (Reynolds) is dead, and two others, Sickles and Hancock, are seriously wounded.

Those who are quick to blame Meade for his sluggishness should understand that in *victory*, Meade has lost 31 percent of his army. In *defeat* at Waterloo, Napoleon lost only 18 percent.

Every house, church, and building in the Gettysburg area has become a makeshift hospital, staffed mostly by untrained volunteers who can do little else but listen to the cries of the wounded until a doctor should happen to find them. The ground itself is strewn with bodies for weeks after the battle, those hastily buried in shallow graves unearthed almost immediately by the torrential rains. The carcasses of horses poison every stream, and the smells make the town almost uninhabitable.

While the cast of characters includes hundreds of notable heroes, certain names survive the battle to find long-lived acclaim. On the Union side, George Greene, the man who saved Culp's Hill, does not receive nearly the attention accorded the savior of the Union's other flank, Joshua Chamberlain. Of the sixty-two men who receive the Medal of Honor, Chamberlain, the college professor from Maine, becomes the most celebrated for his role in holding off Hood's Confederates on Little Round Top. Nearly 150 years later, Chamberlain is overwhelmingly regarded by the public as one of the North's most valiant heroes, despite the efforts of some detractors who seek to label him a self-promoter.

John Buford is given credit as the man who chose the ground and John Reynolds as the man who made sure the ground could be held. Like Reynolds, Buford does not survive the war, succumbing to typhoid fever in December 1863. On July 2, Winfield Hancock might have saved the battle for the Union army by protecting Dan Sickles's right flank and plugging the gap in the Federal lines caused by Sickles's inexcusable lapse of judgment. On July 3, Hancock is primarily responsible for the unbreakable defense in the Union center. Sickles will lose his right leg, and Hancock will suffer a wound that will debilitate him for much of the rest of the war.

Henry Hunt's wise use of artillery was a key to the utter destruction of Lee's final assault against the center, which is known today, of course, as "Pickett's Charge."

One point worth emphasizing is how the death of John Reynolds may have changed history. Beyond the obvious loss to the Union army of a capable field commander, most of the senior officers in the Army of the Potomac believed that Reynolds should have been given overall command instead of George Meade. With so much criticism directed at Meade for his "failure" to pursue Lee, it is entirely likely that Reynolds would have replaced him. In that event, it's possible that the following spring Lincoln would not have felt the need to call upon Ulysses Grant. Reynolds may have been the man to pursue and destroy Lee's army once and for all. Given how the United States tends to reward its military heroes, it is plausible that John Reynolds (and not Ulysses Grant) would have been elected president. Of course, as with so many what ifs, this is just speculation.

On the southern side, there is as much controversy as there is recognition. Stuart's absence, Longstreet's petulance, Heth's impulsiveness, all contribute to the failures of Lee's army to prevail at Gettysburg. Dick Ewell is soundly blamed for not having captured the Union high ground on July 1 (what will become known as Cemetery Hill), yet despite some modern interpretations of the battle, Ewell had no easy task. Federal troops were already moving onto Cemetery Hill in force, and Ewell's men had already endured an exhausting and difficult day-long fight.

Though Lee is regarded with reverential esteem in the South, there are quiet voices in the Confederate government who suggest that Lee bears the blame for the failure. Though some are motivated by jealousy and politics, it is not hard to find some validity to their assertion. For a century and a half since the battle, the question has been asked: Why did Lee order Pickett's Charge? Since his service to Winfield Scott in the Mexican War, Lee had made his career by embracing tactical wizardry. He well understood and appreciated the value of the flank attack, of deceiving his enemy, of feints and surprises. How could this same man order a frontal assault over a mile of open ground against an entrenched enemy?

I wish I could offer a definitive answer, but this question will be debated by historians and military strategists forever. One possible answer is that up until Gettysburg, Lee could rely on the talents and services of Thomas Jackson. At Gettysburg, there is no Jackson to be found. Up until Gettysburg, Lee's army had shown (to Lee's satisfaction, anyway) that when matched against their Union counterparts, the soldiers of the Army of Northern Virginia had almost always prevailed. Whether Lee convinced himself that Pickett's (Trimble's and Pettigrew's) Charge would succeed simply because it *should* succeed is a question only Lee could answer.

As the details of what happened at Gettysburg flow out through the country, there is muted jubilation in the North that for the moment silences some of Lincoln's harshest critics. In the South, there is immeasurable despair. On both sides there is a gnawing sense of wonder that the war has become so devastating that neither army can stop it. In Washington, though Lincoln basks in the glow of the victory at Gettysburg, he is enormously frustrated by Meade's sluggishness in pursuing Lee's staggered army. Then, only one day after Lee's crushing defeat, both Washington and Richmond are stunned by word of yet another cataclysmic event far to the west.

Within a few months of the conclusion of the Battle of Gettysburg, plans are already being made to set aside land to commemorate what happened here. The first order of business is the creation of a cemetery, and the site on Cemetery Hill is dedicated on November 19, 1863, one of the most significant nonmilitary dates in American history. On this day, thousands of onlookers, including government officials, foreign dignitaries, and soldiers in full dress uniform, crowd the new cemetery to witness the official ceremony. After enduring a rousing two-hour speech by former senator and political celebrity Edward Everett, President Abraham Lincoln rises up on the platform, telling those who can hear him that he has been advised to "make a few appropriate remarks." Lincoln then delivers the most famous speech in American history. It consists of only 272 words and takes him barely two minutes to deliver. It is, of course, the Gettysburg Address.

WHAT YOU SHOULD SEE

My first tour of Gettysburg was a life-changing experience. As I noted in the introduction, I was twelve when I first accompanied my father there. Today, it is extremely gratifying to see twelve-year-olds (and those far younger) who are not merely being dragged along by the enthusiasm of their parents. I have met children who already know impressive details of the history of the place, some leading their parents on a tour of their own, the child as the historian. Visitors come to Gettysburg from all over the world, and many of them know the history of this place better than a great many Americans. Others come to participate in the annual reenactments that take place on the anniversary of the battle each year, which for vacationers falls conveniently on the July Fourth weekend.

The first place I visit in Gettysburg is the spot where Lincoln spoke his immortal words. The exact spot is today situated by the large Soldiers National Monument, though most people absorb the spirit of that event by reading Lincoln's words on the National Park Service plaque, an enormously powerful experience. I can only imagine that Lincoln had the same emotions, absorbing the significance of what occurred on this ground. Lincoln had doubts that his speech could do justice to the memory of the fallen, or that his speech would be remembered at all. If you can stand on that spot and feel the emotions, the sense of gravity for what happened on the land around you, I believe that Mr. Lincoln would be greatly pleased.

The cemetery itself now holds some thirty-five hundred Union dead and from the beginning is the focal point for all that follows here. The first monuments are placed on the battlefield within a few years of the war's conclusion, and by the 1880s, the surrounding countryside is populated by a great number of monuments. The park begins to take shape as early as mid-1864 and becomes the property of the National Park Service in 1933.

There is no piece of historic ground in North America that is as widely recognized as Gettysburg. To make a magnificent place even better, a program pushed forward by park superintendent John Latschar was instituted in the past few years to restore the park to its original 1863 appearance. In other words, if a piece of ground was bare then, it will be made bare now. If there was a patch of woods then, trees are being planted now. This program is a monumental success, in that the battlefield now resembles almost exactly the terrain as it was then, an enormous help to understanding the ebb and flow of the battle.

Explaining in detail the sites worth seeing on this field would require a book of its own. The self-guided autotour suggested by the Park Service is in itself eighteen miles long. While I recommend the driving "tape guided" tour, the best way to experience the park is to hire a private guide to accompany you in your own vehicle. A list of these guides can be found at the park's Visitor Center.

There are nearly a hundred original structures, homes, barns, and the like that date to the time of the battle, as well as a great many homes in the town of Gettysburg itself (many are marked with a plaque indicating that they date to the Civil War). The park also has more than thirteen hundred monuments, including tributes to each state, to corps, divisions, brigades, and regiments, even some dedicated to the individual soldier.

The best place to begin a tour of the field itself is . . . at the beginning. West of town are the two parallel strips of high ground, perfectly suited for two armies to face each other for the first time. Standing on McPherson's Ridge, facing west, you are looking at Herr's Ridge. Along this same line is where John Buford placed his Union cavalry, knowing he was about to be assaulted by a considerable force of rebel infantry. Note the low wooded ground between the two ridges, the creek known as Willoughby Run. On July 1, 1863, Harry Heth's Confederates pushed in line through the thickets and approached Buford's dismounted horsemen on this hillside. The battle had begun.

Two monuments are particularly interesting along McPherson's Ridge. One marks the place where Major General John Reynolds was killed, which, as mentioned earlier, might have been a moment that changed American history. The second monument is dedicated to the "Old Hero of Gettysburg." As the battle began, a seventy-year-old civilian, John Burns, walked up to the Union position carrying an old flintlock musket and demanded that he be allowed to fight. Burns was a veteran of the War of 1812 and made such a convincing case that over the course of the three-day battle, he fought in several engagements. He was wounded and eventually captured. Since he lived until 1872, one wonders what kinds of stories he had to tell the townspeople in Gettysburg in those years after the battle.

At the north end of McPherson's Ridge, you can see the imposing Eternal Light Peace Memorial. This is something of an unusual monument for a battlefield, since rather than celebrating the accomplishments of any one group, the emphasis is on the hope that this sort of carnage is never repeated. The monument was dedicated in 1938, during the seventy-fifth anniversary ceremonies. Ironically, the monument stands close to the railroad cut, which saw horrific action on July 1 and is the place where only a few years ago the remains of a Confederate soldier were discovered.

Monument to General George Greene, Culp's Hill,
Gettysburg, Pennsylvania PHOTO PATRICK FALCI

To follow one path of the Union retreat through Gettysburg, drive south on Washington Street. Note the gray house at 107 South Washington Street, at the intersection of South Street. The outer walls of this (private) house show clear evidence of damage from canister, fired by retreating Union artillery on July 1.

The battles that took place on Culp's Hill are not nearly as well-known as those on other parts of the battlefield, and for that reason alone, Culp's Hill is a must-see. If you drive up to the peak of the taller hill, note how the hillside falls away sharply to the north. This explains why the rebels attacked the eastern side of the hills to make their assault. Even there, the steepness of the ground must have made for a brutal fight for the Confederate troops climbing the hill into George Greene's muskets. There is a monument to Greene at the peak of the hill, and though it appears he is pointing out toward the enemy, the grim-faced taskmaster is just as likely pointing at his own men, telling them to get to work.

The Greene Monument sits close beside an observation tower, which was put in place in 1898. Not the prettiest structure on the field, it nonetheless offers a good vantage point for viewing this entire section of ground. Note the lower peak of Culp's Hill, which was heavily occupied by Confederate troops on the night of July 2. Imagine the severe discomfort of the men on both hills, knowing that, in the darkness, their enemy was only a few yards away. Though Chamberlain's bayonet charge on Little Round Top was likely a save-the-day accomplishment, the fight on Culp's Hill had many similarities, including a bayonet charge of its own.

South of Culp's Hill on Colgrove Avenue is the monument to the 2nd Massachusetts, which was placed here in 1871. This was the first regimental monument put in place on the entire battlefield. On the west side of Culp's Hill, near the saddle that connects the two peaks, is Pardee Field. In a strange twist of military lore, this is the spot where, on the morning of July 3, the 1st Maryland (Confederate) fought the 1st Maryland (Union). So much for Maryland being a neutral state.

To stay with the action on the second day of the battle, drive to the far (southern) end of the park. Here, the peach orchard, wheat field, and Devil's Den are prominent features. With the removal of so much of the wooded obstructions, the flow of battle here is so much more visible than it was a few years ago. Devil's Den in particular is much more accessible now and clearly ties in to Sickles's lines farther north. Devil's Den is an extraordinary place to visit whether or not there had been a battle here at all. The enormous boulders seem tossed about at random, and given that a bloody battle was indeed fought here, it is not hard to imagine what kind of struggle men had making their way through

Staged photo at Devil's Den, Gettysburg, Pennsylvania, just after the battle
PHOTO COURTESY OF THE LIBRARY OF CONGRESS

this place from either direction. (Please don't ask a ranger or battlefield guide if the rocks were actually there at the time of the battle. That ranks as one of the most frequently asked stupid questions they hear. There are others, of course; my favorite: "Why aren't there any bullet holes on the monuments?")

Devil's Den is also the location of one of Mathew Brady's most famous photographs of the war, displayed on a plaque you can't miss. As mentioned there, Brady employee Alexander Gardner staged the shot, which, while regrettable, doesn't detract from the impact of what certainly happened in that very spot.

Along the edge of the wood's adjoining wheat field is the Timbers farm foundation. Michael Timbers was a freed slave who worked the land here. Close by, on Brooke Avenue, near the 4th Brigade Plaque, is one place where a battlefield guide is essential. A short walk downhill off the road is the place where Union general John Brooke was wounded. Brooke etched an X into a large boulder, so that in the future he would be able to locate that spot himself. The X is still there.

Near the Loop sits the Irish Brigade Monument. Note the figure of the Irish wolfhound. This particular breed of dog was extremely rare at the time—he was one of only four sires known to exist. The dog represents "faith and devotion to cause and country."

From the area of Sickles's fight, you should now head up toward Round Top. The larger hill is still heavily wooded (as it was then), and there is a zigzag trail for the physically fit to make their way to the top. What few people ever do, though, is walk down, *below* the road. From this point downward, the woods were somewhat cleared at the time of the battle. At the parking area where the trail goes *up* the hill, follow the footpath *down* instead. You will soon come to an amazing outcropping of rock called the Devil's Kitchen. Though this formation of rock is much more compact than Devil's Den, it is equally impressive. This is the first place where Colonel Strong Vincent's brigade skirmishers saw action, attempting to hold Hood's Confederates. Vincent was forced to pull these men back, under severe pressure, and it was then that he situated them on Little Round Top.

I strongly suggest you take your time exploring the different aspects of the ground on Little Round Top. On the face of the hill, with the brush now cleared away, you have a perfect view of Devil's Den and, more to the right, the area where Sickles's men made their desperate fight. There is one obvious statue, the figure of an officer holding field glasses as he gazes out toward the fight below him. This is General Gouverneur K. Warren, who first recognized the crucial value of this hill for the Union army. You can get the same perspective Warren himself had as he stared out across this ground. From Warren's point of view, look to the left. In the distance you'll see a pair of large evergreen trees, standing close together. Those are "witness trees" to the action here on July 2, 1863.

On the east side of the main road (behind Warren), follow the well-worn footpath toward the far end of the Union flank. Anyone who is familiar with my father's classic

Site of the staged photo at Devil's Den today, Gettysburg, Pennsylvania PHOTO PATRICK FALCI

novel, *The Killer Angels,* will find themselves walking in the footsteps of the man whom Michael Shaara helped elevate to iconic status: Colonel Joshua Lawrence Chamberlain, commander of the 20th Maine Regiment. I will not debate the appropriateness of all the attention that has been paid to Chamberlain and his accomplishments on Little Round Top. As is always the case, when one man rises to gain the bulk of attention, others do what they can to bring him back down. There are some historians (and park guides) who stress that what Chamberlain accomplished here was not all that significant, that (of course) there were many other heroes on the field that day. I have no definitive answer to that, except that the Medal of Honor speaks for itself. It is also speculated (by some) that if Chamberlain had failed to hold the flank, the damage might not have been as bad as has often been portrayed. That's a question no one can answer. It seems relatively obvious that a swarm of rebels moving in behind the 5th and 3rd Corps could have caused an enormous problem for Meade's army, especially since, along other parts of the line, the Union army had its hands full trying to hold Longstreet's Confederates away. Regardless of your feelings about the heroism of the 20th Maine, what I hope you will do is walk this ground and see for yourself what those men faced on that sloping hillside.

The small concrete marker that indicates the 20th Maine's right flank is not placed quite accurately. Chamberlain's lines were farther down the hill and ran through the large

View of Little Round Top today, Gettysburg, Pennsylvania   PHOTO PATRICK FALCI

boulders that are perched a few yards above the modern road. The low stone wall you see there was reconstructed well after the battle. Looking down the hill toward the paved road, note the sign indicating Wright's Avenue. This marks the actual *left* flank of the Confederate advance. In other words, from that point, the line of Alabamans coming up the hill would have extended out to Chamberlain's left, along the base of the hill, and with each successive attack moved even farther to Chamberlain's left. As you can see, this eventually takes the Alabamans *behind* Chamberlain's position on the knoll of the hill. The large monument to the 20th Maine is the approximate position of Chamberlain's left flank, so as the rebels kept moving that way, Chamberlain was forced to move with them, to meet their attack. Most people don't realize that most of the fighting actually took place to the left of the large monument. Note the low stone wall in the woods to the far left of the monument. This is called by some the Ellis Spear Wall and indicates the place where Chamberlain's second in command was ordered to turn his left flank back at a ninety-degree angle (called "refusing" the line). But Oates's Alabamans continued to push up the hill, and Colonel Oates himself described quite specifically the place where his flag bearer planted the flag of the 15th Alabama. The spot is beside a large round boulder that today sits behind the small "left flank" marker. Thus, you can see that Chamberlain's men were actually pressed right back against one another. If anyone questions his motive for ordering a bayonet charge, stand on the narrow strip of ground that separated the two sides of Chamberlain's lines. The far *right* flank of Oates's attack actually reached the edge of the modern footpath that runs along the crest of the hill, what most people today assume to be safely in the rear of Chamberlain's position.

Driving north from Little Round Top, you come to a newly cleared knoll on the left called Munchower Hill or Field. For many years, this small hill was hidden by a dense cover of brush and trees, until the park implemented its new restoration program. This is now a perfect illustration of the logic of such a policy. When the hill was cleared, the stone wall you see now was discovered. Though most of the stone walls on the battlefield were re-created after the battle, this one is intact and entirely original.

As you drive north on Hancock Avenue, you will pass the Hancock Monument, which sits out to the left a distance from the road. This marks the place where General Hancock was wounded. North of the Hancock Monument is another witness tree, called the Gibbon Tree, where General John Gibbon was wounded. At that location on the opposite (right) side of the road is a monument to the 13th Vermont Infantry, the only monument on the battlefield depicting a lieutenant, Stephen Brown. Note the "camp axe" on which the man is standing, which replicates the only weapon this lieutenant had as he led his troops into battle.

It's impossible to miss the enormous Pennsylvania Monument, which is the largest

Statue of General G. K. Warren overlooking the face of Little Round Top, Gettysburg, Pennsylvania PHOTO PATRICK FALCI

state monument on the field. This monument has recently been renovated and is worth a visit. Continuing north on Hancock Avenue, you will eventually come to the fenced-in copse of trees on the left, which signifies the high-water mark of the Confederacy. Though there is some debate about how accurate that term really is (there are high-water marks noted on many battlefields), the point is clear. This stretch of ground marks the position of the last gasp of Pickett's Charge. The paved road itself marks a boundary past which no Confederate soldier advanced. This spot probably sees more visitors than any other place on the entire battlefield.

Walk out toward the low stone wall and note the location of the Armistead marker, usually made noticeable by the placement of one or more small Confederate flags. Likely, this marker is too close to the paved road. Armistead was observed as he stepped over the stone wall, and when he placed his hand on a Union artillery piece, he was struck down. It is more likely that he fell in the vicinity of the monument to the 72nd Pennsylvania.

I respect those who care deeply about paying homage to such noteworthy historical landmarks as the high-water mark. I speculate, however, that the copse of trees does not indicate the farthest advance of the Confederate troops that day. Drive just north, to the Bryan House. Walk to the stone wall on the left, peer over, and you will see the newest monument on the battlefield. This marks the spot where the battle flag of the 11th Mississippi was found as it lay across the stone wall. The 11th was part of the brigade com-

The true "high-water mark" at Gettysburg—monument to the 11th Mississippi

PHOTO PATRICK FALCI

manded by Joe Davis, nephew of the Confederate president. By all information, a total of fourteen Mississippians reached this spot, farther into the Union position than the North Carolinians, at what is today labeled the high-water mark. The Mississippi regiment had four color bearers shot down, but the fifth made it, where he and the other survivors were captured. In a note of irony, this property was farmed by a freedman, Mr. Abraham Bryan. Thus did Davis's men see their assault end on the property of a freed slave.

Thus far, most of the places I have mentioned are best seen from the Union point of view. I suggest moving now to the Confederate side of the field. Confederate Avenue carries you along the approximate line of Lee's army, ground known as Seminary Ridge. Note the state monuments, several of which are true works of art. The North Carolina Monument was in fact designed by Gutzon Borglum, who is far better known as the man responsible for the carvings on both Stone Mountain (Atlanta) and Mount Rushmore.

One of the most poignant places on the battlefield is the ground out in front of the massive Virginia Monument. From the paved road, just past the monument is a footpath. This leads out into the open ground to an area that would have been Lewis Armistead's right flank. Somewhere close by is where Lee sat on his horse, Traveller, and watched as his thirteen-thousand-man wave crashed into the impregnable Union position nearly a mile away. It is difficult to imagine the scene, since so much smoke would have shrouded the battle, especially close to the Union lines. Lee could only wait and wonder if he was right, if his great strategy would prevail, if the war might end. Instead, as the smoke cleared, Lee saw the remnants of three broken divisions flowing back toward him, and with that retreat, the dreams of Confederate victory faded away.

Lee could not know that while his army had given so much on this bloody ground at Gettysburg, far to the west, along the Mississippi, another great drama was also drawing to a close.

CHAPTER FIVE

VICKSBURG

Vicksburg, Mississippi

MAY–JULY 1863

WHAT HAPPENED HERE

*W*hile the great tragedy of Gettysburg was unfolding in Pennsylvania, in the west, a battle of equal or even greater significance had been taking shape for several months. With the capture of New Orleans by Union admiral David Farragut, and the capture of the rebel positions farther upriver at New Madrid and Island #10, Missouri, Vicksburg, Mississippi, was the only remaining Confederate stronghold on the river, and in 1862 was the only major strategic position that prevented the Union forces from gaining complete control of the waterway. Control of the river was critical to the economies of both North and South, and Lincoln himself described the importance of capturing Vicksburg, saying, "The war can never be brought to a close until that key is in our pocket."

Command of the area was given to Union general Ulysses Grant, who had made his reputation in several key fights along the

Tennessee and Cumberland Rivers and most recently during the Union's costly victory at Shiloh. As he studied the situation, Grant understood that any attack on Vicksburg would be complicated by the geography of the area. Perched high on bluffs overlooking the great river, Vicksburg provided an ideal defensive position for Confederate artillery to prevent passage of the river by both northern merchant vessels and the Union navy. Sharp bends in the river near the town forced any boat attempting to run the gauntlet of fire to slow down, thus losing the ability to make a rapid dash past the guns that had been dug into nearly invulnerable positions along the bluffs. Inland, east of the river, the town was protected by sharp ravines, numerous small river crossings, and stretches of woods and swamp that made any advance a slow process. From any direction, Vicksburg was a natural defensive position.

Grant also understood that if he was to march an army overland through the rough approaches to Vicksburg, he would have to contend with the deadly nuisance of Confederate cavalry, commanded by the very able Earl Van Dorn. Farther north, the roads and trails that led southward from Tennessee were subject to the lightning raids of the South's most feared cavalryman, Nathan Bedford Forrest.

Grant recognized that his greatest asset was manpower, and from his bases in Tennessee, he planned, logically, to move a great mass of troops southward, directly into Mississippi, beating back the rebel forces in his way. Grant envisioned a two-prong attack—the left, or easterly, prong led by Grant himself; the other, closer to the river, under the command of his subordinate and friend William T. Sherman. It would be a combined force totaling more than seventy thousand men. The march began in November 1862, and at first both drives were successful, driving the Confederates out of Holly Springs, and Oxford to Grenada, Mississippi. But Grant could not escape the torment of the Confederate cavalry, and just before Christmas 1862, in one of the most daringly successful raids of the war, Confederate general Earl Van Dorn stunned Grant by capturing Grant's entire forward supply base at Holly Springs. In addition, farther north, in Grant's rear, Forrest was consistently destroying the railroad lines that supplied Grant's army. By that same Christmas, Sherman actually pushed close to Vicksburg, with a force of nearly forty thousand men, a considerable advantage in numbers to the rebel troops who defended the area. But Sherman unwisely ignored the lay of the land and failed to pay heed to the rebel defenses. He launched several attacks straight into the well-dug-in Confederates, an effort that was a complete failure. Despite enormous political pressure from armchair generals in Washington who saw Grant's initial failures as cause to replace him, Abraham Lincoln instead gave his unflagging support to the man, saying, "I can't spare this man. He fights." Grateful for the president's support, Grant withdrew both wings of his army, and by the end of the year, he began to rethink his strategy.

The Confederate forces in Mississippi were commanded by Lieutenant General John C. Pemberton, a Pennsylvanian who had stayed loyal to his Virginia-born wife and enlisted to fight for the South. Despite considerable experience in the First Seminole War and Mexico, Pemberton had not yet led troops in the field during the Civil War. Though Pemberton's command was technically under the umbrella of General Joe Johnston, who commanded the entire Confederate Department of the West, Pemberton was a friend of Jefferson Davis and had received his assignment, and thus took his orders directly from Davis himself. Everyone in the Confederate army knew of the simmering feud between Joe Johnston and President Davis, a conflict that went back to the earliest beginnings of the war. Thus, Johnston had been sent out west as much to get him out from under Davis's attention as for Johnston's ability to command an entire theater of the war. Though Pemberton commanded the critical Vicksburg defenses, to Johnston, Pemberton was simply Davis's man. That lack of cooperation and authority came to haunt the Confederates and played a key role in the battles to come.

With the Union forces now licking their wounds back in Tennessee, Grant began to work on another strategy for moving his vast manpower closer to Vicksburg. If the direct overland route southward through Mississippi was no longer an option, the only viable alternative was to move west of the Mississippi River and come at Vicksburg from another direction. As far back as June 1862, Union forces had begun several attempts to cut through the dismal network of muddy swamps and meandering creeks that drained into the river opposite Vicksburg, with little success. Now, in early January 1863, Grant tried the same tactic. But after weeks of strenuous effort from Grant's engineers, none of the plans for canals, shortcuts, and artificially constructed levees brought Grant anything more than frustration. Plagued by either too little water or too much, with the troops tormented by the mud, swarms of mosquitoes, poisonous snakes, and the occasional alligator, Grant finally conceded that the only effective way to move his army from Louisiana into Mississippi would be by finding a crossing much farther south, where both sides of the river had firmer ground. But rather than forcing the issue in a direct, undisguised, and extremely dangerous crossing where the Confederates might be waiting for him, Grant ordered Sherman to make a large-scale feint at Vicksburg from the north, while Union cavalry, under Colonel Ben Grierson, began a march southward out of Tennessee, straight into the heart of Mississippi. The key to Grant's crossing would be transport boats, and on the moonless night of April 16, Union admiral David Porter ran the Confederate artillery gauntlet and sent a dozen boats past Vicksburg. The rebels detected the movement on the river and bombarded Porter's boats, but amazingly the Union navy lost only one vessel. In addition, Grant also sent troops toward a strongly held Confederate position at Grand Gulf, south of Vicksburg, holding the considerable Confederate artillery in place

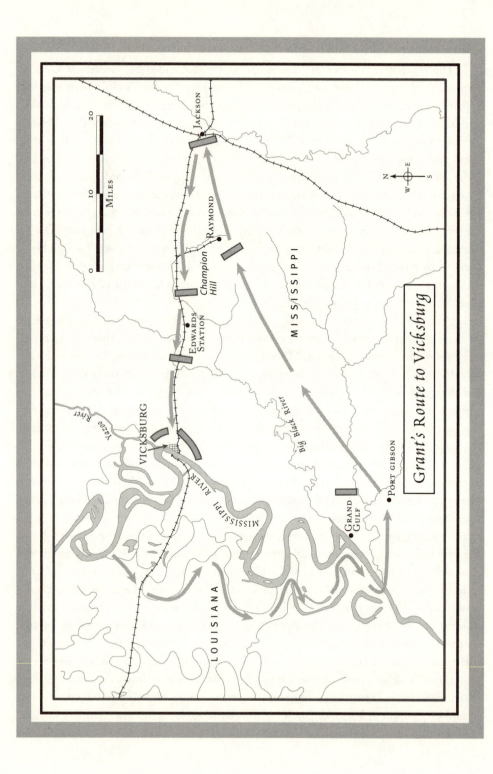

Grant's Route to Vicksburg

there, while Grant began to make his primary crossing of the river farther south. Misled completely by Grant's chess game, a baffled Pemberton failed to predict where Grant was going to make his move. At one point, receiving reports of heavy Union river traffic, the Confederate commander convinced himself that Grant had advanced his enormous army only to reverse course. While Grant continued to put his forces into position, Pemberton suggested to his stunned officers that Grant was, in fact, retreating. Thus, on April 30, 1863, when Grant began to ferry his troops across the river at Bruinsburg, some thirty miles below Vicksburg, the crossing was completely unopposed by Confederate troops. The initial movement of more than twenty thousand Union soldiers over water was up to that time the largest amphibious assault in American history.

As the crossings continued, Grant's base south of Vicksburg grew into a formidable force of more than thirty-five thousand, strength that no Confederates in the area could withstand. The first major contact occurred at Port Gibson, and the greatly outnumbered rebels, under the able command of General John Bowen, made great use of the advantages of the rugged landscape. Bowen had commanded the Confederate defenses at Grand Gulf and had been the one Confederate commander to see through Grant's feints. Though Bowen had sent frequent word to Pemberton to expect the crossing, Pemberton ignored Bowen's desperate request for reinforcements. After a long day's fight, Bowen's Confederates could simply not hold the Union forces back, and Bowen ordered a withdrawal. With the rebels in full retreat, Grant's forces, under the command of General John McClernand, were suddenly ordered to halt so that they could be addressed by Illinois governor Richard Yates, who happened to be along as an observer. To the enormous frustration of the field officers, the rebels made good their escape while the Union soldiers had to endure political speeches from both McClernand and the governor! Needless to say, when an unhappy Grant learned of the delay, he was quick to order his men to resume their pursuit.

The next fight took place May 12, at the small town of Raymond. Again, tenacity could not stand up to numbers, and the Confederates were forced to withdraw. The fight was costly for Pemberton, since the rebel troops engaged were forced to retreat, not toward Vicksburg, but to the east, toward the capital city of Jackson, thus weakening Pemberton's forces.

While Pemberton's intelligence reports continued to be conflicted and confused, Grant learned that Confederate general Joe Johnston had begun to gather what would become a considerable number of troops near the state capital, some forty miles to the east. Grant knew that if Johnston pushed toward Vicksburg, Grant's own flanks could be dangerously exposed. Thus, before Grant could order his men to turn toward Vicksburg, he had first to deal with Johnston.

Joe Johnston had established his reputation since the start of the war as a commander who considered his way of doing things to be the *only* way of doing things. Though Pemberton would have benefited enormously from Johnston's help, even in a delaying tactic, Johnston seemed reluctant to engage a strong enemy force, even if he had the advantage. Instead, Johnston, realizing that Grant was anchored firmly between him and Pemberton, conceded the tactical advantage. Rather than attack the Union forces, Johnston sent a simple message to Jefferson Davis in Richmond: "I am too late." Johnston, however, seemed to contradict his own conclusions when at the same time he sent orders to Pemberton to abandon Vicksburg and march east to link up Pemberton's army with his own.

Grant meanwhile continued to move troops into position east of Vicksburg, and on May 14, he sent a strong force under Sherman toward Jackson, intending to either destroy the Confederates or at least drive them out of the capital city. After a short fight in a savage rainstorm, Joe Johnston accomplished Sherman's mission for him. The Confederate commander withdrew from Jackson, pulling his force away to the northeast. Sherman's men, reveling in the ease of the conquest of Mississippi's capital, set about burning military targets in the city, fires that ultimately burned out of control. Though Sherman deeply regretted his troops' brutality, history (particularly southern history) has recorded that the burning of Jackson was entirely Sherman's idea, a notion fitting neatly into what would become Sherman's exaggerated legend as a man dedicated to the utter destruction of soldier and civilian alike.

Pemberton meanwhile was caught between conflicting orders, first from Jefferson Davis to hold Vicksburg, then from Johnston to abandon the place and move east. Johnston's order was not only contradictory, it made no tactical sense. Besides handing Vicksburg to the Union army, Pemberton could not have marched his troops toward Johnston without placing himself directly in Grant's line of fire. The somewhat confused Pemberton attempted to please both masters and meekly marched a portion of his troops eastward, seeking either some vulnerable place to strike Grant's army or, perhaps wishfully, some open route to link up his troops with Johnston's. Pemberton could only assume that if he was successful in linking his forces with Johnston's, then Johnston would use the combined strength to make a powerful attack on Grant.

(Whether or not Joe Johnston would have made such an attack is a subject left to speculation. From a strategic point of view, had Johnston arrived in Jackson a week sooner, or had he taken the initiative and attacked Grant from the east while Pemberton assaulted from the west, the Union position could have become dangerously squeezed between two Confederate armies. But instead Johnston simply moved away, adding distance between himself and Pemberton.)

With Sherman now occupying Mississippi's capital, the rest of Grant's forces began to consolidate for the purpose of blocking and holding the railroad line that connected

Vicksburg to Jackson. On May 16, Pemberton, still in the dark with regard to Grant's exact disposition, advanced a strong force eastward, trying to find some vulnerability in what he thought might be Grant's rear or flanks. Instead, the Confederates found themselves in direct contact with a large force commanded by two of Grant's senior officers, Generals McClernand and James McPherson. The result was the Battle of Champion Hill, a sharp and brutal fight, where McClernand, by failing to see the opportunity that lay in front of him, might have squandered an opportunity to crush the outnumbered Confederates. The next day, May 17, Grant's forces, now joined by Sherman, pursued Pemberton's troops westward, the fight developing at the Confederate defenses along the banks of the Big Black River. Grant's troops quickly overwhelmed the rebel defenses, capturing nearly two dozen cannon and seventeen hundred rebel troops, men and guns that Pemberton could not afford to lose.

On May 19, Grant was finally in position to launch a significant assault on Vicksburg itself. But the ground strongly favored the outnumbered Confederates, and their defensive position was far stronger than Grant realized. Grant ordered two more straightforward frontal assaults directly into the teeth of the rebel works. The efforts gained the Union soldiers only temporary success, but ultimately every assault was driven back. After suffering heavy losses, Grant recognized the foolishness of his tactics and would not repeat the mistake. He saw that, given the geography and the rebel fortifications, a siege was the most effective and least costly means of capturing the town. Despite his distaste for tying up his army for an extended length of time, Grant knew that a siege could end

Vicksburg, Mississippi, 1863 PHOTO COURTESY OF THE LIBRARY OF CONGRESS

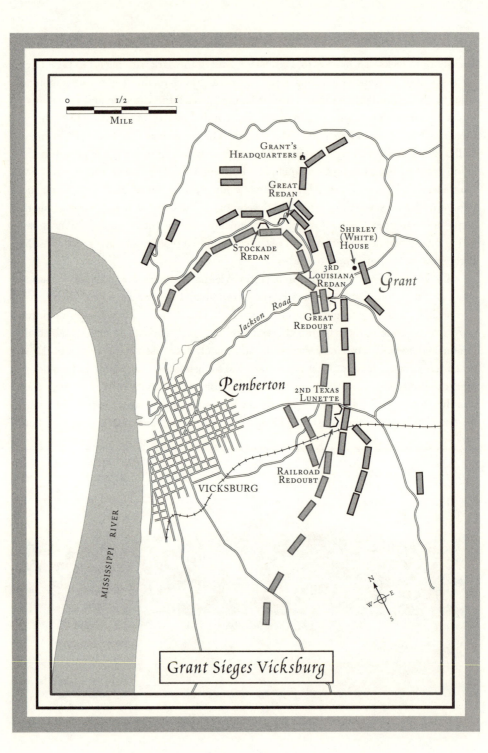

Grant Sieges Vicksburg

in one of only two ways. Pemberton would either surrender or the rebel army and the civilians in the town would starve.

Observing that Joe Johnston's confederate forces were still far to the east, and seemingly content to remain immobile, Grant moved his army into position for his siege. Though Pemberton's own commanders advised him that a siege could result only in tragedy to both the town and the civilian population, Pemberton chose instead to rely on the strong fortifications that ringed the town. Pemberton believed, in a classic case of wishful thinking, that with more than thirty thousand idle troops, Joe Johnston might still come to his aid. But Johnston had already drawn his own conclusions. After advising Pemberton yet again to abandon Vicksburg (just how that could be accomplished, Johnston did not specify), Johnston wired Richmond on June 15 his opinion that Vicksburg could not be saved.

Grant continued to tighten the noose around the town, his army still increasing in size until he confronted the rebels with more than sixty-five thousand troops, outnumbering the rebels by more than two to one. The siege was not a quiet affair, and frequent skirmishes occurred all along the rebel defenses. With Grant realizing that direct frontal assaults were simply too costly, at the encouragement of his engineers, he ordered the dig-

Union bombproof shelters at the Shirley House
PHOTO COURTESY OF THE OLD COURT HOUSE MUSEUM, VICKSBURG, MISSISSIPPI

ging of various mines, to plant explosives directly beneath the Confederate troops. Grant also ordered his artillery to shell the confederate works at regular intervals, and Union gunboats dueled with Confederate cannon along the river. With no house safe from the shelling, the citizens of Vicksburg were forced to seek shelter in caves dug into the banks of the many ravines along the river's edge and within the Confederate defenses. Amazingly, no more than a dozen civilians were killed throughout the siege.

With food running out (Confederate troops had resorted to eating their own mules), Pemberton again conferred with his commanders. Most of them agreed that the situation was hopeless. On July 3, 1863, Pemberton conceded the inevitable and asked for a meeting with Grant. Though Pemberton made various demands as to terms of surrender, U. S. Grant's name was already said to mean "Unconditional Surrender." Pemberton insisted that without suitable terms, his army would continue to fight it out, but both men knew the siege could not go on. Grant finally conceded that the Confederate soldiers would be paroled rather than held in northern prisons (meaning that each man would pledge not to take up arms again unless formally exchanged for an enemy prisoner). On July 4, 1863, Union troops marched into Vicksburg. The siege was over, and Pemberton's army of nearly thirty thousand men had surrendered.

WHY IS THIS BATTLE IMPORTANT?

Since the beginning of the war, the Mississippi River is recognized by both sides as the key to economic survival. Grant's capture of the Mississippi now splits the Confederacy in two, the states to the west severed from direct contact with the east. Though the war will go on in Texas, Louisiana, and Arkansas, the armies there will be fighting in a vacuum. Thus, even if there are victories in the west, the fall of Vicksburg means that the economic collapse of the Confederacy is inevitable. Beyond economics, the double defeats at Gettysburg and Vicksburg are sharp body blows to the Confederate spirit. The losses devastate the morale of the southern citizenry, still reeling from the emotional loss of Stonewall Jackson.

In the North, the midwestern states can now use the Mississippi River to resume their considerable trade with the outside world. In addition, the enormous number of Union troops that are assembled around Vicksburg can now be put to use in other critical areas of the war in the west, including major battles yet to be fought in Tennessee and Georgia. With the Union navy now firmly in control of the great river, the Confederates have no chance to supply their armies in the field except by rail. That situation will of course energize the Union strategists to focus on the South's primary rail centers: Petersburg, Chattanooga, and Atlanta.

The path of the original Jackson Road, Vicksburg, Mississippi PHOTO PATRICK FALCI

The conquest of Vicksburg demonstrates for the first time that the Union army and navy can function as an effective team. Throughout the war, both branches of the service have operated more or less as independent commands. Though the navy has its share of effective leaders, notably men like Farragut and Porter, there have never been any particular reasons for them to cooperate with the army. Rarely has there been a situation where the fight involves both land and water at the same time. Grant has bridged that gap and uses the navy wisely in his overall plan for the capture of Vicksburg. Grant's respect for what the navy brings to the fight is evident to his naval counterparts, and there is very little friction or conflict between them. Without the navy's cooperation, it is unlikely Grant could succeed at Vicksburg.

Though Ulysses Grant makes mistakes during the campaign, he learns from them, a character trait often missing among senior Union commanders. In Washington, much of what occurs in the western theater of the war seems overshadowed by what is happening in the east. In Virginia, Maryland, and Pennsylvania, the thunder of the guns is often heard in the streets of the capital, so the great battles fought against Robert E. Lee are much closer to home. But Grant's accomplishment has elevated his name to particular prominence, especially to Abraham Lincoln, who has grown weary of the parade of inept Union generals. William T. Sherman has proven himself to be far more able as a commander in the field than he was at Shiloh. Both men will have significant roles in the outcome of the war.

On the southern side, Joe Johnston's abandonment of Pemberton must be examined. It is entirely possible that Johnston's strategy is the wisest move, even if his timing is so poor. If Pemberton is able to combine his army with Johnston's, and Grant marches unopposed into Vicksburg, the shoe would then be on the other foot. Johnston could very well have attacked Grant the same way Grant attacks Pemberton. But that kind of speculation is moot, mainly because, for the remainder of the war, Johnston shows himself to be far more effective as an engineer of the good retreat rather than the good assault. Though it is certain that the Union would eventually find a way to capture Vicksburg, the loss of Pemberton's thirty thousand men means that a crucial amount of manpower is lost to the Confederate cause. After the defeat, Jefferson Davis offers Pemberton some words of encouragement, what amounts to feeble congratulations for Pemberton's efforts at saving Vicksburg. But the stains of his failures follow Pemberton for the rest of his career. As might be expected, John C. Pemberton is never again allowed to command in the field.

WHAT YOU SHOULD SEE

*T*wo sites in the town of Vicksburg are worth noting, though they lie outside the boundaries of the park itself. The Old Court House Museum at 1008 Cherry Street was established at the site where, on July 4, 1863, a Union flag is raised on the flagpole there, after the town falls into Union hands. The courthouse, which dominates the Vicksburg skyline (then and now), is established as a museum in 1948 and houses a great many artifacts from the time of the battle, as well as exhibits dedicated to the Civil War era in general. One of the more unique artifacts is a tie worn by Jefferson Davis at his inauguration.

The other site worth visiting is the house that serves as John Pemberton's headquarters throughout the siege. The home, at 1018 Crawford Street, has been a private residence until only recently. After considerable joint effort between the National Park Service and the Civil War Preservation Trust, the house was acquired by the Park Service in 2003.

While a few of the preliminary battle sites around Vicksburg are preserved to one degree or another, particularly in the nearby town of Raymond, the highlight of any tour has to be Vicksburg itself. Much of the battlefield site is established as a National Military Park in 1899, and it becomes part of the National Park Service in 1933. Surprisingly, extensive efforts are not made to preserve the park's many geographical features until the 1960s. The present-day park is an easy driving tour, though, as is the case at so many other military parks, I strongly recommend hiring a guide.

As much as any other well-preserved battlefield, the Vicksburg National Military Park could profit by the example set at Gettysburg for the removal of modern stands of

View from Confederate Fort Hill, toward Louisiana, Vicksburg, Mississippi
PHOTO PATRICK FALCI

timber. Understandably, many people object to the Park Service going into the tree-cutting business, but a historical site like Vicksburg would benefit greatly from having the ground restored to its 1863 appearance.

The first striking aspect of this park is the complicated topography, deep and winding ravines, which give the Confederate troops ample natural obstacles in their defensive lines, and the twist and turn of the ground affords the rebels a great deal of interlocking fields of fire, an enormous defensive advantage. But the ground works to the advantage of the Union as well. In many areas, such as the approaches to the Third Louisiana Redan, it is easy to understand how the Union troops can advance so close to the Confederate works. The steep hillsides allow the Union soldiers to move within musket range, and then, by constructing trenches in a zigzag pattern, they advance quite literally right up alongside the Confederate works. The Third Louisiana Redan is one of the key sites where Union engineers explode an underground mine. Though not as well-known as the "crater" mine explosion at Petersburg, the Vicksburg mining operations are nearly as dramatic and yet almost completely useless as a means of breaking the enemy's lines.

Along the approaches to the Third Louisiana Redan are two important structures. The first is the Shirley House, original to the time of the battle. Though the house has suffered various indignities, the future restoration by the Park Service will bring the house back up to its original appearance. The Shirley House is notable for two reasons: It's the only building in the park that dates back to the battle and it's also the prominent feature in

The USS CAIRO

THOUGH HOUSED WITHIN THE BOUNDARIES OF THE PARK, THE *Cairo* is not technically a participant in the siege of Vicksburg. But it is one of the most significant artifacts of the entire war.

The gunboat is constructed in late 1861, one of several ironclads designed to take the Union navy's fight up the waterways of the South. The technology is then less than a decade old, layering the exterior surfaces of wooden boats with thick plates of iron, making them considerably less vulnerable to cannon fire. But there is genius in the design that goes beyond armor. In order to have any usefulness in the frequently shallow depths of the rivers, the gunboats must have a shallow draft and a relatively flat bottom. The challenge for the engineers is to add the weight of the iron and still allow the boat to float and maneuver in shallow water. Seven gunboats are commissioned by the U.S. government, and the contract is awarded to engineer James Eads. As a testament to Eads's skills at both design and construction, the seven ships are built and delivered within one hundred days from the signing of his contract. Among them is the *Cairo*.

She is 175 feet in length, weighs nearly nine hundred tons, yet can float in only seven feet of water. The boat is well armed, and though slow, with a speed of only six knots, she is considered virtually impervious to any land-based artillery the rebels might throw at her. But the *Cairo* does have a vulnerability, shared by all the boats of this design. Below the waterline, there is no armor.

On December 12, 1862, the *Cairo* accompanies several other small vessels up the Yazoo River, seeking to clear the river of obstructions, part of Grant's cooperative plan with the navy. She carries a crew of 175 men, commanded by Lieutenant Commander Thomas Selfridge, an outstanding naval officer who was first in his class at Annapolis. As the *Cairo* begins its push slowly up the Yazoo River, she is suddenly rocked by a sharp blast from beneath her port side. She has been struck by a Confederate mine. The mine, constructed of a five-gallon glass jug of gunpowder and attached to the shore with a rope and a copper wire, is ignited by an electrical charge by rebels who must surely be astonished and delighted to watch the ironclad settling into the muddy bottom of the Yazoo in only twelve minutes. No lives are lost, and the entire crew escapes to be picked up by another of the Union vessels.

The *Cairo* sinks in thirty-six feet of muddy water, so her smokestacks are still visible. To prevent the rebels from possibly looting what remained below the surface, the other navy vessels destroy any evidence of the *Cairo*'s location, making her difficult to find.

And difficult it is. The *Cairo* lies buried in the mud of the Yazoo for nearly a century, guarded by layers of sunken trees and other debris. But local fishermen have some inkling of the gunboat's location, and rumors abound that at extremely low water, some part of her can still be seen. In 1956, three men, including noted park historian and guide Ed Bearss, locate the *Cairo* and begin the considerable efforts required to salvage her. Funds are raised by a group of private

The USS Cairo, Vicksburg, Mississippi ʋHOTO PATRICK FALCI

citizens, and after extraordinary efforts of time and careful engineering, she is finally raised in 1964.

Though title of the *Cairo* rests originally with the county where the vessel is located, in 1973 ownership is transferred to the National Park Service. In 1977, she is brought to Vicksburg and placed in its current location, just outside the National Cemetery.

Because the *Cairo* is mostly encased in deep mud, the artifacts on board are remarkably well preserved. Incredibly, some of the wooden timbers survive as well, and all can be seen at the site. The skeleton has been preserved in such a way that visitors can actually walk through the interior, where much of what they see is original material. Though the overall structure is supported by modern structural devices, the decks, compartments, bulkheads, gun ports, and much of the mechanical "guts" of the *Cairo* are visible. Adjacent to the vessel itself is the Cairo Museum, which houses the artifacts of the crew. The state of preservation of most of these artifacts is truly astonishing. Among the many dozens of bottles and glassware are medicines and foodstuffs (including one bottle of "hot sauce" for seasoning, which is still edible), as well as medical supplies, dining utensils, the boat's four-hundred-pound brass bell, and artifacts that reflect the everyday life of the men on board, everything from navigational instruments to artillery shells to straight razors. In addition, the museum provides details of the extraordinary salvage operation that brought these artifacts to light.

In the recent past, two other salvage operations have received considerable attention, and rightfully so. The *Hunley,* the Confederate submarine raised in Charleston Harbor, is a remarkable and unique exhibit now housed in its own museum. As impressive as the recovered artifacts are (and they are truly impressive), much of the attention of the exhibit is paid, appropriately, to the tragedy of the men whose ship also became their underwater tomb.

More recently, the turret of the Union ironclad *Monitor* has been brought to the Mariners' Museum at Newport News, Virginia, where it is being preserved and made ready for public exhibition.

Though battlefields, the *lands,* receive the lion's share of preservation efforts, we must acknowledge the dedication and passion required in bringing these naval exhibits to public awareness. The challenges are not just in funding the efforts, but, as well, in finding the (new) technologies required to move such fragile pieces of history from water to land. Far more rare than the battlefield park, these maritime treasures are equally revealing, reminding us that war is ultimately a human endeavor and a human tragedy, no matter what form the battleground may take. Don't miss the *Cairo.*

one of the most widely published photographs of the battle, illustrating how the Union troops had so completely occupied the sloping hillsides around it as part of their siege lines.

The current road that fronts the Shirley House is the original roadbed for the Jackson Road, which at that time led eastward to the state capital some forty miles away. The

Illinois memorial, Vicksburg, Mississippi PHOTO PATRICK FALCI

cuts in the landscape show clearly how the road wound over the crests of the hills that lead into Vicksburg. Past the Shirley House sits the second major structure in that section of the park, the imposing Illinois Monument. The enormous monument resembles the ancient Pantheon in Rome, from which it takes its design, especially the exterior, which is constructed with a massive portico and columns. As you stand inside the monument, look straight up; you can see the circular opening at the peak of the dome, an architectural characteristic perfected by the Romans. Once you get over the dizziness of staring upward, notice the plaques that line the walls around you. These plaques contain the names of thirty-six thousand soldiers who fought here for the numerous Illinois regiments. Some particular notes: On the primary command plaque, where Ulysses Grant's name is displayed, are also displayed the names of his staff officers. Note the name of his son Fred, who had accompanied his father to the field. Obviously, a twelve-year-old boy is not an appropriate staff officer, but clearly someone in Illinois thought that the boy's presence should be made known.

On the far side of the wall, if you locate the plaque listing the soldiers of Company G, 95th Infantry, you'll see the name of Albert Cashier. Cashier survives the battle and around the turn of the century is severely injured in an accident. Only when examined by doctors is it discovered that Cashier is in fact a woman, who after considerable questioning reveals her real name to be Jenny Hodges. Miss Hodges fights as a man all through the war and maintains her secret for decades after, so that she can draw her soldier's pension. After some deliberation (and considerable head scratching), it is decided by the War Department that she continue to be paid.

Note the name of Orion P. Howe, Company C, 55th Infantry. Howe is a fourteen-year-old drummer boy who is awarded the Medal of Honor for his extraordinary bravery under fire.

On the north side of the battlefield is the Stockade Redan, another of the most distinctive landmarks showing how close the Union troops could push forward their trenches. At this spot, Union ladder bearers are ordered to place their ladders against the dirt walls of the redan and are given the description as the Forlorn Hope Battalion. Few survive the attacks, and several receive the Medal of Honor for their astonishing efforts, which ultimately accomplish little. Note as you stand inside the Stockade Redan how simple it would be to roll high-explosive cannonballs right down on the Union troops below and how, if the fuses were just a bit too long, the Union troops could toss them right back over into the laps of the rebels. In many such areas, it was a unique and deadly game of "hot potato."

Near the Stockade Redan is the Wisconsin Monument. Normally, monuments are

The Shirley House today, Vicksburg, Mississippi PHOTO PATRICK FALCI

dedicated to the men who fought from each state or perhaps make prominent mention of a certain regiment. It is rare that a monument emphasizes a bird. And not just any bird, but a bald eagle. The eagle, whose name is "Old Abe" (of course), serves as the mascot for Company C, 8th Wisconsin Infantry. The eagle is so widely known that even the rebels acknowledge the Wisconsin boys and their "Yankee Buzzard." Though wounded at the Battle of Corinth, Mississippi, "Old Abe" survives the war. He lives out his life in comfort, in quarters provided at the Wisconsin State Capitol. He lives, amazingly, until 1881, when he dies from exposure to a small fire in the Capitol building. As a final indignity, his remains are destroyed when the Capitol succumbs to another fire in 1904.

At the far northwest tip of the park is Fort Hill, one of the highest points in the park, overlooking the Vicksburg National Cemetery. The defenses on this hill were so strong that no attack is made here by the Union troops. Today, Fort Hill is a magnificent overlook of the Mississippi River (and the Yazoo River, to the north). Looking west, across the river into Louisiana, note how flat the land is, a complete contrast to the east side of the river where you are standing. The lack of hill country to the west is a clear indication that the terrain on that side of the river is simply a morass of swamp and flood plain that defies Grant's attempts to make his approach to Vicksburg from that direction.

A stroll through the Vicksburg National Cemetery can be something of a physical challenge. Unlike most cemeteries, which tend to occupy fairly level ground, the cemetery here is spread out over rolling and undulating terrain, as is the rest of the park. Some seventeen thousand Union soldiers are buried here, only a fourth of whom are named. As is so typical of Civil War–era cemeteries, most of the bodies are brought here after the war from other battlefields, often having been exhumed from mass graves where identifying the remains is, at best, an unpleasant challenge. The cemetery is also the final resting place for soldiers from the Spanish-American War as well as World War I, World War II, and the Korean War. Ask the park ranger about conflicting stories of how two (and only two) Confederate soldiers came to be buried in the National Cemetery, the burials being illegal (as mentioned previously). The graves belong to Private Ruben White of the 19th Texas and Sergeant C. B. Brantley of the 12th Arkansas Sharpshooters. Most of the Confederate soldiers killed during the fighting here are buried in nearby Cedar Hill Cemetery.

Close to the Park Service Visitor Center is the Second Texas Lunette, an arcing defensive position that sees some of the heaviest fighting of the entire battle. It is here that the rebels learn how vulnerable even stout earthworks can be. Union engineers determine that the soil in this area is of a material so soft, the artillery shells might actually penetrate the dirt walls. Union gunners are able to roll artillery pieces right up to the high embankments and fire solid shot directly into the dirt at point-blank range. To the stunned surprise of the rebels on the far side of the walls, the engineers are right.

Farther to the southern end of the park, the Railroad Redoubt and Fort Garrott are also focal points of particularly vicious fighting. Both offer a bit more open ground to view how the Union troops make their approach with the lines of zigzag trenches.

One of the most striking aspects of the ground at Vicksburg is how close the armies are to each other. From the Jackson Road cut to defenses in the southern section of the park, you can easily see how the men can virtually stare into one another's faces. The comparison between this battlefield and the one-mile stretch of wide-open flat ground at Gettysburg shows the complete contrast between styles of ground and, thus, styles of fighting.

If you are inclined to risk a little poison ivy or the occasional tick, take a walk down into any one of the open ravines that face the Third Louisiana Redan or the Stockade Redan. Imagine it is a brutal July day and that you are a Union soldier ordered to advance down into the ravine. Then you are to charge up the other side, into the guns of an enemy who is firing at you from only yards away. It's easy to imagine that when General Grant ordered his men to cease their assaults and move instead into siege operations, at least someone, somewhere along the Union lines, let out a cheer.

CHAPTER SIX

CHICKAMAUGA

Chickamauga Creek, Georgia

SEPTEMBER 18–20, 1863

WHAT HAPPENED HERE

*E*ven while Grant's army was seeking an effective plan to drive the rebels out of Vicksburg, Mississippi, another great mass of Union troops, based in Nashville, was pursuing a strategy in a different direction. Their commander was Major General William Starke Rosecrans, who had replaced Don Carlos Buell after the campaigns in northern Mississippi. Late in 1862, Rosecrans had been ordered to push the rebels completely out of eastern Tennessee, the goal being the capture of their vital rail center at Chattanooga. In Rosecrans's path lay the Confederate Army of Tennessee, under Braxton Bragg, which was camped close to the town of Murfreesboro. Rosecrans's plan was to reach Chattanooga by sweeping past (or through) Bragg's forces. If it was successful, the gateway would be open for a Federal thrust into Georgia, with the ultimate prize being Atlanta. But Bragg's Confederates would not leave Murfreesboro without a fight, and the result was the Battle of Stones River (also called the Battle of Murfreesboro). The two armies were roughly equivalent in manpower, the Federals bringing just over forty thousand men to the fight, Bragg confronting them with thirty-eight thousand. In a bloody clash that extended from the end of December through the first few days of January 1863, Bragg's army took the upper hand on the battlefield, but neither side had the manpower to crush the other. Since Rosecrans ultimately pulled his army away from the field, Bragg claimed that Stones River was a southern victory. But the Confederates had merely held their ground at a cost of some ten thousand casualties. And even Bragg knew that the "victory" meant nothing if Rosecrans could reinforce his army and simply try again. The Federals had absorbed thirteen thousand casualties at Stones River, but Rosecrans was still operating under the same instructions from Washington: Capture Chattanooga. Bragg could only watch and wait as reinforcements made the Federal army stronger.

Rosecrans was far more cautious now and did not put his troops into motion again until the end of June. Bragg tried to gather reinforcements as well, with some success, but neither commander was anxious for a repeat of Stones River. Bragg blinked first, and as Rosecrans put his army once more on the march, Bragg felt he had no choice but to abandon Murfreesboro. The Confederate forces withdrew some thirty miles closer to Chattanooga, and Bragg anchored them around the small rail junction of Tullahoma, Tennessee.

This time, Rosecrans relied more on maneuver than on direct confrontation. The Federal army divided into several strong columns, thus threatening Bragg's army from several possible points of attack. The strategy worked. Rather than risk throwing his army into another costly fight, Bragg withdrew again. This time he would pull the Confederates back to the safety of the mountainous terrain and the protection of the wide Tennessee River at Chattanooga itself.

Bragg's retreat handed a bloodless victory to the Federal army that Rosecrans had to appreciate, a retreat that was as costly to the southern cause as the loss of so many men. By conceding that the Confederate army could not maintain control of the territory between Nashville and Chattanooga, Bragg essentially gave up a great swath of critical farmland that was enormously important as a breadbasket for southern troops. In addition, the mountainous terrain closer to Chattanooga was rich in natural resources of a different kind, such as copper and other valuable minerals that supplied the South's war machine. The value of the railroads at Chattanooga had much to do with how these crops and raw materials from eastern Tennessee were distributed to southern mills and factories. Despite the good ground that now protected Bragg's army, Rosecrans had learned something about effective strategy. He also had learned something about Braxton Bragg. Rather than attack the Confederates in their strong points at Chattanooga, Rosecrans relied once again on maneuver and deception. In mid-August 1863, the Union forces

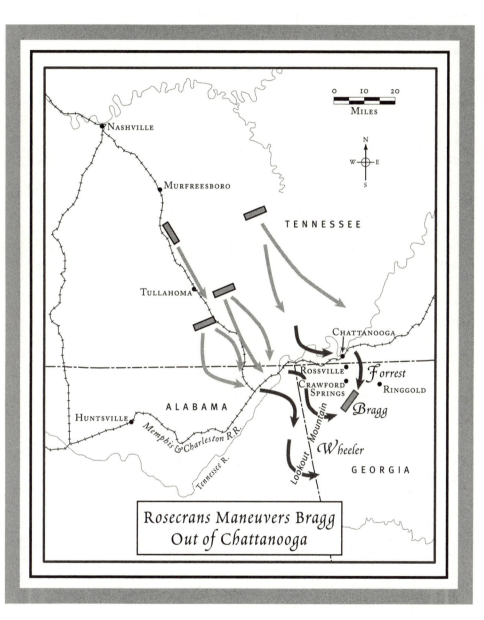

MILES
0   10   20

N
W ⊕ E
S

NASHVILLE

MURFREESBORO

TENNESSEE

TULLAHOMA

CHATTANOOGA

ROSSVILLE
CRAWFORD
SPRINGS

Forrest

RINGGOLD

Bragg

ALABAMA

HUNTSVILLE

Memphis & Charleston R.R.

Tennessee R.

Lookout Mountain

Wheeler

GEORGIA

Rosecrans Maneuvers Bragg
Out of Chattanooga

marched a strong column to the river a few miles north of the city, convincing Bragg that the Federals would make their crossing at that point, a logical plan to sweep down onto Chattanooga from that direction. In addition, Federal artillery began to shell the town, which would typically indicate that the main assault was soon to follow. Meanwhile, far below the town, the actual Federal crossing was taking place. Unlike Burnside at Fredericksburg, Rosecrans had been supplied with adequate numbers of pontoon bridges, and the Federal engineers made considerable use of rafts and floating platforms. By September 1, with most of the Federal army establishing itself downstream on the Confederate side of the Tennessee River, Bragg finally realized that he had been outmaneuvered. On September 7, 1863, Bragg ordered his army to abandon Chattanooga. Once more, Rosecrans had won a victory without forcing a major confrontation.

The Federal army had every reason to feel that all was right with the world. With the fall of Vicksburg, the Mississippi River was fully under Federal control. The Battle of Gettysburg had virtually destroyed the offensive power of Lee's Army of Northern Virginia, and now a major rail center had fallen peacefully into Union hands. Rosecrans was justified in believing that fate was on his side, so he ordered his army to pursue Bragg's demoralized Confederates on their hasty retreat southward into Georgia. But Bragg was not hastily retreating anywhere. He had instead gathered up his army near Lafayette, Georgia, only a dozen miles from Chattanooga.

With Chattanooga firmly under control, Rosecrans's subordinates advised their commander that the Federal forces there should regroup, resupply, and determine what Bragg was actually doing before they pursued him. Rosecrans disagreed. On September 9,

Contrast of open fields to forest, Chickamauga, Georgia PHOTO PATRICK FALCI

Chickamauga Creek, the River of Death, Chickamauga, Georgia PHOTO PATRICK FALCI

a full division of Federal troops under Major General James Negley pushed southward into a valley known as McLemore's Cove. As Confederate scouts reported the movement to Bragg, he realized that the lay of the land made the cove a perfect trap. But by the time Bragg could put his plan into motion, Negley had smelled trouble and successfully pulled his troops out of danger. The problem for the Confederates was that Bragg's orders were often disregarded by his subordinates. Bragg was disliked by his officers as much as any commander in either army.

Bragg's inability to spring his trap at McLemore's Cove allowed Rosecrans to move more of his army through the mountain passes below Chattanooga into position just above the town of Lafayette. Though Bragg had missed his opportunity to cut up the Federals piecemeal, he still believed that Rosecrans would not push for a general engagement. In addition, Bragg had learned that an enormous number of reinforcements was expected at any time to support his Army of Tennessee. James Longstreet and some twelve thousand men had been sent to the western theater to lend vital assistance to the beleaguered Confederates there. Without waiting for Longstreet to actually arrive, Bragg planned to launch a surprise attack on the Federal left (north) flank the morning of September 18. But as had happened at McLemore's Cove, Bragg's intentions were thwarted by poor planning and alert Federal cavalry. Any element of surprise disappeared. The fight

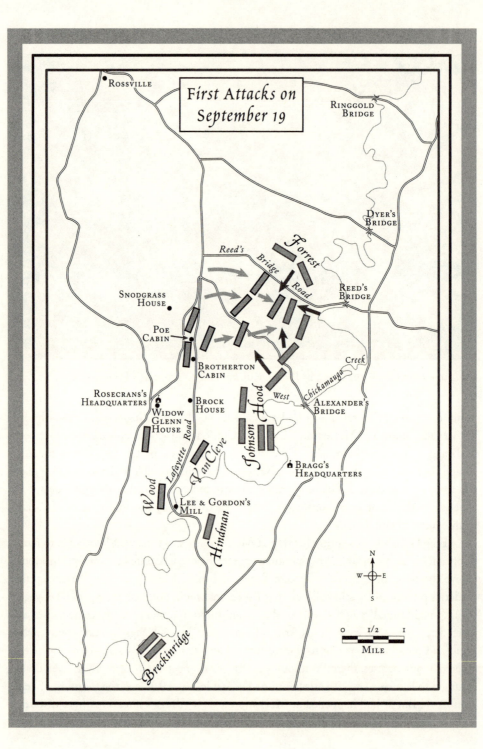

First Attacks on
September 19

ROSSVILLE

RINGGOLD
BRIDGE

DYER'S
BRIDGE

Reed's

Forrest

Bridge

Road

REED'S
BRIDGE

SNODGRASS
HOUSE

POE
CABIN

Creek

BROTHERTON
CABIN

Chickamauga

West

ROSECRANS'S
HEADQUARTERS

BROCK
HOUSE

Johnson

Hood

ALEXANDER'S
BRIDGE

WIDOW
GLENN
HOUSE

BRAGG'S
HEADQUARTERS

Lafayette Road

VanCleve

Wood

LEE & GORDON'S
MILL

Hindman

N
W   E
S

Breckinridge

0   1/2   1

MILE

spread out along the banks of Chickamauga Creek, but it was far from a general engagement. Large patches of woods and the creek itself prevented either side from maneuvering effectively. The battle that developed was instead a haphazard, disorganized affair, and by the end of the day, both sides ended up more or less where they had begun.

Throughout the night of September 18–19, neither Rosecrans nor Bragg was entirely sure just where their enemy would be when the sun came up. With the first light of September 19, the mystery wasn't solved for either side. The vast tracts of forest made visibility difficult at best, and even cavalry had little advantage. The two armies faced each other in a northeast-to-southwest line that roughly paralleled Chickamauga Creek, though the creek was now behind the Confederate position and would play little role in the events to follow. One major disadvantage for both armies was that the creek was the only substantial source of drinking water in the immediate area. Canteens quickly emptied and stayed that way for two days.

The overall line extended for more than five miles. To the north, the Federal position bulged more to the east, and the Federal commanders, notably Major General George Thomas, believed that they outflanked the rebels there. Thus, the first major action came on the far Union left. But Thomas had not counted on Confederate cavalry lurking in the woods, and as the Federal troops advanced, they ran unexpectedly into Nathan Bedford Forrest, whose horsemen actually outflanked even the Union position. In a rapidly expanding and chaotic fight, both sides called upon reinforcements, and both armies reacted by moving masses of troops northward. In the confusion, entire divisions marched blindly through thick woods short distances from their enemy, and in some cases, with their flanks overlapping, lines of troops lost contact with each other in the trees. The woods were broken by a patchwork of open fields, and throughout the day, entire divisions would emerge into a clearing, only to find that they were facing the exact flank of an enemy line or might be flanked themselves. Bragg's control of his Confederate troops was governed by a single philosophy, which he communicated to his commanders: March toward the sounds of the fight. While practical for a small formation of troops, maneuvering an entire five-thousand-man division this way made for confrontations that were haphazard and confused.

The fight eventually engulfed most of the troops in both armies, with very little accomplished on either side. The most distinct boundary that divided the troop positions was the Lafayette Road, along which lay several open fields, farmlands dotted with cabins. The Union left flank remained east of the road all day, hard-fought battles that overlapped one another in the woods. In the center of the action, the road was the pronounced point of attack, and both sides pushed across at various points. But the open fields provided the only place where artillery could be effective, and neither side could sustain any kind of formation in the open ground without absorbing horrific casualties.

The first of Longstreet's men, under John Bell Hood, had arrived on the field, and the added power of Hood's forces gave Bragg a brief advantage. Now slightly outnumbered, Rosecrans spent most of the day embroiled in a feverish chess game, shifting Federal divisions to confront breakthroughs by rebel units who succeeded in punching their way through various points at the center of the Union line. But Bragg did not coordinate his attacks effectively, and more often, Confederate troops would open up a gap in their enemy's position, only to be isolated by a lack of support. Thus the breakthroughs would simply collapse, the rebel troops swallowed up.

The attacks continued until dark, the final battle taking place where it had begun, on the north end of the line. But Thomas's Federals held their position, and by eight o'clock, the guns began to fall silent across the entire field. Neither side had accomplished anything besides the casualties they had inflicted on the other.

During the night, Rosecrans called a council of his senior commanders. He feared that his army had been beaten up so severely that if they resumed this kind of fight the next day, the cost could be catastrophic. But present in the Federal camp was Assistant Secretary of War Charles Dana, who had come from Washington as an observer. Whether or not Dana had his own agenda, the Federal officers knew that ultimately he represented the eyes and ears of Henry Halleck and Secretary of War Stanton. With Dana listening to every word, no officer would dare suggest that the best option was a full retreat. Rosecrans was forced to agree. Late that night, the orders went out all along the Federal position for the men to prepare for another fight. On the north (left) end of the line, George Thomas pulled the men on his far flank into a tightly arcing line three rows deep and ordered them to cut and pile logs to form a strong defensive barrier. Farther to the south (right), the rest of the Federal troops dug in along the west side of the Lafayette Road.

Across the way, Bragg had called no council. He had instead decided to reorganize his army, reducing the responsibility of those commanders with whom he had the least affection. Longstreet arrived close to midnight and immediately learned from Bragg that he, Longstreet, was now in command of the entire left wing of Bragg's army. Though Longstreet and Bragg were far from friends, Bragg acknowledged Longstreet's seniority by placing him over several of Bragg's corps commanders. Never mind that Longstreet had not even seen the ground he would command.

The right wing would now be commanded by Lieutenant General Leonidas Polk. Polk, who, like Bragg, was a close friend of Jefferson Davis, did have seniority, but his dislike of Bragg was well documented. Thus, Polk was nearly as surprised as Longstreet by the sudden change in the army's command structure. The changes in command were perceived by many of the Confederate corps and division commanders as a distinct slap in the face, a lack of faith in their abilities. In addition, no one had ever experienced this kind of administrative change in the midst of a major battle. Whether or not the reorganization made tactical sense, to Bragg it seemed to be necessary given the disjointed efforts of his army throughout the fighting on September 19. Whether or not that lack of coordination originated from Bragg himself was an issue he did not address.

On the Union left, George Thomas expected a repeat of the preceding day, anticipating a major attack on his flank. Such an attack was logical: If the Confederates were successful, they could get between the Union army and Chattanooga, thus cutting off a primary Union supply (and escape) route. As Rosecrans continued to shift his troops into stronger positions, he agreed with Thomas and sent reinforcements to the left flank to shore up Thomas's position. In the predawn, while the Federal troops waited for the inevitable attack, confusion reigned in the Confederate camps. Bragg had decided on the exact plan that the Union generals expected, and as Leonidas Polk prepared his men for their assault on the Union flank, he learned that the orders had not been communicated to several of the division commanders who were supposed to take part in the action. Many of the Confederates on their crucial right flank simply had no idea what they were supposed to do. The result was delay, and instead of launching their assault at five a.m., Polk's attack did not begin until nine-thirty in the morning.

The far right of the Confederate assault was led by Major General John C. Breckinridge, whose men rose up out of the patches of woods with a ferocious push against Thomas's position. Though Thomas's arcing log works held up well, on his far left, the tip of the Union position, Breckinridge succeeded in flanking the Union line. As Breckinridge turned his attack to the south, Thomas's entire position was in danger of being assaulted from behind. Thomas immediately called up reserves to confront the crisis, and because neither Polk nor Bragg had responded to Breckinridge's breakthrough, the Confederate troops there were not reinforced by the strength needed to completely crush the Federal flank. The center of Polk's position was directly in confrontation with the center of Thomas's well-defended arc, and a hot fight there poured heavy smoke through the woods, adding to the confusion. Polk had his hands full, so that he was unable to shift any effective strength to the support of Breckinridge. The troops who should have gone to the Confederate right were instead bashing themselves against Thomas's stout defense of log works. And Bragg had placed the Confederate reserves too far to the south, where they could really only back up Longstreet in the center and left of the line.

Thus far, the Federal commanders had been far more efficient than the Confederates in the handling of their troops, quickly shifting men to where they were most needed. By midday on September 20, all of that was negated by one critical mistake and one extraordinary piece of luck for James Longstreet.

Though Breckinridge's success against the Federal left flank had been brief and, ultimately, ineffective, Rosecrans had responded to that threat by doing exactly what a good

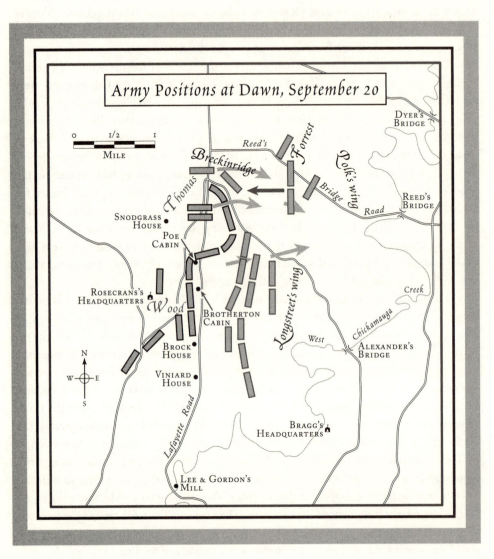

Army Positions at Dawn, September 20

DYER'S BRIDGE

Reed's

Forrest

Breckinridge

Polk's wing

Thomas

Reed's Bridge

Bridge

Road

SNODGRASS HOUSE

POE CABIN

Creek

ROSECRANS'S HEADQUARTERS

Longstreet's wing

Wood

West

Chickamauga

BROTHERTON CABIN

ALEXANDER'S BRIDGE

N
W—E
S

BROCK HOUSE

VINIARD HOUSE

BRAGG'S HEADQUARTERS

Lafayette Road

LEE & GORDON'S MILL

O   1/2   I
MILE

commander should do. He shifted units out of a relatively quiet part of his line northward, where they might be desperately needed. One division in the Federal center, under Major General Thomas Wood, was ordered to pull out of line and shift to its left "as fast as possible," to fill what Rosecrans believed was a gap created by the movement of another division northward. But Wood could see that the area to which Rosecrans had ordered him to move was not a gap at all. No one had abandoned the Union lines there. To add to Wood's dilemma, the wording of Rosecrans's order was confusing in and of itself. Wood was ordered to "support" the troops who were on the far side of this fictional gap. Wood understood that in such an order, "support" meant to move in behind, not beside. Since Wood could see there was no gap, he obeyed Rosecrans's order by pulling his division, some five thousand men, out of line and marching them back behind the division two positions away. Unfortunately for Rosecrans, his confusing order now created a genuine gap in the line—the position Wood's troops had occupied.

On the far side of the Lafayette Road, Bragg had not only failed to take advantage of Breckinridge's success on the flank, but he had failed to coordinate the Confederate assaults in the center. As a result, one division to Longstreet's right had launched an attack of their own without any support, crossed the Lafayette Road, and, after a momentary breakthrough, were engulfed by a Union counterattack. Longstreet had been ordered to attack as well, but Bragg had failed to be specific in his instructions, and Longstreet performed according to his own timetable (something he had become famous for at both Second Manassas and Gettysburg). Just after eleven o'clock in the morning, Longstreet began his own attack. One of his divisions just happened to march into the gap that Wood's division had opened up in the Federal line, a gap that Rosecrans had not yet filled. Longstreet's men quickly made their way far beyond the Lafayette Road, well past the main Union positions. The rest of Longstreet's attack was pushing against several Federal divisions on both sides of the gap, who, while they were being attacked in front, suddenly found jubilant Confederates in their rear. Within minutes, the entire center of the Federal position began to come apart. As the blue-coated troops fell back in disarray, the Confederates kept up their pursuit and quickly overran the Federal artillery positions, capturing a good many cannon along the way. By coincidence, Rosecrans had ridden to a knoll to observe the attack and had put himself directly in the path of his panicked troops. The official observer, Charles Dana, was as easily panicked as the troops who swarmed by him, and Rosecrans himself realized that escape was the better option.

As the fight swirled around the woods and open fields in the Union rear, many Federal soldiers held their ground, and the fight became bloody for men on both sides. But the tide had turned against them, and no matter the courage or resilience of several Union commanders, retreat was ultimately their best option.

To the north, George Thomas's twenty thousand men were still holding tight to

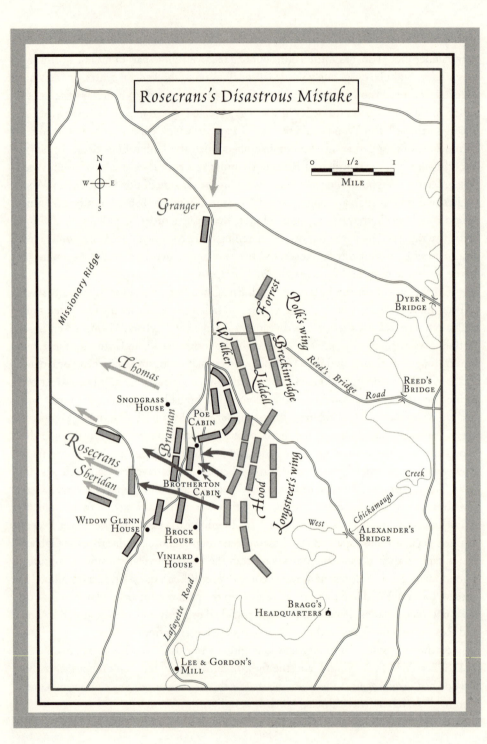

Rosecrans's Disastrous Mistake

N
W—E
S

0   1/2   1
MILE

Granger

Missionary Ridge

Forrest

Polk's wing

DYER'S
BRIDGE

Walker

Breckinridge

Reed's Bridge Road

REED'S
BRIDGE

Thomas

Liddell

SNODGRASS
HOUSE

POE
CABIN

Brannan

Rosecrans

Sheridan

BROTHERTON
CABIN

Hood

Longstreet's wing

Creek

Chickamauga

WIDOW GLENN
HOUSE

West

ALEXANDER'S
BRIDGE

BROCK
HOUSE

VINIARD
HOUSE

BRAGG'S
HEADQUARTERS

Lafayette Road

LEE & GORDON'S
MILL

their stout defensive line. Behind Thomas, on the western side of the Lafayette Road, rose a fat wooded knoll known as Snodgrass Hill. Those Federal troops who had not scampered toward Chattanooga had begun to gather on the hill, which was a natural defensive position. With the southern half of the Union line shattered, Longstreet's euphoric men began to swarm up toward the hill, attempting to drive those Federals back as well. But the momentum of their successful assault began to fade. Throughout the afternoon, Longstreet's men made several costly attacks up the slopes of Snodgrass Hill, but overcome by both exhaustion and thirst, the frustrated Confederates began to understand that the hill was simply too formidable an obstacle and the Federals who held it were determined not to give it up.

Across the Lafayette Road, Thomas's men continued to be pressed hard by Polk, and though the Union line was holding, Thomas realized that his position was no longer tenable. Late in the afternoon, he withdrew his men away from their log works and moved them in good order back to Snodgrass Hill, uniting his men with those who had fought so valiantly throughout the day. Polk and Longstreet united their forces around the base of the hill, and the assaults continued, but Thomas and the Federal troops on Snodgrass Hill stood firm. With half of Rosecrans's army racing through the mountain passes for Chattanooga, Thomas understood that no matter how many attacks they survived on Snodgrass Hill, the battle had been lost. Once the sun had set, Thomas's men and the other Union troops on the hill withdrew, joining the retreat back toward Chattanooga.

Even as the Federal army was making good their escape, Braxton Bragg was not aware that his army had won a significant victory. Throughout the night, he formulated plans for the next day's assault. But with the new dawn on September 21, the Confederate army realized how complete their victory had been. The battlefield was littered not only with dead and wounded men, but with a massive quantity of abandoned equipment. Rather than pursue the Union retreat, the exhausted Confederate soldiers tended to more immediate concerns.

Safely in Chattanooga, Rosecrans immediately began to organize a strong defense, though there was little danger to the Federal troops once they had crossed the Tennessee River. Once the Federal engineers had pulled in their makeshift bridges, the Confederates had no means to cross the river. The Battle of Chickamauga had ended.

WHY IS THIS BATTLE IMPORTANT?

*T*he cost in human terms is staggering for both sides, and the numbers are amazingly similar. During a fight that lasts little more than two days, each side loses nearly 30 percent of its forces, a total of thirty-five thousand casualties. Thus, as Rosecrans

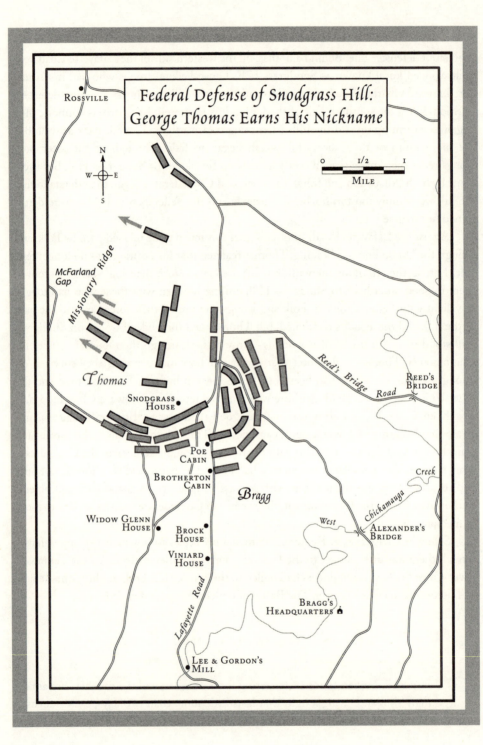

Federal Defense of Snodgrass Hill: George Thomas Earns His Nickname

ROSSVILLE

N
W ⊕ E
S

0   1/2   1
MILE

McFarland Ridge Gap

Missionary Ridge

Thomas

SNODGRASS HOUSE

POE CABIN

BROTHERTON CABIN

WIDOW GLENN HOUSE

BROCK HOUSE

VINIARD HOUSE

Lafayette Road

LEE & GORDON'S MILL

Bragg

West

Reed's Bridge Road

REED'S BRIDGE

Creek

Chickamauga

ALEXANDER'S BRIDGE

BRAGG'S HEADQUARTERS

regroups his army in Chattanooga, neither he nor Bragg is in a position to begin a new campaign.

Though Bragg is the victor, his reputation gains little from Chickamauga. If anything, the subordinates under his command increase their general loathing for the man, which bodes ill for Confederate fortunes later on. Bragg's personality problems have plagued him since his earliest days of command, and despite many official complaints against him, it is his friendship with Jefferson Davis that has kept him in the field. A rigid disciplinarian, Bragg lacks the flexibility required of an effective senior commander, and his insistence on involving himself in the duties best performed by his subordinates has long made enemies of men who were otherwise excellent field generals. Joe Johnston technically outranks Bragg in this department of the war, but given a free hand by President Davis, Bragg has every intention of running things his own way, whether his officers agree with him or not.

Both sides have come to understand that a victory that does not overwhelmingly destroy the enemy's army is Pyrrhic at best. For centuries, the "victor" has been defined simply as the army that holds the battlefield while the enemy withdraws. But this war has changed the definition. Holding on to a piece of ground means little if the "victorious" army has sacrificed far too many good soldiers. Such is Chickamauga.

Bragg is loudly criticized for failing to cut off Rosecrans's retreat into Chattanooga, but as had happened at Shiloh and Antietam and Gettysburg, at Chickamauga the triumphant army is too badly bruised to continue an aggressive fight. In terms of the larger picture, Rosecrans has lost the battle but succeeds with his original plan, which is to capture Chattanooga. Bragg wins the day, but the North has made one more leap toward winning the war.

Some stars rise on the Confederate side of the line, including John Breckinridge, whose troops might have sent the Federal forces reeling much sooner had they been supported on their right flank. John Bell Hood had recently returned to action following his severe wound at Gettysburg, and he proves himself in the field once more. But once again, Hood pays an enormous price. This time he loses his right leg. Amazingly, his leg is amputated nearly in its entirety, an operation that almost no one survives. But Hood lives and will return once more, though many questions will be asked later about his effectiveness. The leg itself is actually sent toward Hood's home in Texas, under the care of a single soldier. But for reasons no one can quite explain, the man doesn't complete the trip, and the leg is left at Tunnel Hill, Georgia. (The question has to be asked if the leg might have begun to emit an odor strong enough to discourage its escort.)

Most other Confederate division and corps commanders acquit themselves well, though some suffer from the same failures that result from a confused and chaotic battlefield. Regardless of the overall competence of the Confederate commanders in the field, their greatest disadvantages are the confused orders and lack of a cohesive plan from their commander. But Bragg immediately and openly blames his subordinates, which only increases the dissension in his headquarters, as well as in the ranks, since many of the Confederate officers are highly respected by their men.

On the Federal side, Rosecrans successfully manages the overall fight, until his one extraordinary blunder (and Longstreet's amazing stroke of good fortune) hands victory to the Confederates. Though most of the Federal commanders perform well under fire, two shine brightly in the midst of the catastrophe of September 20. One is Major General Gordon Granger, whose reserve corps strengthens the Federal last-gasp efforts on Snodgrass Hill. But the most famous name arising out of the fight belongs to Major General George Thomas. Though the successful defense of Snodgrass Hill was conducted by the outstanding work of many Federal brigade and regimental officers, it is Thomas who commands the field and thus receives the acclaim. For his skillful work in holding the Federal left flank, for withdrawing his men in good order, and for holding off the rebel attacks on Snodgrass Hill until his men can be withdrawn successfully, Thomas is forever after known as the "Rock of Chickamauga."

Energized by his victory at Chickamauga, Bragg focuses on what he sees as an opportunity for revenge for the loss of Vicksburg, still a bitter pill for the southern army and its people. Surprised that the beaten Federals are remaining in Chattanooga, he begins to form a plan that could result in another crushing blow to Rosecrans's army, which might help revive the southern spirit. Bragg believes that Chattanooga can be recaptured not through firepower, but through a siege, which might serve to avenge the humiliating loss of Pemberton's army. Since Chattanooga is neatly hemmed in by a deep curve in the Tennessee River, Bragg believes he can starve Rosecrans's army by penning them up in the city. Within two weeks of the conclusion of the Battle of Chickamauga, the Confederates occupy the heights above the city on two sides: along Missionary Ridge to the east, and to the south the high promontory that commands the entire valley around the city—Lookout Mountain. But despite Bragg's grand plans, the siege will work only for a short while. The valleys around Chattanooga are simply too extensive for Bragg's forces to control. And unknown to Bragg, a drastic change occurs in the command structure of the Union army. On October 20, 1863, Rosecrans learns that he has been relieved and that his successor is Ulysses Grant, who has been elevated to command of all Union forces in this theater of the war. Grant makes his way into Chattanooga three days later and immediately puts a plan into operation that will open a supply route to relieve the Confederate siege. By the end of October, Bragg's hopes for avenging the loss of Vicksburg are shattered by Grant's ingenuity.

Grant knows that he does not yet have the strength in Chattanooga to mount any ef-

Castle monument, site of Rosecrans's headquarters, Chickamauga, Georgia PHOTO PATRICK FALCI

fective breakout of the city, and he requests, and is granted, support from Washington. Tens of thousands of fresh troops under Joe Hooker and William T. Sherman are ordered to march their forces to Chattanooga. Bragg cannot prevent the reinforcements from reaching Grant's army, and once they arrive, Grant plans a campaign that will profoundly alter whatever advantages Bragg had gained by his victory at Chickamauga. On November 23, 1863, Grant's plan rolls into action, and Union forces surge out of Chattanooga in a complex (and sometimes disorganized) advance that by November 25 carries them up and over Missionary Ridge, causing a complete collapse in Bragg's army. As part of Grant's plan, on November 24, Union forces under Joe Hooker climb the heights of Lookout Mountain and in one sweeping charge eliminate the Confederate positions there as well. Any celebrations for the southern victory at Chickamauga are thoroughly silenced.

The sudden stunning success of Grant's burst out of Chattanooga is the final straw in Richmond, and Jefferson Davis has no choice but to remove Braxton Bragg from command. Grant's breakthrough cannot be contained, and their success at Missionary Ridge opens the gateway for the Federal army to advance toward Atlanta. Though the Confederates, led first by Joe Johnston and then by John Bell Hood, will make a hard stand to protect the South's most valued rail and supply hub, Atlanta cannot be saved. Once the city falls into Federal hands, the Union army will begin yet another campaign designed to further divide the Confederacy and thus bring the war to a close. It is a campaign that will forever be known as "Sherman's March to the Sea."

WHAT YOU SHOULD SEE

*C*hickamauga is a battle that, because of the nature of the ground, is far simpler to see than to explain. One important aspect of this park is that, as at Vicksburg, the panoramic scope of the battlefield is hidden from view by the expanses of trees. A significant difference, however, is that what you see at Chickamauga is much the same thing the soldiers saw at the time. This was, to say the least, an "inconvenient" place to stage a major battle.

In general, the forested areas today are not the same as they appeared in 1863 in one crucial respect: Today, the woods are pretty clogged with brush, small trees, and vines. In contrast, at the time of the battle, a great many farm animals roamed these woods, and as a result the undergrowth was eaten away. Then, the trees were more of a canopy, with the ground beneath fairly open. Thus, visibility for the rifleman was often a hundred yards or more. However, once the battle began, the smoke from musket fire would quickly fill the open spaces and would be held low to the ground by the tree branches overhead. Thus, the view for the soldiers would be considerably restricted, much as the undergrowth restricts your visibility today.

Whether or not the individual foot soldier could see his enemy, the senior commander trying to maneuver entire brigades or regiments could have no idea who or what might be waiting for them beyond the smoky trees. And imagine you're an artillery officer, aiming your cannon at these woods. With a noisy, blind fight rolling through the trees in front of you, firing your guns into that sort of confusion would be dangerous—you'd be just as likely to kill your own men as the enemy. Thus, for the first day's fight in particular, artillery was practically useless.

The Chickamauga battlefield is the oldest national military park in the country, established officially in 1890. The park came into being just prior to the formal establishment of Shiloh, Vicksburg, and Gettysburg parks, all of this historically valuable ground protected by the efforts of veterans who fought there. Chickamauga remains today the largest of the Civil War battlefield parks, covering nearly 5,600 acres. In 1933, the park fell under the management of the National Park Service.

As at several other parks, I recommend using the services of a Park Service guide and suggest that you make reservations for this in advance. The uniformed rangers who are employed by the park are available without charge, and I strongly suggest you take advantage of the opportunity provided. However, since their services are in frequent demand, prior planning is a good idea. Call to make an appointment.

The best place to start any tour here is the Visitor Center. As is typical of most other parks, the Visitor Center offers a half-hour film that explains the battle, and the one here is far better than most films of its kind. It's actually a multimedia program that makes effective use of three-dimensional images and creative staging. The Visitor Center also contains numerous exhibits and artifacts from the battle, as well as a bookstore. However, at Chickamauga there is a unique exhibit for anyone with an interest in firearms. The park is fortunate to have on display a collection of 355 muskets and other "long guns" on permanent loan from the estate of Claud and Zenada Fuller. This exhibit contains an amazing assortment of firearms from the pre-Revolutionary era up through World War I.

From the Visitor Center, the most logical place to begin your tour of the battlefield is where the battle first began. The far northeast corner of the park can be reached by the Reed's Bridge Road, and actually, you should drive east beyond the boundary of the park itself. Your goal is the Reed's Bridge site at Chickamauga Creek. The modern road sits just a few yards south of where the original bridge was positioned. On September 18, a division of Bragg's Confederates confront a much smaller force of Union troops who attempt first to hold the bridge and then to destroy it. But the Confederates are too numerous for the Federals to accomplish either task. The Reed's Bridge crossing is one of two the Confederates use to reach what will become the battlefield. (The second, at the southeast corner of the park, is called the Alexander's Bridge site.) As mentioned earlier, the creek is the only reasonable source of drinking water for the soldiers during the entire battle. The Battle of Chickamauga draws its name, of course, from this creek, which originates from the Cherokee language, meaning "River of Death." Little could the Cherokees have known just how appropriate the name will become.

Moving back into the northeast corner of the park, you will reach the Jay's Mill Field. This field is roughly one-third the size it was at the time of the battle, but the scene can easily be imagined. It is in this area that the two armies stumble into each other and continue that stumbling for most of the day on September 19.

You may note small unmarked concrete posts at various places in the park, found along the edges of the open ground. These were placed by veterans who returned to the park in later years to accurately designate the corners of the various open fields at the time of the battle. Not all of the posts remain, and most people pass by them having no idea where they came from. Those that survive are of great assistance to the Park Service in maintaining some of these fields to their accurate boundaries.

As you move through the eastern half of the park, much of which is heavily wooded, it's pretty easy to imagine how any battle would be a confused affair. The numerous open fields are more or less accurate to the time of the battle, though the dimensions of those fields have been altered over time. To more easily understand the gruesomeness of the fight, you should focus on the Lafayette Road, which essentially bisects the park on a north-south line. Throughout the day of September 19, this road marks the line of con-

Lookout Mountain

TODAY, MOST PEOPLE WHO VISIT LOOKOUT MOUNTAIN HAVE VERY little awareness of its historical significance. The site is a major tourist attraction for the same reason that it was so useful to the troops who occupied it during the Civil War. You can see for miles. When I was a child, my family made several long drives from Florida to points north, and I vividly recall seeing numerous billboards trumpeting Lookout Mountain and its various attractions (YOU CAN SEE FIVE STATES!). If you are a die-hard tourist, or if you have a car full of restless

Confederate view from Lookout Mountain, Chattanooga, Tennessee PHOTO PATRICK FALCI

children, perhaps those commercial attractions, the fudge and T-shirt stores, are for you. These days, I'd rather pass them by and go straight to the National Park Service property at the summit. Besides the tourist attractions along the summit road, you can't help but notice how much of the property on this mountain has evolved into some of the most valuable residential real estate in this part of Tennessee. (I just hope that some of the people who live here understand the gravity of what took place on their property on November 24, 1863.)

The mountain itself is enormous, extending southward from the Tennessee River for eighty-six miles to its southernmost point near Gadsden, Alabama. But the historical focus is on the northern tip, which overlooks the entire valley that holds the great twisting bend in the Tennessee River. This bend defines the city of Chattanooga. Of course, the city is enormous now compared with the population of fewer than three thousand who lived here during the Civil War. But from the crest of Lookout Mountain, you can understand exactly how and why events unfolded the way they did at the time of the battles here. You can also understand that Braxton Bragg was seriously deluding himself that he could contain and lay siege to the Union army who occupied the city, given the enormous length of the waterway and the miles of mountain passes around the city. He simply didn't have enough men.

After the Battle of Chickamauga, Bragg's Confederate forces occupied the mountain and, as well, the long ridge far to the east (easily visible from the mountain) known as Missionary Ridge. Today, there are artillery pieces on the crest of the mountain that represent the position of a number of Confederate batteries. Bragg intended to drop artillery shells into the city, just as Grant had done at Vicksburg. No matter how effective this haphazard shell fire might be, it would certainly unnerve the Union troops, who could not predict where the next shell might fall. The problem for the Confederate gunners on the mountain, however, is that most of those guns didn't have the range to reach the city itself. From this vantage point, the one benefit the cannon gave

Union troops on Lookout Mountain, 1864
(Company F, 7th Illinois Infantry)
PHOTO COURTESY OF THE LIBRARY OF CONGRESS

Bragg was the ability to destroy any river traffic that might try to move past straight below the mountain, and he had placed a considerable number of troops farther down the face of the mountain to prevent the Union forces from using the river at all. (Other much more effective artillery positions were put into place by the Confederates elsewhere, closer to the river.) As long as Bragg maintained a stronghold on the mountain, he was a threat to Grant's greater plan for the breakout of the Federal forces from Chattanooga. Bragg knew that as long as he controlled the southern banks of the river, he could move reinforcements close to the water and high up on the mountain as well.

Though the mountain has a relatively flat top, the problem for anyone attacking the crest would be reaching the peak in the first place. And from the Confederate point of view, placing a large number of troops high up on the crest made little sense. The purpose of having troops on this mountain was to interfere with Grant's attempts to resupply the city. Putting a large body of men all the way on top of the mountain would take them too far from where they could do any good and, ultimately, would simply strand them there. Getting people up and down the mountain was a formidable challenge. Even today there is just one primary road, which has been carved out of the mountain in such a way as to be somewhat gentle for automobile traffic. In 1863, that road was far straighter and, thus, far steeper. On your way up the road, you can see how vertical the sides of the mountain are just below the crest. But below those sheer cliffs, the mountain has several moderately sloped meadows, which is where the bulk of the Confederate troops were camped.

Early on the morning of November 24, 1863, Major General Joe Hooker was ordered by Grant to attack the Confederate position on Lookout Mountain. This attack was to roughly coincide with Sherman's attack on Missionary Ridge. Hooker was a man in desperate need of redemption for his catastrophic failure at Chancellorsville, and he responded to the task accordingly. With three divisions of fresh troops, Hooker climbed up the southwestern side of the hill, and by ten o'clock in the morning, his men began to sweep along the face of the mountain, driving the surprised Confederates before them. (This attack is represented, somewhat romantically, in a painting on display in the Park Service Visitor Center.) After giving considerable ground, the Confederates finally recovered their composure and gathered enough force to make a stand. On a stretch of relatively flat ground on the north face of the mountain, heavy fighting consumed some two hours, until the Confederates were forced to continue their retreat. As they

Modern view of Chattanooga, Tennessee, from Lookout Mountain; note prominent rock

PHOTO PATRICK FALCI

withdrew toward the eastern side of the mountain, they became engulfed in a heavy fog bank. The Federal troops who pursued them were suddenly facing an enemy who was completely hidden from view. Rather than pursue blindly, the Federals wisely held up their attack and fought only a few skirmishes as the rest of the day passed. By late afternoon, Bragg recognized the hopelessness of his troops' position, and the Confederates were withdrawn toward the passes at Missionary Ridge, leaving the mountain in Federal hands. Early the next day, November 25, 1863, a Union soldier climbed to the highest point on the crest of the hill and planted the Stars and Stripes. The flag could clearly be seen in Chattanooga and was loudly cheered by the Federal troops there. It was seen as well from the crest of Missionary Ridge by the men in Grant's army who were in the process of driving Bragg's forces into a catastrophic defeat.

From the park itself, the perspective of the battle becomes clear. From your viewpoint at the overlook, the fight swept along below you from left to right, beginning on the far left edge of the park (the southwestern side of the mountain). Though thick brush blocks some of the view, and much of what was open land is now shrouded in trees, it is possible to get a clear sense of what Hooker's men accomplished. From that same perspective, move more to the north face, with Chattanooga directly in front of you. If the trees have been trimmed, you can just catch sight of the rooftop of the Craven Farmhouse, which is where the worst fighting took place. The house can be reached from the main road on the drive down the mountain, a well-marked turnoff. The rebuilt house has been preserved by the Park Service, and a photograph on a plaque in the yard shows the house at the time. You can clearly see some of the same boulders and can tell exactly where the photographer stood to take the picture.

Though the Battle of Lookout Mountain has always been referred to as the "Battle Above the Clouds," the major portion of the fighting occurred in relatively clear air. Accounts written by people in the city itself mention the flickers of light they could see, the flashes of musket fire that appeared at that distance as "so many thousands of fireflies."

Though the Park Service property on the crest of the mountain is a relatively compact area, the small admission price there is well worth the experience. If you are fit enough for a healthy climb, I recommend taking the steps that descend the mountain just above the site of the battle. Besides the obvious vantage points, which are pretty spectacular, there is a plaque with a photograph of Ulysses Grant, standing in front of a large rock, plainly evident today. One final note: Lookout Mountain is well over two thousand feet above the valley of the Tennessee River and can absorb some pretty harsh winds. Take a jacket. Even if the temperatures are mild down below, at the crest you can be surprised by the chill.

As you take in the amazing perspective from the mountain, pay special attention to Missionary Ridge. The passes there were the routes used by desperately retreating Confederates and their Union pursuers, in what would result in an entirely new campaign that would contribute to another seventeen months of war.

tention on the southern flanks of both armies. At the Viniard Field, near the Heg Monument, there is a narrow, shallow drainage ditch visible in the field to the west of the road. This becomes known as the Ditch of Death. The Federal troops are positioned in the woods to the far west and have the enormous advantage of the most modern repeating rifles. As numerous Confederate troops attack, they are cut down all across this field. The storm of both rifle and artillery fire causes the rebel attack to fall apart, and many seek whatever shelter they can find. For hundreds of men, this ditch is it. But as is plainly obvious, the ditch can offer very little protection. The Federal artillery responds to the stagnant position of the men here by shifting the position of several cannon so that they can fire canister charges straight down the ditch, thus greatly increasing the slaughter on this field. The Confederate troops who survive here make a rapid escape back across the Lafayette Road to the safety of their original lines.

Note the "castle" monument behind the Federal lines. This marks the spot of the Widow Glenn House, which serves as Rosecrans's headquarters and is the place where he calls his council of war during the night of September 19.

Along the Alexander Bridge Road and the Battle Line Road, in the northern sector of the park are positioned the monuments that indicate George Thomas's Federal position on the morning of September 20, the area along which Thomas has his men construct their log breastworks. Though Thomas arranges his men in rows three deep, note that the monuments today are placed virtually side by side. This is a vivid example of pride and perhaps competition. Even the men who fight in the third line want their unit to be memorialized along the front row. Note too that the monuments are placed in a curving line. This marks the "curve" in Thomas's position that is so effective in holding back repeated Confederate attacks.

Note one monument in particular, to the 15th U.S. Infantry. This is a regular army

Grave of Georgian John Ingraham, the only grave on the battlefield, Chickamauga, Georgia PHOTO PATRICK FALCI

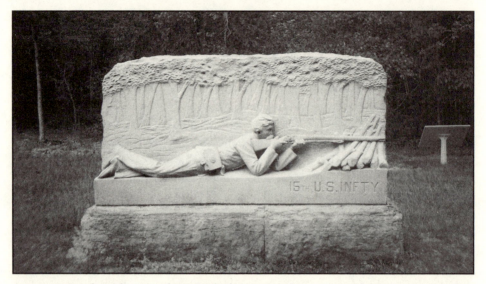

Monument to the 15th U.S. Infantry, Chickamauga, Georgia   PHOTO PATRICK FALCI

unit, as opposed to most other regiments, which were designated by the states where they originated. This same regiment has had a long history in the U.S. Army and participates in the march into Baghdad during the Iraq War.

At virtually the center point of the park, just west of Lafayette Road is the short loop of the Poe Road. Directly across from the Georgia Monument is the point where Rosecrans mistakenly believes he has a gap in his line. So he orders the unfortunate Union general Thomas Wood to pull his division out of line. Wood's men are positioned farther south, the area marked clearly near the Brotherton Cabin, at the Dyer Road intersection. Wood's obedience to the confusing order opens up a gap at this point that Longstreet's men just happen to attack. With almost no opposition in front of them, Longstreet's men race into the rear of the Union position, which marks the beginning of the end for Rosecrans's army. Note the open ground behind the Federal lines, where John Bell Hood drove his men. The hill that rises just to the west is the position from where Rosecrans observes the disaster firsthand. Consider that, from that point, Rosecrans has a choice of going to his left, north, toward Thomas's position, or to his right, toward the smaller portion of his army. Logic would tell you that he should stay with the greater part of his command. But he goes south instead and thus separates himself from communication with the greater part of his army. As the right flank of his command melts away, he has no choice but to melt with it.

From the location of the breakthrough, travel north on the Glenn-Kelly Road. Snodgrass Hill will be clearly evident on your left. To many, this is the most important spot on the battlefield. The hill allows the retreating Federal troops (who still have some fight in them) to form up on good defensive ground and make their stand. This defense holds off attacks from the Confederate forces for several hours. The wooded crest of the hill closely resembles how it appeared in 1863. This is also the place to which George Thomas withdraws his troops (who had been positioned to the east, on the far side of the Lafayette Road from this point). It is, thus, the place where Thomas receives his moniker, the "Rock of Chickamauga," though some maintain that Thomas's troops deserve the name more than Thomas himself. That's one of those contentious points that historians love to debate.

There is no cemetery at Chickamauga battlefield. The National Cemetery for the Union troops killed here is in Chattanooga itself. Since the battlefield was in Confederate hands after the battle, most of the Union dead were put into mass graves. Thus, when they were moved to the National Cemetery, 90 percent of the Union dead were unknown. But there is one, and only one, marked grave on this battlefield. Just east of Battle Line Road, off the Alexander Bridge Road, rest the remains of John Ingraham, Company K, 1st Georgia Volunteers. Given that this field lies in Georgia, the grave is quite well maintained and symbolizes the attention paid by the southern states to their own dead from this battle, most of whom have been scattered into family plots and other cemeteries throughout the South.

Along the northern boundary of the park is McFarland Avenue. If you follow this westward, it will take you through McFarland Gap, which is one of the primary routes of escape used by the Union troops on September 20. Had Bragg's men not been as beaten up as their enemy, they could have pursued the retreating Federals and possibly captured huge numbers of troops, troops who later would get their revenge marching through Georgia.

CHAPTER SEVEN

THE WILDERNESS
and
SPOTSYLVANIA

West of Fredericksburg, Virginia

MAY 5–21, 1864

WHAT HAPPENED HERE

*I*n early spring 1864, Ulysses S. Grant received the recognition he had earned by his accomplishments in the western theater of the war. On March 9, 1864, he was promoted to lieutenant general (becoming, up to that time, the third man in the history of the United States Army to be awarded that rank, after George Washington and Winfield Scott). Abraham Lincoln had purposely elevated Grant to overall command of the entire army, in all theaters of the war. This move took administrative power away from Henry Halleck, a man who already disliked Grant. But Grant had no intention of moving to Washington and replacing Halleck by assuming command from some comfortable office. Halleck was named chief of staff, which soothed his ruffled feathers, and thus he would remain in Washington to handle many of the army's administrative duties, while Grant would put his own headquarters in the field. Grant placed himself right in the middle of the Army of the Potomac, which was still commanded by George Meade. To say that Meade was uncomfortable with Grant suddenly pitching his tent next door is an understatement. But Grant had little patience for the intrigue and bouts of temperamental behavior that seemed to infect many of the Federal commanders, Meade in particular. Whether Meade was comfortable with his presence or not, Grant was in charge and intent on using the latitude Lincoln had given him. Lincoln made it clear that his recognition of Grant had not come from some decision based on politics. The president had put Grant in command because the president sensed that the Union army might *finally* have found the right man for the job. Lincoln vowed that official Washington would keep its nose out of Grant's business. All Grant had to do was fight. For the first time, the massive Union war machine was in the hands of someone who appreciated the value of a broad, large-scale strategy and had the temperament to put that strategy in motion.

Grant possessed a strategic philosophy that had eluded his predecessors. Up until his promotion, every major campaign in the east had as its ultimate target the capital of the Confederacy: Richmond. It was a game as old as warfare itself: Capture the flag. But Grant realized that the rebellion would survive and the war would continue no matter where Jefferson Davis's office happened to be. What allowed the South to wage war was its army, and what drove that army had for the most part been Robert E. Lee. The war was still bisected into two primary theaters, and many observers in both the North and the South believed that unless the Confederate forces could pull off some kind of miracle, the war in the west clearly belonged to the Union. The challenge for Grant now lay in the east. If Grant could destroy Lee's army, the Confederacy would collapse.

Throughout April 1864, Grant designed a plan to engulf Lee's army from different directions, a multipronged pincer putting pressure on Lee that his limited manpower could not overcome. The Army of Northern Virginia was camped in the vicinity of Orange Court House, just south of the Rapidan River, some forty miles west of Fredericksburg. Grant's plan was to pressure Lee from both the Shenandoah Valley and the Virginia peninsula, while Grant himself, with Meade's Army of the Potomac, would move straight into the heart of Virginia, posing a direct threat to Richmond that Lee could not ignore. If Grant had his way, Lee would be forced to confront Grant on the field of battle, where Grant would have overwhelming numbers. Even if Lee was moderately successful in holding Grant away, he would soon be pressed from both east and west by the other two prongs of Grant's attack. Knowing that Lee did not have the resources to fight a war on three major fronts, Grant was convinced that, as he told his subordinates, the end of the war was "just a matter of time."

Grant put his plan into operation on May 4, 1864. In the Shenandoah, some ten

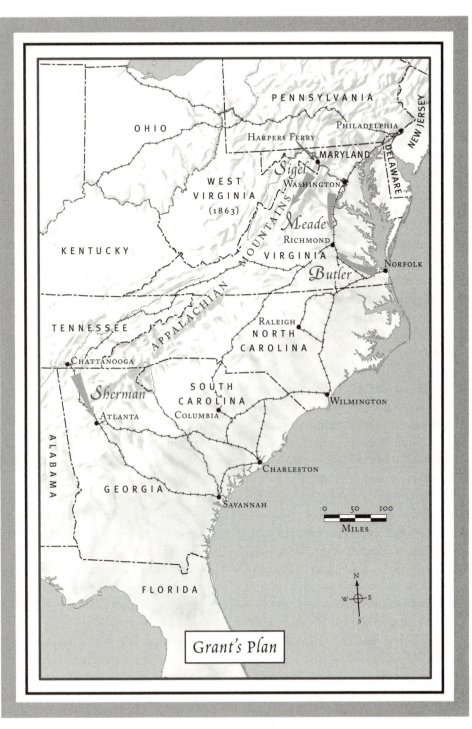

OHIO

PENNSYLVANIA

NEW JERSEY

HARPERS FERRY

PHILADELPHIA

MARYLAND

DELAWARE

Sigel

WEST
VIRGINIA
(1863)

WASHINGTON

APPALACHIAN MOUNTAINS

Meade

Richmond

KENTUCKY

VIRGINIA

Butler

NORFOLK

TENNESSEE

RALEIGH

NORTH
CAROLINA

CHATTANOOGA

Sherman

SOUTH
CAROLINA

WILMINGTON

Atlanta

Columbia

ALABAMA

Charleston

GEORGIA

Savannah

0   50   100
MILES

N
W   E
S

FLORIDA

Grant's Plan

thousand men under Major General Franz Sigel began their march southward, slicing directly into Virginia's most valuable breadbasket. On the banks of the James River, southeast of Richmond, Major General Benjamin Butler put an even stronger force ashore, close to thirty thousand men, who would directly threaten Richmond. If Butler actually captured Richmond, all the better. Meanwhile, Grant brought Ambrose Burnside's 9th Corps from Kentucky to join with Meade's Army of the Potomac. On May 4, more than 120,000 Federal soldiers, a force nearly double the size of Lee's army, began crossing the Rapidan River.

The crossings took place at shallow fords that led Grant's forces directly toward the site of the Battle of Chancellorsville. As the Federal soldiers marched southward, they entered the Wilderness. Along the way, they could not avoid glimpsing the barely concealed skeletal remains of soldiers who had died on this same ground only one year before. The veterans, the men who had actually fought here, quickened their steps, warily eyeing the dismal stretches of blind forest that seemed to press in tightly around the narrow roads. As they passed by more remnants of the horror of that battle, low talk spread through the column, word passing that this ground was no place to fight and that if they were to meet Lee's army again, it would be best if these tangles and thickets were long behind them. Grant agreed with his nervous soldiers and did as much as he could to drive his army out beyond the Wilderness before daylight ran out. But the crossings took time, and the coordinated movement of such a large force of men and equipment consumed the day. They would camp within the boundaries of the Wilderness after all. On the evening of May 4, Grant was far more comfortable than the men in his command. He believed he had sprung a surprise on Lee and that with one more day's march, he could move swiftly out of the tangled countryside and push hard toward the unsuspecting Confederates before Lee could do anything about it.

But Lee was not surprised at all. On a high promontory below the Rapidan River, Lee had seen firsthand the movement in the Federal camps. Anticipating Grant's advance southward, Lee had put his men into motion as well. Grant expected a battle to be fought beyond the boundaries of the Wilderness; Lee had other ideas.

Early on the morning of May 5, 1864, Union pickets stared into a misty haze across a wide field and saw an unexpected sight: Confederates. The pickets assumed that the rebels had sent out a few scouts of their own. Very quickly, they realized they were mistaken. What they saw was Richard Ewell's entire corps. Lee was attacking.

Lee's army was divided into thirds, with two of his corps under Ewell and A. P. Hill, each marching toward Grant's position along the two parallel routes that ran east and west through the Wilderness. The third part of Lee's army was under Longstreet, who had returned east to bolster Lee in the expected spring campaign. Longstreet's corps had been camped much farther away from Lee, but he had been ordered to march as quickly

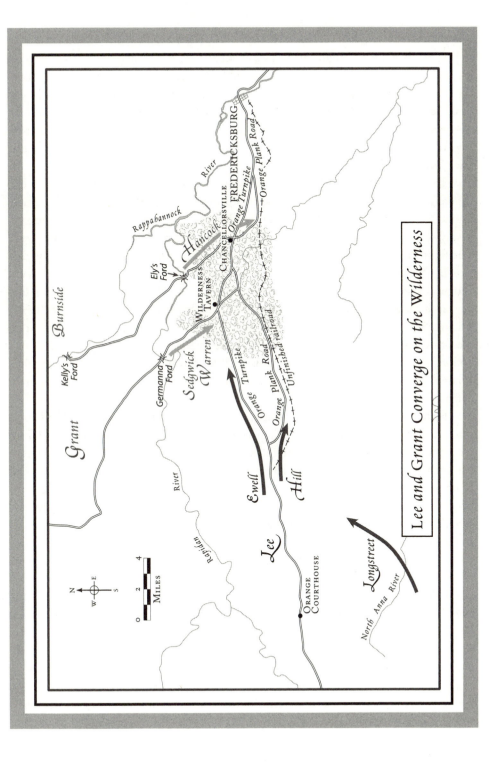

Lee and Grant Converge on the Wilderness

as possible to add his strength to the assault. Lee's plan was simple: Pin Grant down in the Wilderness, where the rough terrain would eliminate the numerical advantage that the Union forces enjoyed. With Grant's men virtually blind to what faced them, Lee could launch attacks from two or even three directions and possibly drive the Federal troops away, just as Stonewall Jackson had done the year before. The obvious danger to Lee was that on May 5 he was attacking the Army of the Potomac with a force a third the size of his enemy.

The Federal units positioned along the route of Ewell's attack moved quickly to meet the danger, and a fight soon spread across the open ground, into the thickets on either side of the main roadway (the Orange Turnpike). Ewell's men began to dig in, throwing up hastily constructed defenses, as Federal units of Warren's 5th Corps drove toward them. The fight was vicious and costly, the lines wavering, ground lost and gained. As the day passed, Warren called desperately for reinforcements, and Grant supported him with Sedgwick's 6th Corps, men who were only now arriving on the field. But Sedgwick did not reach the fighting until mid-afternoon, and the battle had already exhausted itself. Though Sedgwick pressed an attack toward Ewell's left flank, the fight grew stagnant in the dense woods, and no progress could be made by either side. Sedgwick realized that nothing could be accomplished, so by nightfall he had pulled his men back alongside Warren's corps, and the Federal soldiers did as their enemy had already done: They built defensive works.

Farther south of the Orange Turnpike, the parallel road (the Orange Plank Road) was the scene of another equally vicious confrontation. A. P. Hill's Confederates had moved toward Grant's left (southern) flank, hoping to roll up Grant's position there. But Meade had received word of Hill's advance, and Hancock's 2nd Corps was rushed into position to confront Hill. As had happened on the Orange Turnpike, the two sides collided along the Plank Road in the blind morass of brush and undergrowth, both sides absorbing huge losses in a fight that was nearly impossible for the commanders to manage. In the dense thickets, the fighting was occasionally hand-to-hand, men suddenly facing their enemies only a few yards apart. Frustrated artillerymen had no real targets and often simply fired their cannon into the brush regardless of whom they might hit, blasts of canister killing and mangling men on both sides. As night fell, Lee's position along the Orange Turnpike was as strong as that of the men he faced. But to the south along the Plank Road, A. P. Hill made a deadly mistake. With Hill's men scattered all through the woods, there was little organization, officers having no idea where their commands were. Instead of pulling back, reorganizing out of range of the muskets of the Federal troops, Hill chose to keep his men where they were. Throughout a dismal, exhausting night, Hill's troops had no food other than what they might, by chance, be carrying. They had no water beyond the small creeks that wound close by. Most of the men had no choice but to attempt

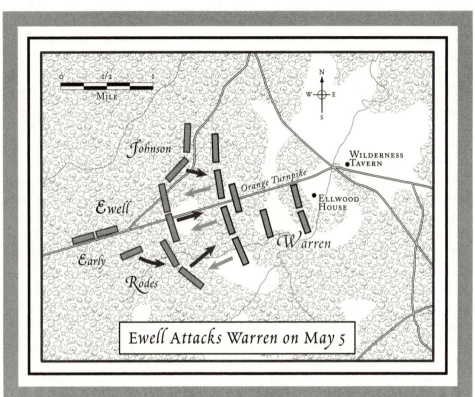

N
W E
S

0   1/2   1
MILE

Johnson

Orange Turnpike

Ewell

WILDERNESS
TAVERN

ELLWOOD
HOUSE

Early

Warren

Rodes

Ewell Attacks Warren on May 5

to find sleep right where they were, since any sound brought musket fire from an enemy (or a friend) that no one could see.

Far worse for the wounded, small fires had broken out in the brush, ignited often by the flashing muzzles of the muskets or the blasts from artillery shells. In the blind spaces between the two sides, these fires consumed a number of wounded men, men who could not escape. Throughout the night, those who survived the awful ordeal of the fight had to endure an ordeal of a different kind: the screams of the men they could do nothing to save.

Grant and Meade realized that their position on the Orange Turnpike was a stand-off, that if any attack was to be made, it should come down below, on the Plank Road. Hancock's 2nd Corps was fully in place, prepared to advance into Hill's disorganized position, while Burnside, with his 9th Corps, would move into the Wilderness to Hancock's right and add enough strength to the attack that Hill's corps might simply be destroyed.

Lee felt no sense of urgency about Hill's position, because he believed that by dawn on May 6, Longstreet's corps would arrive in time to relieve Hill's miserable men. But with the first light, Lee's urgency began to grow. Longstreet was nowhere to be seen. Couriers confirmed to Lee that Longstreet was on the march and could arrive at any time, but across the way, Hancock would not allow the Confederates the luxury of time. At first light, Hancock's men surged westward into the thickets and engulfed A. P. Hill's disorganized troops. In minutes, the force of Hancock's attack drove most of Hill's corps back in disarray. Lee, near his headquarters, was suddenly surrounded by retreating Confederates. Across a wide field, Lee could see the advance units of Hancock's men surging out of a dense tree line, pressing toward him. Lee immediately mobilized a battalion of artillery, under William Poague, to form up in the field; but despite Poague's efforts, his guns were no match for the power of the blue wave that was pressing toward them.

Though Lee's line was collapsing in front of them, Hancock's assault began to slow, the men exhausting themselves as they drove through the underbrush. There were still pockets of fighting in the woods, some of Hill's men either trapped, lost, or simply refusing to retreat. But the momentum was clearly on the Federal side, and Lee could see that the entire right flank of his army was being swept away.

In a moment that only a scriptwriter could create, Lee suddenly realized that fresh troops were streaming up the road behind him, rushing forward. Lee asked who they were, what unit they belonged to. The response was that they were Texans, which Lee knew meant only one thing. They belonged to Longstreet. The final third of Lee's army had suddenly reached the field.

Within minutes, Longstreet's men had blunted the Federal wave and turned them back. Hancock's troops had given all they had in the dense underbrush, and with fresh troops suddenly pushing into their ranks, the fight became too hot to absorb. Hancock's men were pushed back, Longstreet now taking the momentum. As the morning passed,

The Wilderness, Virginia, after the battle, 1864   PHOTO COURTESY OF THE LIBRARY OF CONGRESS

the fight drove the Federals back to their defensive lines. But Longstreet wasn't through. By late morning, one of Lee's engineers had discovered an unfinished railroad cut that led toward the Federal left flank. Quickly, Longstreet sent a strong force down the cut, completely undetected by Federal lookouts. When Longstreet's men were astride Hancock's flank, he ordered them forward. A great mass of Confederates suddenly rose up out of the hidden railroad cut in a burst that completely surprised Hancock's troops. The attack was an overwhelming success. Hancock's line crumbled, and panicked Federals poured past their own lines, the flank rolling up, in Hancock's words, "like a wet blanket."

Both Lee and Longstreet knew that the Confederate assault would soon bog down in the Wilderness, just as every other attack had done. With such an astonishing success at hand, Longstreet had to make sure his troops continued their push. At midday, Longstreet himself rode forward, accompanied by several of his staff and subordinate commanders, including twenty-nine-year-old Micah Jenkins, who commanded one of

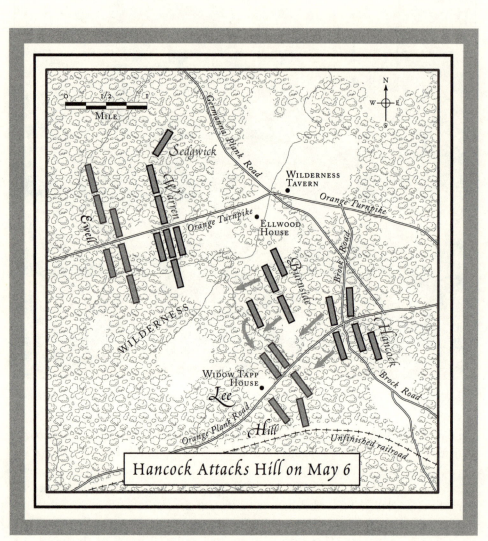

Hancock Attacks Hill on May 6

Longstreet's brigades. As the men rode toward the sounds of the fight, they surprised a group of weary Confederates moving through the jumble of brush. The Confederate troops had been surprised too often, and their jumpiness caused them to open fire on the group of horsemen. Micah Jenkins was killed, and Longstreet was severely wounded, shot in the throat.

Without the push from their commander, the Confederate assault began to lose steam, and with Hancock's men regaining their composure and their defensive lines, the effects of the masterful flank attack began to fade. Before Lee could put Longstreet's troops back into motion, any chance of continuing their success was gone. Worse for Lee, the Army of Northern Virginia had once again lost its best field commander.

At the Orange Turnpike, on Lee's left flank, the day had passed mostly without major incident; but late in the day, Ewell authorized Brigadier General John B. Gordon to attack the Union right flank, which Gordon believed was vulnerable. The attack worked as Gordon had planned, driving the startled Federal troops back into the woods. Had there been sufficient daylight, Gordon's attack might have posed a serious threat to that part of Grant's army. But darkness prevailed, and Gordon's attack succeeded only in scattering two Federal brigades.

As the fires spread once more through the thickets, the two armies lay like two wounded beasts, each angrily eyeing the other. But throughout the day of May 7, there was little fighting, neither side having much interest in venturing out beyond its own strong defensive works. Though his army was resting, Grant was already forming a new strategy.

Several miles to the south, Federal cavalry under Philip Sheridan had spent May 6 scouting out a route that would lead the Federal army away from the Wilderness and put them back on a route that would threaten Richmond. A small force of Confederates had blocked Sheridan's way, forcing a brief but bloody engagement, but Grant ordered Sheridan to continue the southward push. Grant wanted the road cleared of rebels so that the Army of the Potomac could place itself between Lee and Richmond, a situation Lee would have to respond to.

On May 7, Sheridan's men engaged in several cavalry fights with Lee's horsemen, commanded by Major General Wade Hampton and Lee's son W. H. F. "Rooney" Lee. As the fights spread out over roadways and open pastures, the rebels were driven far enough out of harm's way that Grant could now begin his new campaign.

Previously, after every major fight, whether victory or defeat, the men of the Army of the Potomac had become accustomed to either inactivity or rapid retreat. With the awful two-day fight in the Wilderness now growing quiet, the blue-coated foot soldiers began to look back toward headquarters. It had become a dismal custom in the Union army that, since they had been bloodied and embarrassed by their enemy, the order would come for

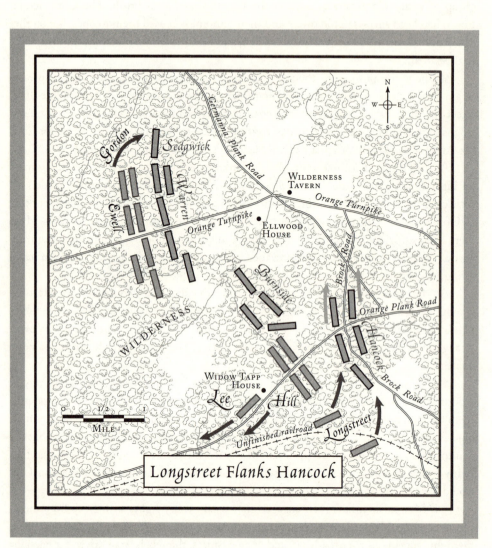

Longstreet Flanks Hancock

them to skulk back to their crossings on whatever river was behind them. As had happened so many times before, the Federal troops expected that they would return to their camps to wait for some new decision maker to descend on them from Washington. But when marching orders came, the men were put into columns facing south, not north. By nightfall on May 7, they began to march not back to their camps, but farther into the enemy's territory. Even in the darkness, it didn't take long for the meaning of this new march to be understood. Along the columns, the enthusiasm returned, beaten and bloodied men no longer cursing the officers who had failed them so many times before. If they were moving south, the meaning was clear. Grant was not retreating. He was still on the attack.

Lee was nearly as surprised as Grant's own men. When he realized that Grant was in fact moving south, Lee recognized that he could not allow the Federal forces to get a significant head start. Lee knew he had one advantage. Given the sheer bulk of the Army of the Potomac, their progress would be slow, marching at night over unfamiliar roads. But Lee had no parallel route to keep abreast of Grant's march. To keep pace, Lee had to force open a pathway through the woods. During May 7, Lee's engineers, led by artillery commander William Nelson Pendleton, created a road on their own, chopping and cutting open a route that allowed Lee's army to march southward as well. For Lee, the march was a desperate race to reach the primary roadways and intersections that controlled the route toward Richmond. Lee knew the countryside, and he knew that Grant's route of march would take him eventually to a crucial intersection, a small village surrounded by open farmland called Spotsylvania Courthouse.

On the morning of May 8, the cavalry clashed again, but the Confederates, under Lee's nephew Major General Fitzhugh Lee, had built and reinforced barricades that lay across the Federal line of march. By now, Federal infantry, Warren's 5th Corps, had reached Fitzhugh Lee's defenses, and faced with overwhelming opposition, the rebel cavalry was forced to fall back. As Warren drove the rebels southward, there was little to prevent the Federals from seizing the intersections that would give Grant the advantages he had sought. A short distance northwest of Spotsylvania Courthouse, Warren's foot soldiers confronted Confederate cavalry again, dismounted horsemen who were using a fence line, hastily converting it to an effective defensive position. But to the surprise of the Federals, a heavy line of rebel troops was filing in behind the dismounted cavalry. They were infantry, led by Major General Richard Anderson, the man Lee had selected to replace Longstreet. Lee had won the race.

Throughout the day on May 8, the two armies gathered to face each other, and fights erupted across a high mound known as Laurel Hill, where the two armies met on mostly open ground, a field of battle completely opposite the Wilderness. Grant pushed the offensive, but the Federal attacks were disjointed. The bulk of the Federal forces moved in clumsy fits and starts, with poor coordination among Grant and his commanders. As

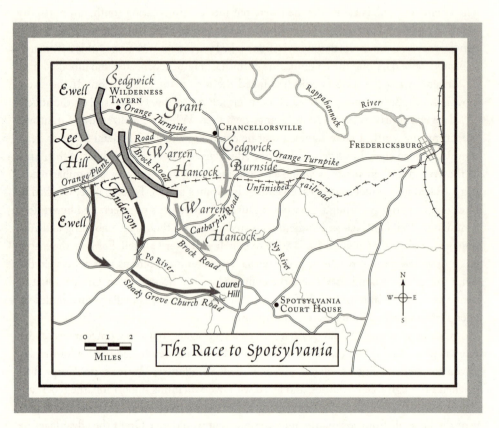

The Race to Spotsylvania

Grant's army struggled to unite, Lee's men had grabbed possession of the best ground, the lessons learned from Gettysburg. At the end of the day, Lee's men were rapidly construct-ing a stout defensive line, while Grant's commanders squabbled with one another about confused positions and lack of support. Though most of the Federal corps commanders seemed to accept that Lee had put them on the defensive, Grant insisted he had the man-power to launch another assault.

On May 9, as the two sides prepared for the inevitable, Major General John Sedg-wick was inspecting his 6th Corps's defenses. Around him, the air was cut by the occa-sional zip and whine of rebel musket fire, and Sedgwick was amused by those of his troops who flinched and ducked at the sound. As he scolded one man, dismissing the rebel marksmanship, saying, "They couldn't hit an elephant at this distance," a musket ball struck Sedgwick in the face, just below his left eye. In an instant, the man affectionately known by his men as "Uncle John" was dead.

Sedgwick's death was a serious blow to Grant, but with the two armies strengthening their position, face-to-face, there could be no delay in Grant's strategy. On May 10, the Federals attacked Lee's army in two major engagements. But Grant had misread Lee's de-fenses, and once again the attacks were snarled by poor coordination and poor execution, which cost the Union forces horrific casualties. With miserable timing, the Federal 6th Corps, now commanded by Sedgwick's replacement, Horatio Wright, launched a limited assault of five thousand men against a point near the center of Lee's lines. The attack, led by Colonel Emory Upton, was designed as a spear, to make a sharp narrow thrust into the Confederate position, the men charging rapidly without firing, so as to hammer a rapid breakthrough before the Confederates could reinforce the position. Upton succeeded bril-liantly, opening a gap in the rebel defenses. But Upton was not supported; no reinforce-ments rushed forward to take advantage of his success. It was as though no one on the Federal side of the line had planned for the possibility that the attack might actually work. By dark, Upton's men were either killed, captured, or pushed back out of the Confederate breach. One of Grant's worst days in command had come blessedly to an end.

All the next day, May 11, Grant reviewed the flaws that had plagued his army. With Lee seemingly content behind his defenses, Grant began to formulate the final assault that could possibly destroy Lee's army where it sat. Grant still had the numbers, and Up-ton's disastrous assault had one silver lining: Upton had proved that what appeared to be an unassailable position could be broken by a heavy and direct attack. If five thousand men could create a breakthrough, then twenty thousand or more might open a breach that Lee could not seal.

Lee's lines followed the lay of the land, with the defensive works constructed along the higher ridgelines. The result was that in the Confederate center, the line extended outward in a bulge some half a mile across. This was referred to as a "mule shoe," given its shape on the maps. As Grant knew, such a bulge could be the weakest point in any line, since it could be attacked from three sides. With an entire day to prepare, Grant made certain that there would be no more failures of coordination, no more lapses in general-ship. Throughout the day, the Federal units shifted their positions, so that Hancock's 2nd Corps would be the spearhead of the attack directly on the bulge in Lee's line, directly on the mule shoe.

It was then that Robert E. Lee made his greatest tactical mistake of the battle.

Rumors had reached the Confederate position that Grant had begun to withdraw his army and had put the Federal troops on the march toward Fredericksburg. There was some logic to the rumors, since Lee knew that a strong force moving in that direction could once again become a serious threat to Richmond. But Lee did not wait for confir-mation of the rumors, and in response, he began to shift as well, moving artillery and men so that they would be prepared to march rapidly to the east if the rumors proved true. With Hancock preparing to launch a massive attack on the mule shoe, that would be the one place on the field where the Confederate troops would most need their artillery. That was precisely the area from which Lee had ordered his guns to be withdrawn.

On the afternoon of May 11, rain had begun to fall, and the defensive positions on both sides became a miserable, mud-filled swamp. In the predawn hours of May 12, as Hancock's men prepared to move forward, the rain had slackened, but now a heavy driv-ing mist had smothered the field. At four-thirty in the morning, the order flowed along the Federal lines. Moments later, some twenty thousand blue-coated soldiers surged out of their cover toward the closest rebel position at the tip of the mule shoe. They were un-detected at first, their sounds muffled by the misery of the weather, heavy rows of troops cresting the rolling ground as they moved toward the bulging salient. The Confederate lookouts were the first to notice the ghostly tide rolling toward them, and muskets came up; but instead of a hard volley of fire, the Confederate troops along the mule shoe heard the light chatter of so many popping percussion caps. To the horror of the sharpshooters, the weather had soaked their powder. The muskets simply wouldn't fire.

Word passed quickly, and more Confederates awoke to what was coming toward them. As Hancock's men grew closer, the undulating terrain would suddenly hide great ex-panses of their lines, making them invisible to the anxious rebels. Shrouded by the mist and the darkness, the Federal troops would appear again, cresting a hill, closer now, close enough that every man along the mule shoe knew that they were about to be swallowed up.

The Federals swarmed completely over the tip of the mule shoe, Confederate units in their path simply obliterated. Gradually, muskets on both sides began to fire, flashes of light cutting through the mist, the ground behind the Confederate works teeming with

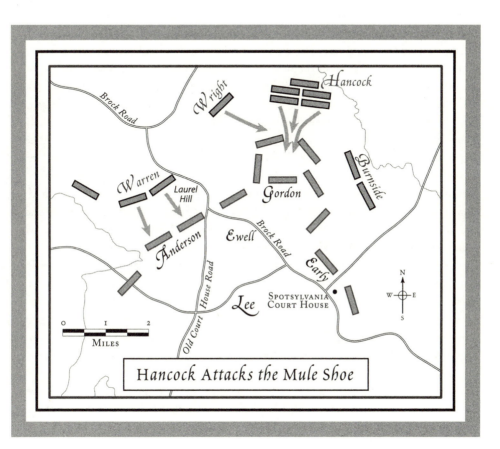

Hancock Attacks the Mule Shoe

men on both sides. Behind the barricades, Lee's men had cut numerous trench lines at varying angles, and the fight spread through the chopped ground. Quickly, the firing of the muskets gave way to bayonets and fists. All order disappeared, but the momentum was still with Hancock, and the tip of Lee's salient was entirely in Federal hands. Behind the mule shoe, Lee had constructed defensive lines that cut straight across the base of the salient, and led by John B. Gordon, men charged forward to hold back the breakthrough, adding to the chaos in front of them. With no order, Hancock's men simply fought any-one who faced them, the rebels doing the same; but the fight began to slow as exhaustion and lack of ammunition took hold. With Gordon's reinforcements, the rebels began to push back the Federal troops until most of the salient was cleared of their enemy. But Hancock's men did not retreat, most staying right at the mule shoe embankment, hunker-ing down along the outside of the Confederate wall. The Federal troops were reinforced as well as Grant sent in Wright's 6th Corps. The log-and-earthen wall gave protection to men on both sides, and the fight engulfed the wall of the mule shoe itself. Men fired at their enemy through gaps in the logs, and others jumped up on top, firing point-blank into men on the other side, until they were cut down as well. To the shock of the men who continued to flow into the fight along the mule shoe, the slaughter would not abate; the fight settled into a horrifying stalemate as greater numbers of men packed together in a swirling, confused mass. As the hours passed, no one gave ground, no one could push the enemy away. Men stood on the lifeless bodies of their comrades, while wounded men drowned in the deepening mud. In some trench lines, the dead were piled four deep, but still the fighting continued. It continued for twenty-two hours. Finally, Lee recognized that little more could be gained from this galling confrontation, and early the next morn-ing, he withdrew his men from the mule shoe, pulling the survivors into a more compact defensive line. The Federal troops who hugged tightly to the works at the tip of the salient now began to call the place the Bloody Angle, a name that everyone who fought there would remember.

While Hancock's men endured some of the most vicious fighting of the war, out on both flanks of the Federal army, Grant ordered his commanders there to assault what he had to believe were the weakest positions in Lee's defenses. Yet while Hancock and Wright fought along the mule shoe, the troops on the Federal flanks under Warren and Burnside accomplished almost nothing.

On May 13, Grant went into motion again. Resting Hancock's exhausted corps, Grant ordered most of his army to slide eastward, seeking to get around the flank of Lee's posi-tion. In driving rain that continued for several days, both armies clumsily sparred with each other without either side gaining an advantage. With the roads churned into deep mud, Grant finally realized that outmaneuvering Lee in those conditions was impossible. On May 21, after more inconclusive and costly confrontations that accomplished nothing more

Confederate dead at Spotsylvania, Virginia   PHOTO COURTESY OF THE LIBRARY OF CONGRESS

than bleeding both armies, Grant finally moved away. Once more, Grant pulled his army toward the east and south, again forcing Lee to accept that Richmond was threatened.

Grant's plan now was simple: Draw Lee out into a fight. Despite Lee's successes at the Wilderness and Spotsylvania, with the resources Grant could call upon, Grant knew that a Union victory was still "just a matter of time."

As the two sides maneuvered toward their next confrontation, word began to spread of a fight that had taken place a few miles from Richmond. The confrontation had occurred May 11 and had involved cavalry, Sheridan's Federals against Jeb Stuart's Confederates. The place was called Yellow Tavern, and it had been a fairly decisive victory for Sheridan. But to Robert E. Lee and the entire Confederacy, the results of the fight had been far more devastating than any military defeat. The refrain had become too familiar in both camps, the good men, the valuable leaders who had been swept away. At Spotsylvania, the Federal troops had mourned the loss of John Sedgwick. At Yellow Tavern, the Confederacy lost the finest cavalryman in either army. Jeb Stuart was dead.

WHY ARE THESE BATTLES IMPORTANT?

$\mathcal{I}$n the two-week period from May 5 through May 21, the cost to Grant's army is astonishing. The Army of the Potomac suffers thirty-six thousand casualties. Lee loses some twenty-one thousand men. Despite claims of southern victory, Lee understands that, as it has been throughout the war, the northern losses are far easier to replace.

The battles are Grant's first tests in handling and coordinating separate commands, and he certainly makes mistakes. Burnside's 9th Corps is not a part of Meade's Army of the Potomac, and Burnside in fact outranks Meade. Though Meade commands a far larger body of men, Burnside has to receive his orders directly from Grant. It is a clumsy system that often breaks down. But the system is not as bad as the men who manage it, and Burnside in particular performs poorly throughout both major fights. On May 6, when Hancock assaults A. P. Hill, Burnside is ordered to support Hancock's right flank. Instead, much of the 9th Corps spends the day lost in the thickets of the Wilderness. At a time when Hancock's exhausted men are being repulsed by Longstreet's timely heroics, Burnside, who could have turned the tide of the battle, makes little if any impact.

At Spotsylvania, Burnside anchors Grant's left flank and has several opportunities to strike Lee in severely vulnerable points. But Burnside is slow to act (or does not act at all). Given his level of frustration with the various failures of his subordinates, it is something of a mystery why Grant does not remove Burnside altogether. (Stay tuned.)

The other Federal commanders have a mixed record in their various fights. While Hancock's 2nd Corps deals out the hardest blow to Lee's army, they absorb it as well. The men of the 2nd Corps deserve the highest praise, but their commander makes several errors. The most damaging occurs on May 6, when Hancock allows Longstreet to turn the Federal flank by the surprise attack from the hidden railroad cut.

The death of Sedgwick is a sharp blow to Federal morale, but the loss of Jeb Stuart is a crushing blow to Lee, one that equals the loss of Stonewall Jackson. James Longstreet proves himself to be the shining star for the Confederate effort at the Wilderness, saving the day for the Confederate right flank and possibly saving A. P. Hill's corps from complete destruction. It is an odd bit of payback for the man whose own flank was rescued by A. P. Hill at Antietam. Hill's mistake in not preparing his men for the assault of May 6 is a painful reminder to Lee that the level of excellence in his command has suffered severely as the war has dragged on. Longstreet is clearly Lee's finest field commander, yet Longstreet's wound will incapacitate him for nearly eight months. The irony of the tragic event is unmistakable to Lee and his troops: first Jackson, now Longstreet. Once again,

Lee's best man on the spot has been shot down by his own muskets, what we now refer to, of course, as "friendly fire."

Though both Lee and Grant make tactical errors, the two weeks of fighting symbolize what is to come. Grant makes leadership mistakes, but he has the resources to overcome them. Despite Grant's tactical errors, his overall strategy is sound: Grant knows that Lee cannot hope to win a war of attrition. He tells Abraham Lincoln, "I propose to fight it out on this line if it takes all summer."

The astonishing carnage that takes place May 12, 1864, at the Bloody Angle reinforces what the men in both armies have come to accept. The war has changed. The days of chivalry, of politeness, of any sort of "gentleman's war," have been wiped away. What occurs at the mule shoe is a horror that, three years before, no one could ever have imagined. Those who witness it realize that the two armies are now capable of carrying their fight to a new, horrifying level. Mutual respect, which has shown itself on nearly every battlefield, has been replaced by an astounding level of viciousness. The shock of so much blood and so much grisly horror has become dulled by the unending duty to destroy the enemy. At Spotsylvania, the two armies demonstrate in graphic terms that they have grown to hate each other.

As the two armies begin to shift southward, maneuver becomes Lee's greatest asset. Both Lee and Grant learn from their mistakes by taking greater control of their forces. To Grant, it is expedience. To Lee, it is survival. Despite loud criticism of Grant in the northern newspapers for his supposed "butchery" of the Union troops under his command, Grant presses forward, renewing the spirit of his army. On Lee's maps, Grant's goal would seem to be Richmond, which is exactly the interpretation Grant hopes for. What the Federal commander wants more than anything else is for Lee to stop maneuvering, to come out from behind his carefully laid out defenses and face Grant on the battlefield. Grant knows that despite the condemnation from his critics, his duty is to wage war, to crush his enemy with as much power and as much brute strength as the North's resources will provide. A mistake by Grant might prolong the war. But a mistake by Lee might end it.

WHAT YOU SHOULD SEE

*A*t the Wilderness and Spotsylvania, the territory under control of the National Park Service falls within the administrative boundaries of what is called the Fredericksburg and Spotsylvania National Military Park. Thus, it is possible, and probably desirable, to experience all four major battlefields there during the same visit: Fredericksburg, Chancellorsville, the Wilderness, and Spotsylvania. There are no actual Visitor Centers at the

Site of the Widow Tapp Farm, the Wilderness, Virginia PHOTO PATRICK FALCI

Wilderness or Spotsylvania sites, though there are "exhibit shelters" with maps. The main Visitor Centers at Fredericksburg and Chancellorsville serve as the focal points for all.

The actual Wilderness battlefield, where much of the fighting of May 5 and 6 takes place, is located roughly five miles west of the Chancellorsville site. In fact, Ellwood, which I detailed in the Fredericksburg chapter, is located adjacent to an area that saw fighting during May 1864.

There is one primary site in the Wilderness battlefield that I strongly recommend. On the Orange Plank Road (Route 621) is an open field marked by a sign indicating the location of the Widow Tapp Farm. This is the site of Lee's headquarters for much of the battle there, and the open field is more or less original in boundaries to the time of the battle. There are several good reasons to park in the designated parking lot and take a walk through the field. When you leave the parking lot at the Confederate (southwesterly) end of the field, the open ground lies roughly toward the northeast. I will use that direction as a point of reference. What remains of the Tapp Farmhouse is marked by a sign, which directs you to a thicket of woods that juts out into the field on your left (west). It is possible to shove your way through the thick brush to reach the foundation site, but it's not an especially good idea. Besides the thorns and tangles (which certainly resemble what most of the Wilderness was like for the soldiers), there is a significant amount of poison ivy in these woods. Be forewarned.

As you walk toward the northeast, facing the far end of the field, you will see a stand of trees roughly a hundred yards in front of you, somewhat to the left (north). This is approximately the area where one of the more remarkable events of the battle occurred, one that had very little to do with the fight itself. Early on the morning of May 6, 1864, Lee, his staff, and Jeb Stuart were meeting in this field. From the patch of forest, a small formation of Federal soldiers suddenly appeared, led only by a sergeant. The Union troops were obviously lost and just as obviously surprised to be facing a cluster of Confederate officers. As Stuart slowly maneuvered his horse in front of Lee, acting as a protective screen, Lee reached into his own saddlebag to retrieve a pistol. The Federal troops, having endured the misery of the Wilderness, were apparently in no mood for a fight. Just as quickly as they had appeared, they vanished back into the woods. It was the Federal sergeant's decision not to order his men to fire a volley. In that single moment, he could have changed the history of the war. It is reasonably certain that he had no idea exactly who the Confederate officers were that his men had stumbled into.

If you walk farther out into the field, you will see a row of cannon, which represents the position where Poague's Battery attempted to hold back Hancock's massive assault on A. P. Hill's beleaguered troops. The woods at the far (northeast) end of the field are where Hancock's troops appeared and the direction from which Hill's men were making their desperate retreat. From behind you, on the paved road itself, is where Longstreet's men suddenly appeared, thus turning the entire attack around. Near Poague's cannon is the most famous episode of "Lee to the rear," the cry that went up from the Confederate troops as they moved toward the fight. As desperate as the situation had been, when Longstreet's men appeared, Lee responded to his commander's instincts and seemed determined to lead the men into the fight himself. His men would have none of that, and before they would join the fray, they insisted quite vocally that Lee remain behind.

Along the paved road is a granite marker to the Texas troops who "saved the day" here. Notice the clear evidence close by of several grave sites, where the bodies of a number of soldiers were exhumed after the war.

Across the road, on the far (east) side is the site where Longstreet was wounded. That site now sits behind a fence and is on private (and vigorously "posted") ground, part of a subdivision. With all respects to the rights of private property owners, this is a particularly galling instance of modern encroachment onto a historically valuable piece of ground. It's a marvelous advertisement for the efforts of those who have a passion for battlefield preservation.

Signs clearly mark the route that Grant's army took as they disengaged from the Wilderness the night of May 7, 1864. The Brock Road (Route 613) runs south from the Plank Road and will take you directly to the Spotsylvania battlefield.

The driving tour of Spotsylvania can be brief, but, as on most ground where such a momentous event occurred, I suggest parking at the signs that indicate the Bloody Angle. There are several interesting sites nearby, including the marker where John Sedgwick was killed and a footpath that follows the route where Emory Upton made his ill-fated attack on May 10. But the highlight of this ground is the apex of the Bloody Angle. Signs will guide you, and once you face out toward the wood line where Hancock's men emerged on May 12, try to imagine the darkness, made worse by the rain and the heavy mist, and then notice the undulating ground. Hancock's men came in thick lines that followed the sloping ground so that to many of the Confederate observers, they seemed to suddenly disappear. Then, when they appeared closer at hand, imagine that, as a Confederate soldier, your gunpowder was too wet for your musket to fire. Not a good way to begin your day.

It might be difficult to absorb the unspeakable horror of what occurred on this ground, since there is no reconstructed wall or trench works to illustrate the point. Whether or not your imagination is up to the task, realize that you are standing on ground that still holds the blood from one of the most tragic days in American (and human) history. If you do little else here, just take a moment to ponder that.

The original trench line of the Bloody Angle is still visible. You can see a trench line

Reconstructed Confederate works at Spotsylvania, Virginia PHOTO PATRICK FALCI

in the grass that extends out to the left, forward of the angle. This is not the original, but was dug after the battle by Federal troops who occupied this ground. Back behind you a few yards into the woods are the remains of a Confederate artillery lunette (so called because of its half-moon shape), where a cannon had occupied a place in line. Farther back in the woods you can find a log-lined trench, which was constructed as an exhibit in the 1960s. Unfortunately, no remains of the original log wall at the Bloody Angle exist, since in this climate, with so many insects and so much moisture and humidity, logs simply don't last.

When you leave this area, notice the open farm country, the simple farmhouses (and try to ignore the modern development). Both armies left this place knowing that they would meet again, very soon, perhaps, on some piece of ground that neither of them could yet predict. What was certain to both Grant and Lee, and the men in their commands, was that what had occurred at Spotsylvania could never be forgotten. It was one more horrifying chapter in a war that had simply gone on for far too long.

CHAPTER EIGHT

NEW MARKET

The Shenandoah Valley, Virginia

MAY 15, 1864

WHAT HAPPENED HERE

As Grant drove his massive army into a confrontation with Lee at the Wilderness, in the Shenandoah Valley, what was to have been a tightly compact hammer blow was moving south as well. This right wing of Grant's pincer was entrusted to Major General Franz Sigel, a forty-year-old German American. Though Sigel had shown some promise at the Battles of Wilson's Creek (Missouri) and Pea Ridge (Arkansas), many of his senior officers believed his greatest talent was his ability to keep his men organized in a retreat. But as the highest-ranking German American immigrant in the army, Sigel held considerable political pull in Washington. A large number of German American troops had joined in the Union effort because of their high regard for Franz Sigel, and the War Department was justified in believing that Sigel's prominence in the field was essential to keeping up enlistments from that part of the northern population. Though Grant and Henry Halleck had only minimal confidence in Sigel, Grant could not avoid the fact that Sigel's current seniority among the troops positioned at the mouth of the Shenandoah Valley made him the logical choice to command the right wing of Grant's grand plan. Grant had every reason to expect Sigel to be successful, since Lee's army would have their hands full east of the mountains. Though Sigel's force was the smallest of Grant's three prongs, Grant knew that there was no effective Confederate defense in place to block Sigel's way. The potential reward of Sigel's success seemed to Grant to outweigh the risk of putting a man in charge who had not necessarily demonstrated tactical brilliance. Sigel's occupation of the Shenandoah would place the South's most productive farmlands in Union hands, and more, would give the Union troops access to the only major east-west route that passed directly through Massanutten Mountain. The road was a gateway that could allow Union forces easy access through the passes of the Blue Ridge Mountains, to bring serious pressure to Lee's army from the west. It was known as the Luray Road, and west of Massanutten Mountain it intersected the main Shenandoah Valley Pike at a small town called New Market.

The Confederates who were quickly gathered in the southern part of the Shenandoah were led by Major General John C. Breckinridge, who had shown considerable skill at Shiloh and whose flank attack had nearly won the Battle of Chickamauga. Breckinridge had been vice president of the United States under James Buchanan, and in 1860, he finished second in the election that put Abraham Lincoln in the White House. In May 1864, Breckinridge received orders from Robert E. Lee to march his own command to the valley and to gather whatever additional forces could be quickly assembled. While Lee focused on the massive threat of Grant and the Army of the Potomac, Breckinridge would be the man to confront Sigel, to hold not only the crucial Luray Road at New Market, but the valuable rail centers all throughout the Shenandoah and thus preserve the bread-basket of the Confederacy.

Sigel outnumbered Breckinridge by a margin of roughly eight to five, and as a precaution, Breckinridge accepted an offer from Francis H. Smith, superintendent of the Virginia Military Institute (VMI) in Lexington, that the VMI cadets be allowed to add their muskets and one section of artillery to the defense of the valley. Breckinridge was well aware that Jefferson Davis opposed such a move, that the VMI cadets, many of whom were below the age of enlistment, were not yet fully trained as soldiers. Lee had long suggested that the cadets be used in battle only as a last line of defense, should VMI or Lexington come under direct assault. But Breckinridge knew that he was outnumbered, and though he fully intended that the cadets be held back as reserves, he accepted Smith's offer and approved the order for the cadets to march northward to join up with his army.

In May 1864, Lexington, Virginia, was engulfed by the emotion of the first anniversary of the death of the Confederacy's greatest hero, Thomas "Stonewall" Jackson. None were as inspired by the memory of their finest commander as the VMI cadets, who revered Jackson as one of their own. On May 11, 257 cadets marched northward, and after slogging their way through a dismal rainstorm, they made the thirty-five-mile trek to Staunton in two days.

To the north, Sigel continued to approach, crossing the Shenandoah River several miles north of New Market. Along the way, he began to make critical mistakes. He divided his forces, responding to nuisance raids from Confederate cavalry, and once across the river, he peeled off two regiments of his troops to stand guard at the bridge, now in his rear. Veteran officers in his command knew the symbolism of that kind of decision. An aggressive commander would burn the bridge to prevent the enemy from circling around behind him. A timid commander would guard the bridge carefully, keeping it intact—in case he needed to retreat.

On May 15, the two armies converged at New Market. Breckinridge intended to remain on the defensive, and Sigel obliged him by attacking. But Breckinridge had placed his troops on high ground, Shirley's Hill, just southwest of the town of New Market. Sigel's assault was quickly pushed back, and Breckinridge realized the momentum had shifted. He ordered the Confederates to attack. The two sides pushed back and forth across the open farm country west of New Market and in and out of the town itself, and by late morning, Sigel had pulled his troops to a defensive position alongside their artillery, on a ridge that stood high above a farm owned by Jacob and Sarah Bushong. The Confederates advanced northward through the farm and reached a fence line at the far end of the Bushong orchard. But Sigel's artillery had the range and opened up on Breckinridge's men with canister, the most brutal form of artillery fire. Great gaps were ripped in the Confederate lines, particularly weakening the center. It was at that moment that Breckinridge faced the agonizing decision of whether or not to employ the VMI cadets. Just after noon, Breckinridge sent word:

"Put the boys in, and may God forgive me for the order."

When the cadets had first arrived, they had been assigned to guard the supply train in the Confederate rear, and most were frustrated at being kept away from the fight. Though the march had inspired considerable dread in some of the boys, the sounds of the growing battle began to inspire them. Only a handful of the boys, some as young as fifteen, had ever seen combat, and none had any idea what they would find when they marched northward through the Bushong Farm.

As the cadets advanced in the thick mist and soaking rain, they were led by a VMI faculty member, Lieutenant Colonel Scott Shipp. Shipp led them directly around the Bushong Farmhouse, then quickly advanced through the orchard, where they were put into position at the split-rail fence line. Shipp was wounded almost immediately, and al-

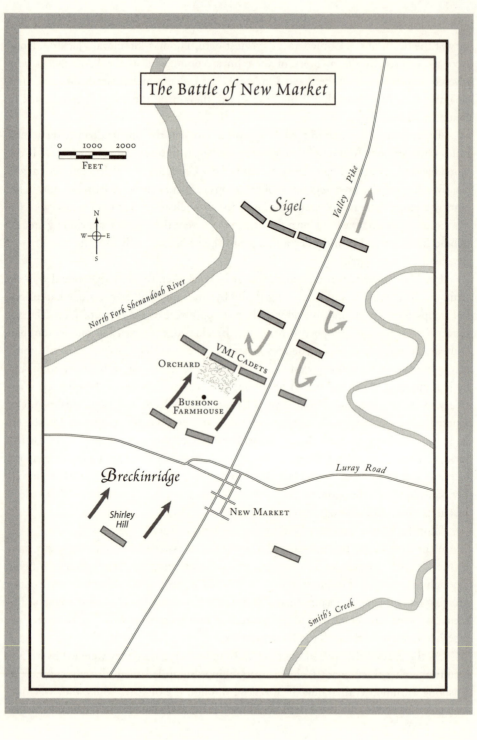

The Battle of New Market

ready the boys had seen some of their own fall: At least five of the cadets had been struck dead. Kneeling amid the bodies of the men who had been so brutally shattered by the Union canister, the cadets faced the massed enemy who lined the high ridgeline 250 yards to their front. There, for the first time, the cadets fired a volley of their own.

Sigel's field commanders were not as shaky as their leader, and the Union troops, behind the continuous fire of their mass of artillery, were ordered to charge down the wide, sweeping wheat field into the line occupied by the cadets. But as the Union troops advanced across the field, they were met by effective Confederate artillery fire as well as the musket fire of the cadets and other troops along the fence line. The attack quickly bogged down, the Union lines breaking up, many of the troops retreating back up toward their artillery.

The wheat field in front of the VMI cadets had now seen two Union advances, and with the rain soaking the ground, the wheat had been trampled into mud. Directly in front of the cadets, the field had a bowl-

"Virginia Mourning Her Dead,"
Virginia Military Institute campus,
Lexington, Virginia PHOTO PATRICK FALCI

like depression, which was now little more than a knee-deep bog. With the enemy in front of them pulling away in some disorder, the officers in command of the fence line ordered the Confederates to pursue—making a charge of their own. The cadets stood with the rest of the soldiers and began to advance through the mud. As they moved across the boggy depression, the boys began to lose their shoes, but they continued the assault, and though ripped by Union artillery and musket fire, they eventually reached the enemy guns. Along the way, the cadets would ultimately see ten of their own killed and forty-seven wounded.

As Sigel learned of his failure to sweep away the Confederates, the chaotic fight caused him to become considerably agitated; losing his composure, he began to shout his orders in German. Sigel's agitation only added to the confusion, and since his orders could not be understood, the Union forces could offer little organized resistance to the Confederate advance. By midafternoon it was over, as Sigel finally ordered his soaked and weary troops to retreat to the carefully guarded bridge on the Shenandoah River. While the Confederates could certainly have pursued, and possibly have crushed Sigel's forces, they were held in check by a Union officer, Captain Henry duPont, who, without orders, executed a masterful retreat using artillery and musket fire to hold the Confederates at bay, delaying them long enough to allow Sigel's men to reach the safety of the river. For his actions that day, Henry duPont was awarded the Medal of Honor.

WHY IS THIS BATTLE IMPORTANT?

*W*ith Sigel pushed out of the Shenandoah, the Virginians will be able to safely harvest the considerable bounty of their farms in the valley, thus feeding themselves as well as Lee's army. Though Franz Sigel claims (incorrectly) that he is greatly outnumbered by Breckinridge's forces, Grant has seen enough of failure, and barely a week after the battle, Sigel is replaced by Major General David Hunter. Though Grant's original strategy for punching at Lee's army through the Blue Ridge is thwarted, Hunter will eventually push his men southward through Lexington and, in the process, shell and burn VMI, a brutal and needless destruction that holds no strategic importance for the North and forever taints Hunter's reputation.

The Battle of New Market is the Confederacy's last major victory in the Shenandoah, the last chapter of a legacy that had begun two years earlier, under the brilliant guidance of Stonewall Jackson. Jackson had engineered the defeat of four separate Union armies and had kept the valley free of Union occupation against overwhelming odds. On May 15, 1864, the valley is protected again, not by the genius of a superior commander, but by the helping hand of a group of boys who leave behind a tragic story of their own on that field.

WHAT YOU SHOULD SEE

*W*hile the exploits of Stonewall Jackson are memorialized on several battlefields throughout the Shenandoah Valley, much of that ground has been obliterated by modern growth. I know of no single piece of ground in the valley that surpasses New Market in terms of poignancy and as a place where families can visit not only to walk in the footsteps of those who fought, but to gain a clear understanding of what the experience must have been like. The ground is that well preserved.

Today, the land that encompasses a sizable part of the New Market battlefield is owned by the Virginia Military Institute. Much of that land was donated to the institute in 1964 by one of the alumni, George R. Collins. Since then, VMI has been able to secure

The Virginia Military Institute

TO ABSORB THE FULL EXPERIENCE OF THE NEW MARKET BATTLE-field, you must certainly make the journey southward to Lexington, roughly an eighty-five-mile drive down Interstate 81. The VMI parade ground appears virtually identical to the ground in 1864, but today, the far (eastern) end is dominated by the imposing statue of Thomas "Stonewall" Jackson. Beneath Jackson's gaze are four artillery pieces that were used to instruct the VMI cadets. They were named Matthew, Mark, Luke, and John by the devout Jackson, a bit of lore carried by every VMI alum. These guns have been restored to their original condition and color. Visitors (and VMI alumni) often ask why the cannon are red. The color indicates that they are not regulation army ordnance, since the barrels are slightly smaller than specifications required for a six-pound cannon of the time. Below the guns is a plaque explaining their history.

Buried close by are the remains of Little Sorrel, Jackson's horse.

The VMI Museum, adjacent to the parade ground, is a must-see for anyone visiting the institution. On display is the Henry Stewart Gun Collection, an extraordinary collection of firearms, including very rare examples of early experimental technology, most of which were never used on a large scale. The museum

Statue of Thomas "Stonewall" Jackson, overlooking the Virginia Military Institute parade ground, Lexington, Virginia PHOTO PATRICK FALCI

holds Jackson's original field desk, and no one can miss viewing, and contemplating, the original raincoat that Jackson was wearing on May 2, 1863, the night he was shot by his own men. The bullet hole in the left upper sleeve is plainly visible.

There are two other points of interest in this museum that must be seen, which have nothing to do with the Civil War. The first is the collection of VMI class rings, dating back to just after the school's founding in 1839. But more important is the small anteroom in the back of the museum housing numerous collections of medals awarded to VMI alumni for military heroism, including an astounding seven Medals of Honor.

The museum resides in the basement of Jackson Memorial Hall, and the hall itself is a remarkable site, used for various official services as well as private functions. Take a moment to examine the large mural against the back, depicting the Battle of New Market.

Outside the hall, along the sidewalk that parallels the parade ground, you can view the graves of six of the ten VMI cadets who died at New Market. They rest beneath an extraordinary bronze statue, named "Virginia Mourning Her

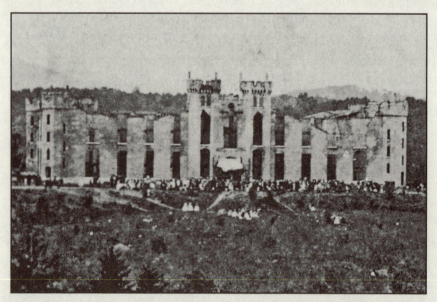

Ruins of the Virginia Military Institute after Union general David Hunter's rampage, Lexington, Virginia PHOTO COURTESY OF THE VIRGINIA MILITARY INSTITUTE

Dead." The statue is the creation of Moses Ezekiel, a VMI graduate and one of the cadets who fought at New Market. Ezekiel was the first Jewish cadet to attend VMI, and his career is among the most notable in VMI history. Ezekiel was a sculptor of considerable fame and accomplishment, who created, among some two hundred works, the statue of Thomas Jefferson at the University of Virginia in Charlottesville, the Confederate Memorial at Arlington National Cemetery, and the bronze statue of Edgar Allan Poe in Baltimore.

If you walk across the parade ground and along the grave sites of the fallen cadets, invariably you will see cadets moving past, some in uniform, some engaged in various athletic games out on the field. In all my contact with VMI cadets and their families, I have come to understand how important the relationship is between the history of the place and the young men and women who attend this institution. No matter their awareness of VMI's history when they arrive, when they leave, the legacy of New Market, of General Jackson, of Moses Ezekiel, and of all who have come before them is a significant part of their educational experience. It is said that when the cadets made their charge at New Market, they left behind any sense of their individuality, that their training had made them parts of a whole, that it was "corps forward" across that muddy field. The cadets today at VMI seem to understand that they are carrying on an important tradition, that they are part of a legacy of sacrifice and heroism, that the history of the place is something they will carry with them long after their education is complete. While the same is certainly true for other service academies, such as West Point, one distinct difference that VMI (and the Citadel in Charleston, South Carolina) has from the various U.S. military academies is that the cadets here are being trained as "citizen-soldiers." Though the training at VMI is military in nature, the cadets are not necessarily being trained to be soldiers. Upon graduation, they do not necessarily receive a military commission, and their instructors are not necessarily officers of the U.S. military. (The faculty members at VMI are designated by rank in the Virginia Militia.) It is understood that the cadets will use their experience at VMI in ways often quite different from traditional military activities. It's easy to forget that when you watch them at drill or observe their decorum, a polite "sir" as they pass by, a crisp salute toward a passing officer. It's easy to forget that these cadets are also college students, but I'm confident that whether or not they have a particular passion for studying history, they are well aware of the legacy of those who came before them.

Washington and Lee University

DIRECTLY ADJACENT TO THE VMI CAMPUS SITS THE CAMPUS OF A school that is in many ways a direct contrast to VMI. Instead of buff-colored military architecture, Washington and Lee is a serene place, with tree-covered walkways and redbrick buildings. The students look much more like . . . well, students.

Lee Chapel, campus of Washington and Lee University, Lexington, Virginia
PHOTO PATRICK FALCI

Among the antebellum homes on campus is one occupied today by the president. Though not open to the public, it was in fact constructed for Robert E. Lee when he assumed the presidency of the school (then called Washington College) in the late 1860s. In the dining room of this home is the place where Lee spent his last days, confined to a bed after suffering a stroke. At the north side of the house, on what is now a patch of (private) open yard, throngs of Lee's veterans and other citizens gathered to view Lee through his dining room window as he lay dying, paying their last respects to their general. (The window is today a set of French doors.) Alongside the home is an older, slightly smaller house, which had served as the president's home prior to Lee's arrival. It is in this house, occupied by Washington College founder George Junkin, Thomas Jackson's first father-in-law, that Jackson endured the devastating loss of his first wife, Ellie, when she died giving birth to his first child, who was stillborn. Understandably, since that house is also a private residence in use today, it is not open to the public.

Down the long, sloping hill from the row of residences is the Lee Chapel. This is a must-see, for several rather emotional reasons. The chapel was constructed in 1867 under the guiding hand of Lee himself and was used as a place of worship. In the basement, Lee maintained his administrative offices. The basement today is a museum, housing the Washington-Custis-Lee Collection, with artifacts dating back to the time of George Washington, for whom (of course) the school was originally named. One room of the museum is Lee's office, left exactly as it was the day he died in October 1870. The papers, books, and furniture are original and placed precisely where Lee left them.

In the rear of the museum is the Lee family vault, where the general and many of his family are buried. Included in the marble vaults are his father, Henry "Light Horse Harry" Lee; his mother, Ann Carter Lee; and Lee's many children. On the chapel level is the stark white marble statue of General Lee at rest, sculpted by Edward Valentine. Just outside the chapel, beside the southern exit to the museum, is the grave of Lee's horse, Traveller. It is a charming and touching tribute to the faithful horse that people continually place various foods on the stone marker, usually carrots. However, for reasons no one seems able to explain, the stone is also a repository for a great many pennies.

The Stonewall Jackson House

LOCATED AT 8 WASHINGTON STREET, IN LEXINGTON, VIRGINIA, THE only home Stonewall Jackson ever owned is now fully restored and serves as a museum for his personal and family life. Jackson and his second wife, Anna, occupied the house in 1859. Built originally in 1801, the house was not restored until 1979 and more recently has been renovated with a sharper eye toward historical accuracy. The house offers a simple, no-frills slice of life from Thomas and Anna Jackson's perspective. From the backyard outbuildings framing Jackson's beloved garden to the wallpaper, furniture, and flooring, the details provide an almost eerie sense of calm, a complete contrast to the battlefield monuments and artillery pieces that more often symbolize Jackson's life.

The house is open to the public daily, except major holidays, and tours are offered every half hour.

Stonewall Jackson Memorial Cemetery

SOME WHO TOUR OUR NATION'S HISTORIC SITES ARE DEDICATED TO the exploration of old or historic cemeteries in general, but this one has an aura and a roster of inhabitants that will appeal greatly to anyone with a particular interest in Confederate history. Spread over a peaceful hilltop just south of the center of downtown Lexington, the cemetery is dominated by the imposing figure of General Jackson, a monument placed over his grave site with considerable ceremony in 1891. Resting with the general is his wife, Anna, and their young daughter, who died at barely a month old. At the site as well, which is encased by an iron picket fence, are the graves of Jackson's only child to reach adulthood, Julia,

Stonewall Jackson's original grave site, Stonewall Jackson Memorial Cemetery, Lexington, Virginia PHOTO PATRICK FALCI

and her progeny. In several visits to this monument, I have observed that more often than not, someone has placed a lemon at the foot of the monument, a poignant tribute to Jackson's well-known quirkiness, including his much portrayed love of lemons.

As profoundly impressive as is the Jackson Monument, if you look westward from that point (toward the center of Lexington), you will find Jackson's original grave site, dating from his death in May 1863. Though the newer monument was designed as Jackson's final resting place, the simple headstones of his first burial plot were left in their original location, for which we should be grateful. It is noted that at the time of his death, the body of Jackson's infant daughter was placed in the coffin with him. Just beyond Jackson's original grave site is the family plot of the Junkins, wherein rest Ellie Junkin Jackson, the general's first wife, and her sister, Margaret Junkin Preston, one of the most literate and respected women of the nineteenth century. George Junkin's remains were interred at this site, though as a staunch Unionist he had left Lexington at the outbreak of the Civil War and moved to Pennsylvania. George Junkin founded Washington College and later became president of Lafayette College and Miami University, Ohio.

Other graves spread throughout the cemetery have enormous historical meaning both for the Confederacy and for Lexington and its institutions. Among many are the grave sites of Jackson's staff officer, Colonel William "Sandie" Pendleton. Interestingly, Sandie's wife, Kate Corbin, is buried elsewhere in this same field, alongside the man who became her husband after Sandie's death in 1864. Kate Corbin is the aunt of the charming five-year-old Jane Corbin, who so captured Jackson's affections while he was camped in winter quarters in early 1863. I portrayed the story of their relationship in *Gods and Generals,* every detail of which is true. But while Jackson was being completely charmed by the five-year-old, Colonel Pendleton was pursuing a somewhat more mature relationship, which, sadly, lasted only until his death in battle barely a year later. Sandie is buried alongside his father, General William Nelson Pendleton, who commanded much of Lee's artillery in the early part of the war, and the man who brilliantly commanded the efforts that allowed Lee to win the race to Spotsylvania.

Several other prominent graves here include Virginia governors John Letcher and James McDowell; Confederate general E. F. Paxton; J. T. L. Preston, the founder of VMI; and General Francis Smith, who commanded the institution during the Civil War—and who, in May 1864, offered the service of his cadets at what would become known as the Battle of New Market.

additional acreage and continues to work with local preservation groups so that eventually some six hundred acres will be under its protection.

Though Interstate 81 runs more or less directly through the site of the battle, and separates the town of New Market from the VMI property, the site is a magnificent place to visit. Fortunately, the preserved land encompasses much of the Bushong Farm, including the farmhouse, several outbuildings, and the location of the orchard. The apple trees there now are not original but consist of varieties of apples found on this land in the nineteenth century, a nod to authenticity that most caretakers of a site such as this would ignore and most visitors would miss. In addition, the split-rail fence line where the cadets made their first stand is faithfully reproduced, and most poignantly of all, the bowl-like depression, where the cadets made their advance, is clearly apparent. That part of the field has become known as the Field of Lost Shoes, a name given the ground by one of the young participants in that day's tragic battle.

If you take a walk northward (if it's raining, you might lose your shoes as well), you can follow the exact steps of the cadets as they moved up the long rise in front of them. The two artillery pieces there on the ridge represent the cannon captured by the cadets but as well show the proximity of the two sides. At the time of the battle, the Union cannon were lined up virtually hub to hub along the clearly visible ridgeline. It's easy to imagine how devastating the artillery would be from guns that close to a line of advancing troops.

The Bushong Farmhouse is open for view and contains several original artifacts

The Field of Lost Shoes, New Market Battlefield, Virginia PHOTO PATRICK FALCI

The Bushong Farmhouse, circa 1880, New Market, Virginia
PHOTO COURTESY OF THE VIRGINIA MILITARY INSTITUTE

belonging to the family. Note that the Bushong family remained in their own basement throughout the battle, a testament to stubbornness. The house became one of many hospitals after the fight, and it's not hard to imagine the gruesome scene repeated in homes all through this part of the valley. The Bushong Farmhouse is just one more place where outside, the surgeons stack grotesque piles of amputated arms and legs.

Just south of the Bushong Farm, at the entrance to what is now a Virginia State

Modern view of the Bushong Farmhouse, New Market, Virginia   PHOTO PATRICK FALCI

Park, VMI has constructed the Hall of Valor Civil War Museum, conceived as a tribute to the fallen cadets. The museum contains a large number of exceptional artifacts from the battle. (Notice in particular a musket that has been shattered by an artillery shell, a nearly unique artifact.) The poignancy of the youthfulness of the cadets who fought there is unmistakable, as evidenced particularly by the letter on display, written by nineteen-year-old Cadet Beverly Stanard, who actually died on the steps of the Bushong Farmhouse. (Since the time of the battle, every generation of the Stanard family has always had at least one child named Beverly, man or woman, as a memorial tribute to the young cadet.)

The museum also houses an exceptional bookstore and numerous other exhibits that rival many of the much larger facilities on other battlefield sites. Notably, on sale in the museum store is the DVD version of *Field of Lost Shoes,* an Emmy Award–winning documentary on the battle and its young participants, one of the best documentaries of its kind. As well, there are living history guides who offer frequent programs for schoolchildren. The museum is open daily 9:00 a.m. to 5:00 p.m., except Thanksgiving, Christmas, and New Year's Day.

CHAPTER NINE

COLD HARBOR

Old Cold Harbor, Virginia

MAY–JUNE 1864

WHAT HAPPENED HERE

*G*rant's grand strategy of crushing Lee's army within the vise grip of a three-pronged assault had begun to unravel. While Sigel was being embarrassed in the Shenandoah, Major General Benjamin Butler's foray along the Virginia waterways was an adventure of the absurd. Butler, whose longevity in the army depended on his political connections, had demonstrated once and for all that he had no place either at the planning table or leading troops into battle.

Butler was as disliked by his subordinates as Braxton Bragg had been. The Confederate forces in north Georgia had already learned how an inept commander could defeat his own army, and now the Federals southeast of Richmond were finding out as well. Butler stumbled and staggered his way through several engagements, none of which produced any significant gains. All the while, he issued a self-congratulatory torrent of messages, telling Washington that Richmond would soon be well in hand.

His opponent, P. G. T. Beauregard, had been summoned from the Carolinas by Jefferson Davis, and though Beauregard had a tendency to suggest strategies that seemed far more fantastic than workable, he was clearly superior to Butler. By May 18, as Grant began to maneuver away from Spotsylvania, Butler was busy recoiling from a costly defeat that Beauregard had inflicted on the Federal troops at Drewry's Bluff, southeast of Richmond. Butler seemed to believe that by pulling his army together into a compact position, he could make some effective show of confronting the outnumbered rebels and at the same time fulfill the boasts he was sending the War Department. But Butler had no appreciation for the geography of his position. He withdrew his army into his well-defended base at Bermuda Hundred, a peninsula below Richmond wrapped by the James and Appomattox Rivers. The mouth of the peninsula was pinched into a narrow stretch of land, which Beauregard immediately recognized as a perfect place for an outnumbered force to contain a much larger one. The Confederates rushed forward and dug a stout trench line across the narrow opening to Bermuda Hundred. Butler's army was thus hemmed in by the wide river and unable to dislodge Beauregard's troops. Instead of rolling a powerful threat toward Richmond, Butler had allowed himself to become (in Grant's words) corked in a bottle.

With Butler now unable to divert Lee's attentions, Grant returned once more to the strategy of maneuver. Grant's ultimate goal had not changed. By again marching the Army of the Potomac toward Richmond, he knew that Lee would be forced to abandon the rebel trench lines, and once more, the Army of Northern Virginia could be brought out into the open. Between Spotsylvania and Richmond, the next major rail center in Grant's path was Hanover Junction, which sat just below the North Anna River. Should the Federals capture that rail junction, Lee's supply lines to the south would be seriously impaired. Naturally, Grant assumed that Lee would do everything he could to protect Hanover Junction, and the place to do that most effectively was along the line of the North Anna.

As the two armies moved along parallel routes, both sought the advantage, a chess game of deception and feinting moves that for the most part simply didn't work. Numerous fights erupted along the way, none having any major effect. Nothing had altered Grant's intentions to force Lee into a major engagement, and nothing had changed Lee's desire to avoid one. Once again, Lee had the advantage of speed and maneuverability, and the race to the banks of the North Anna was won by the Confederates.

Lee recognized that the only means to defeat Grant was a sudden surprise blow that might crush a significant, and separate, portion of the Federal army. At both the Wilderness and Spotsylvania, Grant's commanders had demonstrated sluggishness and the utter

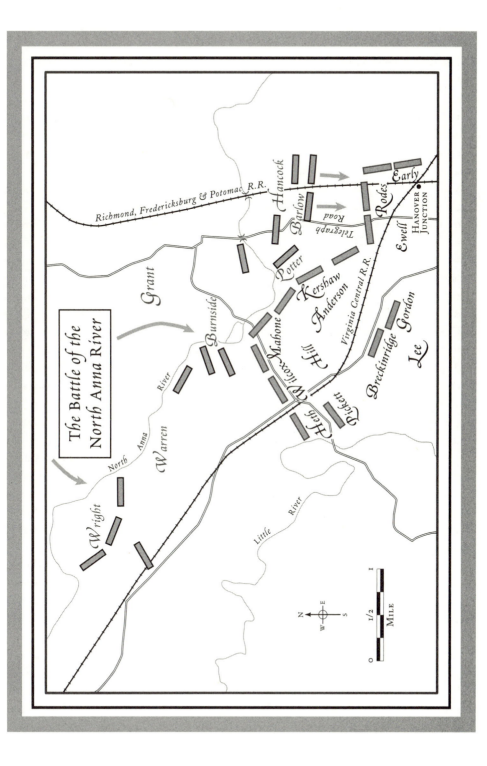

The Battle of the North Anna River

Richmond, Fredericksburg & Potomac R.R.

Hancock

Barlow

Early

Rodes

Telegraph Road

Hanover Junction

Ewell

Grant

Potter

Kershaw

Anderson

Virginia Central R.R.

Burnside

Mahone

Wilcox

Hill

Breckinridge

Gordon

Lee

North Anna River

River

Warren

Pickett

Heth

North

Little River

Wright

N
W — E
S

1/2
MILE

0

failure to coordinate with one another. If Lee was to strike effectively, he had to rely on a repeat of that same kind of performance. Lee devised a plan where his army would fold back on both flanks, so that only the tip of an upside-down V would actually rest on the river. If Grant attempted to cross the North Anna, a direct attack on Lee's troops would cause Grant to split his army along the V. Lee relied on Grant's lack of familiarity with the terrain, which along the river could be heavily wooded, rocky, swampy ground. It was the perfect place for Lee to spring a trap on a sizable portion of Grant's army.

On May 24, Grant's men began to fall right into Lee's trap. The Federal commanders had wholly inaccurate maps, and as Lee had hoped, the two flanks of Grant's army became divided. The geography near the river and Federal confusion created a dangerous situation for Grant. Once they moved south of the river, the two halves of the Federal army could support each other only by a circuitous route that would require two river crossings. It was exactly the situation Lee had planned for. But both commanders knew that a perfect plan on paper is rarely sustained on the battlefield. Lee's grand opportunity was to dissolve by the mismanagement of his subordinates and by a stroke of fate Lee could not avoid. As the battle began to unfold, Lee was struck down with a severe case of diarrhea that so debilitated him, he could not ride his horse. Lying prostrate in his tent, he had to rely on the efficiency of his three corps commanders, A. P. Hill, Dick Ewell, and Richard Anderson. But none of the three showed the skill or initiative to take advantage of the opportunity Grant had offered them. Lee responded with uncharacteristic fury to the failures of his subordinates, knowing that a magnificent chance to crush Grant's army had been squandered.

Grant quickly realized the precarious position his army was in, and by the next day, May 25, the Federal troops had pulled into a strong defensive line. But Grant saw no good reason to confront Lee on such difficult ground, and once more, Grant's overall strategy went into motion. On May 26, the Federal forces were withdrawn from the North Anna River and shifted out to the east. Once more, Grant would try to force Lee into the open by marching toward Richmond.

Lee responded the only way he could. Moving to parallel the Federal march southward, Lee put his army between Grant and the crucial rail junctions that led to the city. As Grant marched southeast, he followed the path of the Pamunkey River, a natural defensive line that prevented any surprise attacks from Lee. But the Pamunkey actually took the Federal army to the northeast of Richmond, a move that somewhat baffled Lee. Lee took advantage and marched his army into position directly between Grant and the capital. With the two armies drawing up into a new arena, to Lee, the symbolism of his position was obvious. The two armies were now turning to face each other on the same ground where some of the Seven Days' Battles had been fought two years prior. Then, Lee had faced a reluctant and sluggish George McClellan. But Grant had already demonstrated that he was far from reluctant and that the Federal commander sought only an opportunity to fight. Lee also realized that despite his victories at the Wilderness and Spotsylvania, with all of his careful maneuvering, Richmond was now less than ten miles behind him.

Grant finally crossed the Pamunkey River, and though Lee made every effort to scout Grant's movements, the network of good roads and intersections in the open farm country made Lee uncertain just what Grant was intending to do. On May 28, after a sharp cavalry fight near a key intersection known as Haw's Shop, Lee correctly guessed that Grant was about to make his major thrust forward. As the Federal forces pushed toward Lee, the two armies were extended into parallel lines along Totopotomoy Creek that ran roughly north and south. On May 30, Grant's left (southern) flank confronted Ewell's corps at Bethesda Church, resulting in a hard fight that bloodied both sides. (Ewell was absent owing to severe illness. Lee had named Jubal Early to command Ewell's corps.) That night, Grant extended his left to protect the troops there from being turned by a Confederate flank attack. The reinforcements to that part of the line were summoned from Butler's army. They were the 18th Corps, commanded by Major General William "Baldy" Smith (so called because even as a cadet at West Point, he had begun to lose his hair). Smith's men had left Butler's beleaguered army by steamship, following the water route of the James that brought them within marching distance of Grant's position. But Lee had sought reinforcements as well, and Beauregard had been persuaded to send a seven-thousand-man division under Major General Robert Hoke. While Hoke marched rapidly to support Lee's right flank, Smith's Federals received confusing orders and marched the wrong way. Grant, recognizing the potential for disaster on his flank, ordered Horatio Wright's 6th Corps to extend the flank. Both Lee and Grant aimed their reinforcements toward an intersection that loomed large on the maps of both sides. The place was a traveler's rest stop called Old Cold Harbor (the name signifying that no hot food or fire was available). On May 31, the intersection was precariously held by Phil Sheridan's Federal cavalry, who valiantly held off pressure from repeated efforts on June 1 by Lee's horsemen to drive him away. That same day, with Hoke's Confederate infantry now on the field, Lee ordered an attack aimed at capturing the vital intersection. But Sheridan held on, and by the end of the day, the Federal cavalry was rescued by the arrival of the Union 6th Corps. Then, Baldy Smith's men arrived as well.

Grant could clearly appreciate the value of the intersection. A network of roads spread out in all directions, and one led directly into Richmond. Late in the day on June 1, Grant ordered that the attack be continued by the two full corps now forming his left flank. Despite a blistering and devastating response from well-entrenched Confederates, the Federal troops succeeded in driving the rebels back far enough to secure complete Federal control of the Old Cold Harbor intersection.

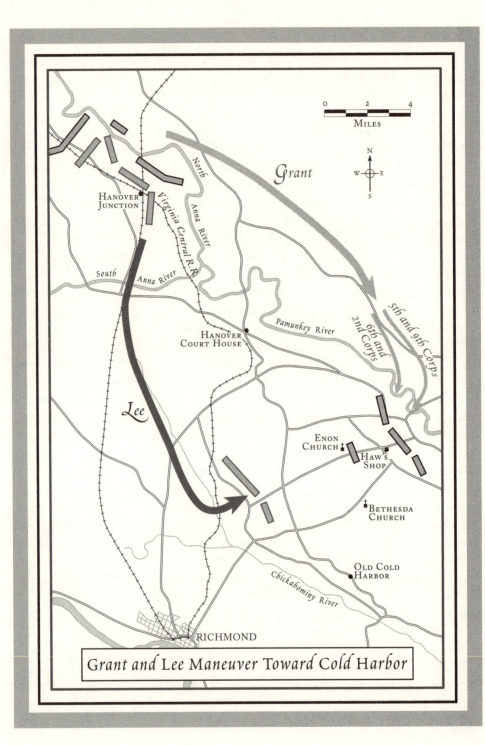

Grant and Lee Maneuver Toward Cold Harbor

Grant believed he now had the momentum and planned to drive forward another heavy assault the next day. To add strength to the Union left flank, Meade suggested that Hancock's 2nd Corps be shifted there from its position on the far right. But there was no simple route to be followed by weary troops on a night march, and Hancock did not reach his designated place in line until the late morning of June 2. The men of the 2nd Corps were in no shape for battle, and Grant was forced to rethink his strategy. To allow time for Hancock to rest his men, Grant called for the attack to be put off for one day. Whether or not Hancock's corps would give Grant the added weight he needed to crush the enemy position there, the one-day delay was a catastrophic mistake.

Throughout the day on June 2, Lee took full advantage of the inactivity from the Federal troops. The Confederates shifted their lines as well, moving strength against strength, and with their enormous luxury of time, they constructed a formidable defensive position. The lessons of Fredericksburg had been learned by Lee's engineers, and the rebel soldiers dug a primary trench line deep enough for men to fire their muskets while standing up. To add to the effectiveness of their defense, Lee's troops placed fat logs on top of the earthen embankment, supporting the logs so that there was a gap just beneath. This allowed the rebels to fire their muskets through a narrow slit of an opening, while the men themselves were almost completely impervious to enemy fire.

Though Grant had ordered his corps commanders to make a careful reconnaissance of what lay in front of them, no one seems to have taken the order seriously. All preparation was for an attack that would begin at four-thirty in the morning, well before anyone could actually see what kinds of defenses waited for them. At precisely four-thirty, three Federal corps, nearly fifty thousand men, rose up out of their works and poured in several unconnected waves toward Lee's waiting soldiers. The result, according to Confederate general Evander Law, was "not war, but murder." In less than twenty minutes, more than five thousand Union troops were cut down in front of the nearly invulnerable rebel line. In many places, the ground between the two armies was open woodlands, flat land, with no escape for anyone who approached the carefully aimed rebel muskets and artillery. In others places, the ground fell into swampy gullies, low-lying washes of mud and marsh that trapped men by the hundreds, massacred by the enemy they couldn't see. As the Federal officers drove their men forward, entire companies were wiped out in a single instant, officers and men falling like some grisly game of dominoes. The Federal troops who survived the first volleys had virtually nowhere to go, no escape route, no hope of actually breaking through the rebel position. With so many officers simply wiped away, any cohesion, any coordinated attack, simply dissolved. Survivors dropped to the ground, digging frantically with bayonets or tin cups, digging themselves into shallow one-man rifle pits, anything to allow them even a few inches of protection from musket fire that blanketed the entire field. Those who tried to retreat did so at enormous cost, men shot down no

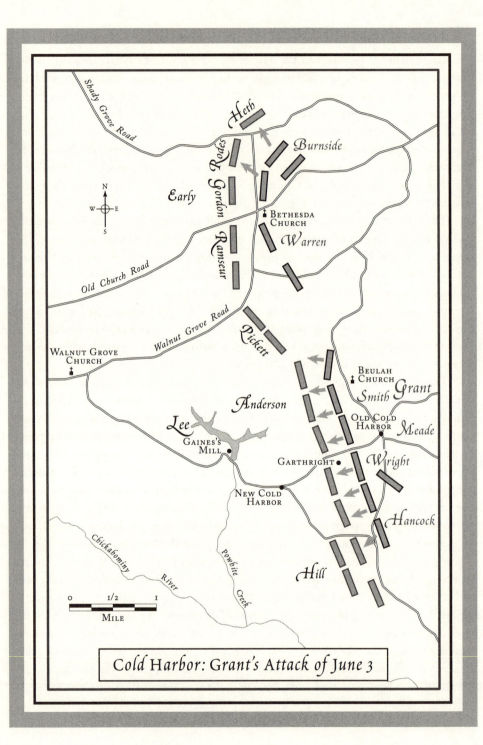

Cold Harbor: Grant's Attack of June 3

matter which way they were running. On the far left, Hancock's men made a brief break-through but could not hold the ground, driven back by Lee's reserves.

On the Federal far right flank, the only supporting attack came from Burnside's 9th Corps, which accomplished nothing at all. On Burnside's left, Warren's 5th Corps did virtually nothing. By eight a.m., it didn't matter. Though Meade ordered the attacks to resume, all three corps commanders on the left flank responded that no further attack was feasible. It was a grotesque understatement. Horatio Wright in particular simply refused to give his men the order. By midday, Grant conceded that the attack had failed. But for the men caught between the lines, the horror did not end. From the safety of their unbreakable defense, the Confederate troops stared in horror at the carnage that spread out in front of them. Even those who had witnessed the slaughter at Marye's Heights or the Bloody Lane at Antietam could not fathom what the Federal soldiers had been made to do. In places, the dead lay stacked like firewood or spread out in neat formations, entire rows of men just falling as they marched. The wounded lay thick around the men who still crouched in their shallow pits, so many good troops simply unable to move. Despite the horror in the eyes of the Confederates, the men with the muskets still held their aim, still scanned the ground for movement, for any man who showed himself. For the rest of the day, hundreds of Federal troops lay within yards of the rebel line, desperately counting the minutes until nightfall.

All night and into the following day, trenches were dug along the original Federal lines at a feverish pace. The Union commanders fully expected Lee to take advantage of his overwhelming victory and launch a counterattack. But Lee had no intention of sending his men out from behind the protection of their earthen wall. Instead, the Confederate commanders put their sharpshooters to work, riflemen who sought out any target. Some called out to their enemy, taunting them to show any fleck of blue. On the Federal side of the line, the response came from their sharpshooters as well, and very soon, the two sides were huddled into a stalemate.

Between the lines, the wounded lay helplessly under a scorching sun, and as hours became days, the odor from the carpet of dead bodies sickened the survivors on both sides. But even more horrible was that nothing was done to retrieve the wounded who might still be alive. In a tragedy born more of diplomacy than combat, Grant and Lee could not agree on the terms by which the wounded could be taken safely from the field. After three days, Grant finally conceded to Lee's demand for a "formal truce." This meant that, in official terms, Grant was acknowledging that it was his army that had suffered the defeat, his army that had the greater need for the temporary armistice. Grant's reluctance to accept the terms was not so much a demonstration of pride as a practical necessity for the Union commander. The presidential election was five months away. Grant was painfully aware that a declaration of defeat at Cold Harbor would give enormous momentum to Lincoln's enemies or those who favored ending the war at any price. Finally, on June 7, at the urging of his senior commanders, the need for humanity overcame the political pressure, and Grant agreed to the terms required by Lee that would allow the wounded men to be collected. When the men in blue ventured out, they discovered the inevitable horror. An enormous number of wounded had simply not survived. Though Grant had been forced to bend to Lee's diplomatic one-upmanship, the potential for a political crisis in Washington could not compare with the tragedy of Grant's battle plan. As he rode through his lines, he saw it for himself and realized finally what the men in both armies already knew. Cold Harbor had been a Union disaster.

Despite the catastrophic failure and the enormous cost to his army, Grant responded the only way that made military sense. He immediately began planning his next move. Though Richmond was temptingly close, with Lee blocking the roads, Grant never gave serious thought to making another drive toward the Confederate capital. His plan would be the same as it had been every step of the way, and the disaster at Cold Harbor would not change that. The goal was still to destroy Lee's army, and if that army stayed behind an unassailable wall, then Grant would maneuver away and find another route, another means to accomplish the task. To the south of Grant's position lay the wide James River, which most believed could be crossed only by boat. Below the James sat the critical rail center of Petersburg, a junction where communication and supply routes converged from those parts of the South not yet under Federal control. If Petersburg could be captured, Richmond would be virtually severed from the rest of the Confederacy. The same strategy that Lee had attempted in Pennsylvania, a roundabout threat to Washington, would, in Grant's mind, work just as well in Virginia. The difference was that Grant still had far superior resources and could supply and reinforce his army from the waterways along the coast, all of which were under Federal control. All Grant had to do was disengage his army from Lee at Cold Harbor and slip to the shores of the James River without leaving his army vulnerable on the march. Lee's best chance to do damage to the Army of the Potomac had always come when the great mass of Union troops had been on the move. Though Grant had the manpower to place formidable roadblocks along their route of march, he understood how important it would be to first remove Lee's most effective intelligence-gathering source: the Confederate cavalry.

Grant ordered Sheridan away with two full divisions of Federal horsemen, to make a strong raid toward the west, destroying rail lines and supply routes that led toward the Shenandoah and central Virginia. As Grant predicted, Lee had to respond accordingly, and Confederate cavalry moved quickly to follow. At a time when Lee was urgently trying to determine Grant's next move, he was suddenly without his eyes.

During the night on June 12, 1864, the Army of the Potomac began its stealthy march toward the James River. Grant ordered Warren's 5th Corps to act as a screen, blocking a key intersection, while the rest of Grant's forces moved along parallel routes toward the boat landings on the James.

On June 13, Lee was dismayed to learn that Grant had indeed slipped away from Cold Harbor. The only evidence of the location of any sizable number of Federal troops was the obvious location of Warren's corps, who had positioned themselves to the south of Cold Harbor at an intersection known as Riddell's Shop. From Riddell's, Warren had a direct route into Richmond, and Lee had to recognize the threat. But Warren was doing exactly what Grant wanted him to do: occupy Lee's attention while the rest of the army made good its crossing of the James. Though Lee scrambled to discover Grant's plan, at the same time he was forced to do Grant yet another enormous favor.

With Sigel's Federal troops banished from the Shenandoah Valley, Lee had called upon John Breckinridge to march his Confederate division to bolster the Confederate lines at Cold Harbor. But the Federals were not yet through with the valley. In early June, a new Union threat had rolled southward into the fertile farmlands, led by Major General David Hunter. Hunter not only threatened to accomplish what the hapless Sigel could not, but in so doing, Hunter committed several outrageously brutal acts against the civilian population. Among other depredations, Hunter had shelled and burned the Virginia Military Institute. Whether or not he approved of Hunter's brutishness, Grant's original plan for forcing pressure on Lee from the Shenandoah was finally working. To deal with the new threat, Lee ordered Jubal Early to detach from Lee's army and march an entire corps toward the valley.

With much of his cavalry and a third of his infantry now gone from his Cold Harbor position, Lee could pursue Grant's escape in only a halfhearted way. The Confederate command could not ignore the threat that Warren posed to Richmond, and quickly, Lee's hands were tied in a way that Grant could only have wished for. Once Warren's mission was accomplished, the 5th Corps slipped away to join the rest of Grant's army.

Though his plan was working almost perfectly, Grant was still wary. Simply reaching the James River was not enough. Any army gathered haphazardly in a confused mass, backed up by a wide river, was an invitation to disaster. Transporting the massive army by boat across the wide river would be a slow and laborious process that could leave a sizable number of Federal troops in vulnerable positions. It was Grant's engineers who solved the problem.

Though some of Grant's troops made the crossing by steamship, many more made use of an extraordinary pontoon bridge. Federal engineers had devised a technique to anchor what would normally be a flimsy structure so that it would stand up to the roughness of the open water. The bridge was an amazing feat of engineering, spanning more than two thousand feet. By June 15, with Lee unable to do anything to prevent it, Grant's army was entirely across the James River.

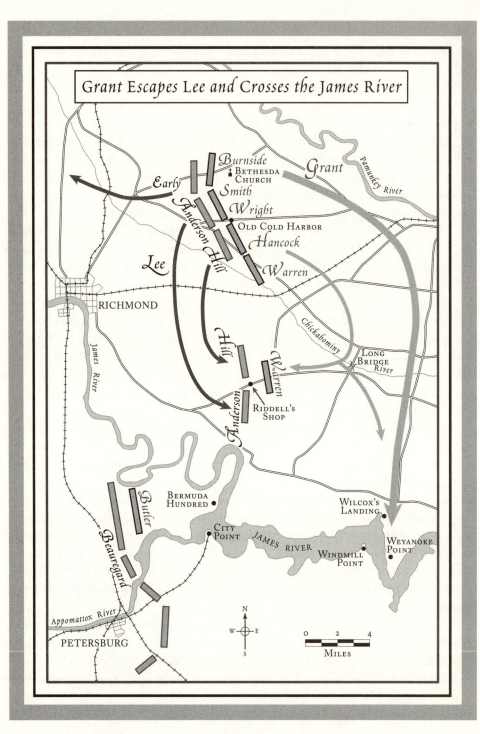

Grant Escapes Lee and Crosses the James River

Burnside
Bethesda Church
Grant
Pamunkey River
Early
Smith
Anderson Hill
Wright
Old Cold Harbor
Hancock
Lee
Warren
Chickahominy
RICHMOND
Hill
Warren
Long Bridge River
James River
Anderson
Riddell's Shop
Butler
Bermuda Hundred
Wilcox's Landing
Beauregard
City Point
JAMES RIVER
Weyanoke Point
Windmill Point
Appomattox River
PETERSBURG

N
W—E
S

0   2   4
MILES

WHY IS THIS BATTLE IMPORTANT?

Simply put, Cold Harbor represents the worst single day of Ulysses Grant's career as a military commander. During the primary predawn assault on June 3, the cost to the Union army is staggering: more than five thousand casualties in less than twenty minutes, seven thousand for the day as a whole. Including the fight on June 1, the Federal army loses twelve thousand men, compared with a combined loss of fifteen *hundred* Confederates. On the Federal side, the failures at both North Anna and Cold Harbor are many: the failure to scout Lee's defenses, failure to secure accurate maps, failure to maneuver troops in a timely manner. But the final responsibility at Cold Harbor lies with Grant himself. His order to launch an all-out assault across open ground, into the massed fire of an enemy protected by stout defenses, produces a volume of slaughter that might compare only to Lee's culpability in ordering Pickett's Charge.

As had happened to Lee, Grant's detractors erupt with loud voices, calling for Grant's head. Grant recognizes the magnitude of his failure, and later he writes in his memoirs that he "always regretted that the last assault at Cold Harbor was ever made." Despite the pressures of the impending election on Abraham Lincoln, the president stays true to his word and will not condemn a man who continues to press the enemy. Grant receives no official censure from Washington. To Grant's credit, he recognizes and accepts responsibility for the failure but does not allow it to distract him from his ultimate goal. With Grant now below the James River, even Lee concedes that "it is just a matter of time."

One bright light presents itself in the Federal army. To replace some of the losses from the devastating

Monument to the 2nd Connecticut Heavy Artillery, Cold Harbor, Virginia PHOTO PATRICK FALCI

fights of early May, Grant summons regiments of untested troops from their secure defenses around Washington. They are called "Heavy Artillery," men who have spent the war in clean uniforms, manning artillery batteries that have never been fired at the enemy. As they march south to join the Army of the Potomac, they are subjected to ridicule from the veterans, referred to as "band box" soldiers, men fit only for parades, "fresh meat" for the battles that lie ahead. They join the fighting at Cold Harbor having no idea what they will face, led by officers who have no idea if any of these men will actually obey the order to fight. Two regiments in particular will find themselves in the lead of attacks where they will charge the enemy with as much courage and gallantry as any unit on the field. Both regiments will lose their commanders, both will see an enormous percentage of their men shot down. And both will have their heroes. The men of the 2nd Connecticut and the 7th New York Heavy Artillery will forever sweep away the label of "band box" soldiers. To anyone who believes the North can no longer offer up fresh troops, or that the untested soldiers lack the resolve to see this war to its conclusion, the message is unmistakable.

The period from May 4 to June 15, 1864, becomes known as Grant's Overland Campaign, and the cost to both armies is horrific. Lee's army loses half its strength, some forty thousand men. The Federals lose fifty-four thousand, and though Grant has succeeded in moving his army deep into the heart of Virginia, critics point out that he could have accomplished the same thing if he had simply put them on ships and, like McClellan, brought them by water. Had Grant avoided Lee altogether and landed his enormous army along the James, he thus could have avoided several of the bloodiest fights of the war. But those who insist on labeling Grant as a "butcher" miss the point, a point that Grant has embraced. Like his friend and subordinate William T. Sherman, Grant understands that this war has become something no one could have predicted. Few had any notion just how dedicated the southerners would be in fighting for their cause and just how dedicated Lincoln and his supporters would be in defeating it. The visceral horror of the war has not overcome that dedication on either side. Grant understands that there is no longer any moral argument, any haggling with conscience. He has one responsibility, which is to crush his enemy. In order to succeed, a great number of men on both sides will die. Lee's army is the goal, and despite various failures from Grant and his command, Lee's army has been decimated. Though Cold Harbor is a disastrous Union mistake, both sides now understand that the entire war is disastrous. It is Grant's responsibility as a commander to force his opponent to commit more disastrous mistakes than he does.

For Lee, the fight has become one of desperate survival. If there is any hope for the Confederacy to prevail, Lee must seek out glimpses of opportunity and strike effectively. Cold Harbor is, thus, a perfect success. But the loss of so many of his capable subordinates is a disaster of a different sort, and Lee has been forced to take one step closer to the hands-on management of his army. Those who are left in the east—Early, Anderson, and

A. P. Hill in particular—simply do not measure up to the men they have replaced. As Lee maneuvers his army to counter Grant's crossing of the James, he is a fifty-seven-year-old man who has already suffered from sickness and age. Increasingly, the weight of responsibility for the survival of the Confederacy settles hard on his shoulders.

One final note: During the day on June 7, when the formal truce allows Union troops to collect their wounded, they are met in many places by Confederates who wander out to mingle with them. The scene has been repeated many times on many fields, but here, the conversations and camaraderie completely belie what has just occurred. With so few wounded men to care for, the soldiers gather with their enemy in a strangely peaceful meeting. Throughout the day, they trade goods, speak of home, share their experiences. Despite all that lies around them, the men seem driven by the need to comfort one another, an expression perhaps of hope that this will soon be over. By nightfall, the truce concludes, and the men return to their trenches. The sharpshooters pick up their muskets, and it all begins again.

WHAT YOU SHOULD SEE

*I*n terms of acreage, Cold Harbor is a far smaller battlefield than many less significant historical sites. The park itself is part of the Richmond National Battlefield Park, which consists of eleven unconnected sites spread throughout the Greater Rich-

Jeff in a Union trench at Cold Harbor, Virginia PHOTO PATRICK FALCI

Confederate entrenchments, Cold Harbor, Virginia PHOTO PATRICK FALCI

mond Area. These sites include battlefields of both the Seven Days' Battles of 1862 and Grant's Overland Campaign of 1864. As is the case in Nashville and Atlanta (to name but two), there is an enormous challenge in preserving any of these kinds of sites around a major metropolitan area, and the reality is that development usually takes the upper hand.

Though several sites in this conglomerate of parks are worth a visit, Cold Harbor stands alone by the very nature of what happened here. Situated a few miles northeast of downtown Richmond, the area outside the National Park Service land is relatively pristine, though privately owned, and much of the farmland is similar to its appearance in 1864. (Of course, much of it is not.) The Cold Harbor park itself covers roughly 180 acres, and efforts are ongoing to acquire adjoining land and nearby parcels, which would greatly add to the park's historical value. But don't overlook what is there now.

One interesting side note: The route to the park, Cold Harbor Road (Route 156), passes directly by the original location of Gaines's Mill, one of the battlegrounds of the Seven Days' Battles. A sign indicates the location, and there is actually some form of modern mill there now. Unfortunately, there is no record, no photograph, no sketch, that shows us what the original mill looked like, though it is likely that the modern building sits on more or less the same site. A bit farther east, there is a turnoff to the right, noted by a sign that indicates a piece of the Gaines's Mill battlefield: the recently restored Watt

Hollywood Cemetery

LOCATED OFF THE BELVIDERE STREET EXIT OF INTERSTATE 195 IN Richmond, the cemetery is the final resting place for two centuries of Richmond's most prominent citizens, businessmen, and civic leaders. But as a repository of Civil War history, this place is not to be missed.

Though the cemetery was founded in 1849, it is somewhat confusing that you can find graves here that date back prior to 1800. (Those remains were relocated here well after the fact.) Before its establishment as a cemetery, this property passed through the hands of some notable landowners, including Henry "Light Horse Harry" Lee. Included among the graves are two U.S. presidents, James Monroe and John Tyler, as well as the president of the Confederacy, Jefferson Davis.

Hollywood Cemetery, circa 1849, Richmond, Virginia
PHOTO COURTESY OF THE LIBRARY OF CONGRESS

In terms of Civil War interest, there are two themes at work here. First, of course, are the famous names. Besides Davis, you will find the prominent grave sites for Jeb Stuart, Dr. Hunter McGuire, who was Stonewall Jackson's physician, and Lee's nephew, cavalry commander Fitzhugh Lee. In an interesting twist, I was caught off guard by the grave site of the man who in the 1930s won a Pulitzer Prize by doing more to bring Robert E. Lee to the public's attention than any other man: Lee's biographer, Douglas Southall Freeman.

Each time I have mentioned the various National Cemeteries that accompany battlefield parks, I have noted that, with rare exception, only Union soldiers are legally allowed to be buried there. Thus has been suggested one logical question: Where are the Confederates? Beyond the grave sites of so many prominent names in the Hollywood Cemetery, there is one memorial marker here that stands above all the rest. It is a ninety-foot-high stone pyramid that memorializes the *eighteen thousand* Confederate soldiers buried nearby, most of whom are unknown.

The Museum of the Confederacy

THOUGH NUMEROUS CIVIL WAR MUSEUMS HAVE EMERGED OVER THE past several years, none exceeds this marvelous facility, in terms of collections, resources, and in general a cooperative spirit toward anyone who researches Civil War history.

The collections are numerous and outstanding, including the largest existing collection of Civil War–era regimental flags. Altogether, the museum holds some 550 flags, which include many prewar banners as well. There is also a collection of some six thousand photographs, which is an extraordinary resource for anyone seeking some definition of just what the era of the mid-nineteenth century *looked* like. Many other extraordinary artifacts are contained in the museum's permanent collection, including, for example, Robert E. Lee's letter of resignation from the U.S. Army, written in April 1861, the frock coat Lee wore at Appomattox, and an enormous assortment of weaponry, artwork, and personal artifacts of the era, both military and civilian. The museum also contains the Jefferson Davis papers and the second largest collection of Confederate currency (exceeded only by that of the Smithsonian Institution). There are also an enormous number of uniforms from the war. Most who have examined exhibits of these uniforms (here and elsewhere) have made the observation that those uniforms seem to our eye to be amazingly small. That's not because they've shrunk. The physical body size of men from the 1860s was far smaller on average than that of men today. Interestingly, one artifact among the museum's uniform collection stands out for that very reason: the uniform of Confederate general John Bell Hood. From eyeing the coat, it seems pretty apparent that Hood's coat would fit me, and I'm over six feet tall. Obviously, the references to Hood being a "large man" for his day are well-founded.

Immediately adjacent to the museum facility, at the corner of 12th and Clay Streets, is the White House of the Confederacy, which was the Civil War–era home of Jefferson Davis and his family. The mansion was built in 1818, and Davis occupied it for the first time in August 1861. When Davis was forced to abandon Richmond in April 1865, he abandoned many of his possessions, which he never saw again. The house survived many attempts to tear it down, but by 1889 those conflicts had passed, and the house was finally designated a National Historic Landmark. The White House was the original site of the Museum of the Confederacy itself, but the collections grew to exceed the space, and in 1976 the museum relocated to its current facility next door. The White House today contains artifacts of the era that show a slice of Davis's civilian life and showcase his administrative office where, later in the war, illness forced him to spend much of his time. I recommend taking a guided tour, which lasts roughly forty-five minutes, though you will need to book a reservation for the tour in advance.

The Museum of the Confederacy has been in something of a crisis for some time now, primarily because of its location. Parking and accessibility are increasingly a challenge, since the facility is tightly squeezed by Virginia Commonwealth University, which surrounds it. Efforts are under way to relocate the museum, and I heartily support such a move.

I've been asked if the museum is in fact an anachronism, that in the (annoying) world of political correctness, some have wondered if anyone should support a museum dedicated to preserving artifacts of the Confederacy. No matter where your loyalties (or your politics) may lie, this facility is a gem of historical preservation. Political correctness had reared its ugly head even in the 1860s: Consider the earlier point about the government in Washington making no effort to preserve any photographic record or even speak openly about the disaster of Cold

Harbor, lest it inflame sentiment against Lincoln and his war policies. But the ground at Cold Harbor was not erased from view and was instead (partially) preserved. Efforts toward that goal continue, as they continue at the museum.

When this New Jersey–born "Yankee" first visited the museum in the early 1990s, I was curious if I would run smack into a wall of uncomfortable politics, exhibits slanted toward diatribes against the North, trumpeting the "righteousness" of the Confederate cause. That is not the purpose of this facility, and anyone who makes that assumption simply hasn't visited the place. I urge you to take the time.

House. Through enormous effort, the Park Service has succeeded in convincing politically powerful preservationists that this land should be at least partially cleared so that it will appear as it did at the time of the battle. I like a good tree as much as the next person, but on other stretches of historical ground such as this, so much of which is threatened by development and urban sprawl, I wish the Park Service could be given the latitude as they were here, to preserve and interpret the history of the place by showing us and our children just what the land looked like at the time of the event. Unfortunately, as was explained to me at Vicksburg, there are those who strongly believe that the Park Service should never be in the business of cutting down trees.

Unlike most of the parks I have outlined in this book, Cold Harbor is best seen on foot. The entire walking tour loops approximately one mile through an area that saw some of the most brutal combat of the war. Whether or not the "mystical" element of that affects you, there are sights that bring the poignancy of this battle to heart.

From the Visitor Center, follow the trail north, paralleling the gravel road. Your route takes you along a section of the line where Lee's troops had built their nearly perfect defenses. Once you move into the woods, you will notice that the land to the right (east, facing the Federal position) is relatively flat, marked by a scattering of tall trees. The land here has very little underbrush. This is remarkably similar to what the land between the lines looked like in 1864, the low vegetation having been consumed by livestock (as at Chickamauga). Remnants of Lee's earthworks are plainly visible, and though they are worn with age, the sheer depth and magnitude of the works is pretty evident. Consider as well how close you are to the Union lines, clearly visible a short way to the east. It is not hard to imagine the "target practice" enjoyed by the sharpshooters on both sides.

At the far northern end of the looping road, you can see a swampy pond. The pond itself is part of the Park Service property, but beyond (to the north) the land flattens out again into open farm fields, which are privately owned. The pond was more of a swampy drainage at the time of the battle, and many Federal troops seeking shelter from the blistering musket fire gravitated naturally to the low ground. Unfortunately, it simply made them a more massed target and led to enormous confusion in the Federal ranks. In the fields beyond, Federal soldiers who advanced along that part of the line were massacred by both musket fire and artillery from the Confederate positions farther to the north and west.

Following the looping road to the Federal side of the field, you can begin to put yourself into the footsteps of some of the men who made this disastrous attack. If you walk out into the ground between the lines, particularly near the thicker brush, you will find several small depressions. These are the remnants of the "pot-hole" trenches that were dug frantically by individual soldiers, usually with their bayonets or anything else they happened to be carrying. If you are immune to poison ivy and don't mind getting pretty dirty, you might try curling yourself up into one of these depressions. Then, peer up toward the Confederate works. It is amazing to me that anyone survived in this field at all.

Back in the woods to the east of the road, behind the Union front lines, are rows of trenches, all of which are original. Some of these are in amazingly good condition, and

The Killing Field, Union perspective, Cold Harbor, Virginia PHOTO PATRICK FALCI

again, the depth indicates how much effort was expended to shelter the troops who were within musket range of their enemy. Many of these trenches were dug immediately after the main fighting here, after the worst of the slaughter. There is one primary walking trail that will take you straight through one of these trenches.

Back on the main road, walk south, toward the Visitor Center. You will come to the monument to the 2nd Connecticut Heavy Artillery. The regiment was half again larger

Collecting the remains of the dead, Cold Harbor, Virginia
PHOTO COURTESY OF THE LIBRARY OF CONGRESS

than the typical combat regiment, some fifteen hundred men, part of the "fresh meat" Grant had ordered down from their comfortable fortifications in Washington. As they made their attack on June 1, they suffered nearly 25 percent casualties, including the death of their commander, Colonel Elisha Kellogg.

When you return to the Visitor Center, drive east on Cold Harbor Road a short distance and you will see the Cold Harbor National Cemetery on your left. Across the road sits the Garthright House. The cemetery contains the remains of approximately two thousand Union soldiers, two-thirds of whom are unknown. At the time of the battle, many of the Union dead were buried in mass graves; their remains were relocated here after the war. One of the few photographs taken on this ground shows a burial party carting piles of skeletons to their new resting place. Interestingly, the photographic record of the Cold Harbor battle is almost nonexistent. There was enormous political sensitivity in the North to the upcoming election and the effects that this devastating defeat would have on Lincoln's chance for reelection. Unlike the interest evinced in the aftermath of Antietam or Gettysburg, little encouragement was offered to Mathew Brady or his contemporaries to photograph what happened here.

The Garthright House sits on fifty acres of preserved land, and though closed to the public, it offers one unique perspective to the battle. Near the parking lot, there is a large plaque that displays a sketch drawn by noted artist Alfred Waud. This sketch was published in *Harper's Weekly* in July 1864—only six weeks after the battle. Though the outbuildings have changed, the house itself remains, and through Waud's eyes we can get a sense of the land as it appeared then, two armies facing each other on one of the most tragic days of the war.

CHAPTER TEN

PETERSBURG

Petersburg, Virginia

JUNE 1864–APRIL 1865

WHAT HAPPENED HERE

*P*etersburg was as valuable to the Confederate cause as any city in the South. The city itself was a booming metropolis, with a population approaching twenty thousand (six times the size of Chattanooga), and served as the most important eastern rail center north of Atlanta. Five separate rail lines fed into the city, creating a hub that supplied most of Richmond's needs as well. The capture of Petersburg meant that the Confederate capital would be sealed off from every rail link but one, and Grant knew that if he could control Petersburg, he would have driven one more hard stake into the heart of the Confederate economy.

The first attempt to capture Petersburg had come while the battered Grant and the victorious Lee still snarled at each other at Cold Harbor. On June 9, 1864, Benjamin Butler had managed to transport a force of close to five thousand men across the waterway that hemmed him in at Bermuda Hundred. The troops were a combination of infantry and cavalry whose mission was to occupy the still lightly defended city. But true to form, the coordination between foot soldier and horse soldier was virtually nonexistent, and a small force of local rebel defenders, including old men and boys too young for service, drove the confused Federals away. Butler's plan dissolved.

Despite Butler's inept handling of the affair, Grant stayed focused on Petersburg. Suspecting that Lee simply didn't have the manpower to adequately protect both Richmond and Petersburg, Grant reasoned that Petersburg would continue to be lightly defended until Grant showed his true intentions. Lee had seemed to be more concerned with protecting Richmond, and if Grant could make a bold stroke—a sharp, decisive advance straight into Petersburg—he might catch Lee completely by surprise.

Though Lee had inflicted a major defeat on Grant's army at Cold Harbor, Grant's proven aggressiveness meant that no Confederate could allow himself to relax and celebrate. In mid-June 1864, while Lee remained close to Richmond, P. G. T. Beauregard held command south of the James River. Neither man could make offensive plans until it was known what Grant intended to do. On June 15, they got their first major clue.

Grant ordered Baldy Smith's 18th Corps to move toward Petersburg and confront whatever opposition they would find there, knowing that Smith's Federal troops would certainly outnumber anything that stood in their way. Unlike Butler's force of five thousand, Smith's corps numbered close to seventeen thousand, and Grant ordered Hancock's 2nd Corps, another twenty thousand men, to back Smith up. As Smith's forces drove toward the outskirts of Petersburg, they came upon the same line of earthworks and fortifications that Butler's troops had faced. It was known as the Dimmock Line, named for the Confederate engineer who two years earlier had responded to fears about the vulnerability of the city by constructing a ten-mile loop of defensive positions along Petersburg's eastern perimeter. Though Dimmock's defenses were strong of construction and soundly designed, they lacked the one thing that would actually make them effective: *soldiers.* As Baldy Smith's Federals approached the ring of fortifications, Beauregard could confront them with a total defensive force of only twenty-two hundred soldiers and militia. Smith's men quickly pushed the rebels out of their lines, and Beauregard recognized that Petersburg was in serious trouble. Working frantically, the Confederate commander pulled troops away from their "cork" at Bermuda Hundred and withdrew them into Petersburg. While the Confederates were scrambling to deal with the crisis, Smith's Federals were poised at the edge of a virtually undefended city. But Smith's men were slow to advance, and yet again, coordination between infantry and cavalry simply fell apart. Hours passed, and Smith became deeply concerned, since Hancock's men had not yet arrived on the field. As the afternoon drifted toward evening, Smith realized that his primary attack could not begin until very late in the day. Baldy Smith then made his worst decision as a commander. He simply stopped.

Hancock's efforts to reach the field in time to assist in the attack had been doomed by the now common failures of the clumsy communication system in Grant's army. Baldy Smith was under Butler's command and received his orders through a different channel from that of Hancock, whose orders came through George Meade. Though Grant knew exactly what he intended the two Federal corps to accomplish, he put his plan into action with a flawed and inefficient system. Hancock arrived on the field well after dark, and his entire corps was not available until midnight. Instead of adding Hancock's strength to his own, Smith decided, on his own initiative, that Hancock should make the attack instead. Smith thus requested that the 2nd Corps move up to take the place of the 18th. Hancock outranked Smith, but he had received no clear orders from Meade about what he was expected to do, so he bowed to Smith's decision making. Very late that night, Hancock received word directly from Grant that Hancock and not Smith was to command the two corps in a combined attack. All through the night, while confusion reigned on the Federal side of the lines, Petersburg was filling rapidly with Confederate troops.

Instead of launching the two-corps attack, Hancock hesitated when he received word that additional reinforcements were on the way. (Whether Hancock actually needed them is doubtful.) Throughout the day on June 16, the Federals strengthened their position with the addition of two more corps, Burnside's 9th and Warren's 5th. By nightfall, Meade himself had arrived on the field to take overall command. The following morning, June 17, the Federals prepared to assault the Petersburg defenses with a force totaling seventy thousand men. Facing them, Beauregard had fewer than fifteen thousand to put into place.

The attack was driven hard, and all along the line, Confederate positions collapsed, overrun by far superior numbers and, finally, well-coordinated assaults. But the Confederates used their strong defensive positions to their greatest advantage, and though Meade's troops made significant advances, they were unable to force a breakthrough that would allow them to swarm into Petersburg itself. But the Federals clearly had the upper hand, and by day's end, Beauregard was once again facing a major crisis.

Just before dawn on June 18, the Federal forces resumed their attack, both Grant and Meade confident that no rebel works could hold back the combined assault. When the Federal troops reached the enemy's lines, they were shocked to find them empty. Though Beauregard continued to add fresh troops into his defenses, he had recognized the inevitable, so during the night he had quietly pulled his men farther back, into a new line of solid trenches. The Federal field commanders, realizing they didn't actually know where the enemy had gone, began to slow their advance. Aides were sent scurrying back to headquarters, seeking orders. In some parts of the line, the blue-coated troops attacked anyway, driving forward until they actually reached someone to fight. But those fights were scattered, with no cohesion on their flanks. Throughout the day, the Confederates continued to strengthen their lines, throwing back one disjointed attack after another. As the sun set, the attacks stopped, the sullen Federal troops returning to their lines cursing their officers, who cursed the commanders above them. They knew exactly what Grant knew. Their best chance to capture Petersburg had been frittered away. Already frustrated, Grant then learned one more piece of information, passed along by rebel prisoners through their captors. Since Grant had made his move, Lee had responded accordingly. Along with the columns of Confederate troops who continued to strengthen Beauregard's lines, Lee himself had ridden south and was now in Petersburg. Though Beauregard had performed an admirable, if not heroic, task in saving Petersburg, once more, Grant would face Lee. This time, instead of maneuver and flexibility, Lee would have to rely on the same kind of defensive position that had won him the day at Cold Harbor. But Grant had learned his lesson. There would be no more massive full-scale frontal assaults against a well-fortified enemy. Grant might finally have had Lee right in front of him. But for the first time, Grant seemed to appreciate the value of patience. With Lee forced to hold tight to Petersburg, Grant's superior numbers would give the Federal army an even greater advantage than before. The wisest strategy for Grant now was the same strategy that had worked at Vicksburg: a siege. But Petersburg gave Grant one enormous advantage over Vicksburg. There was no great barrier that protected one side of the city, no Mississippi River to challenge Grant's maneuverability. Grant's army outnumbered Lee by roughly two to one, odds that could only increase in Grant's favor. If the Federals could force Lee to extend his trenches, lengthening them so as to spread his army over a much broader defensive position, then gaps or weak points in the line would become inevitable. It would be up to Grant to exploit them.

Almost immediately, Grant ordered his troops to begin pushing out to the south and west of the city. The immediate goal would be the roads and railway lines that linked Petersburg to points farther south. These operations began on June 21 and continued for months afterward. At few times during the ten-month siege was Grant ever able to force a major breakthrough of the Confederate defenses, but that was rarely the point. Nearly every attack or every threat to the city's crucial lifelines pushed Grant's army a little farther west and thus forced Lee to dig new trenches, extending his earthworks, stretching his manpower, weakening his lines just a bit more.

In many places, the enemies faced each other from deep trench lines little more than a hundred yards apart, the soldiers accepting that the most useful man now was the sniper. On both sides, carefully hidden sharpshooters scanned the enemy position for any fleck of movement, for the foolish, the careless, or the unlucky man who should linger at a small gap in his own defenses. In one area, on the southeastern bend of Lee's lines, the two armies faced each other at a place called the Taylor Farm. There, the Federal troops held ground that sloped back away from the rebel position, which held nearly impregnable

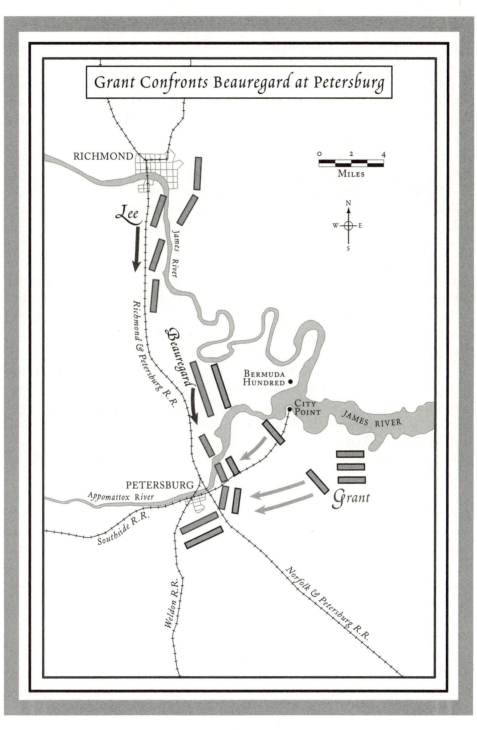

Grant Confronts Beauregard at Petersburg

RICHMOND

Lee

James River

Richmond & Petersburg R.R.

Beauregard

BERMUDA
HUNDRED

CITY
POINT

JAMES RIVER

Grant

PETERSBURG

Appomattox River

Southside R.R.

Weldon R.R.

Norfolk & Petersburg R.R.

0   2   4
MILES

N
W   E
S

earthworks on the crest of the ridgeline. The lay of the ground sparked an idea in the mind of Federal lieutenant colonel Henry Pleasants, who commanded a regiment of troops from the coal-mining country of eastern Pennsylvania. On June 24, Pleasants took his idea to his commanding officer, Ambrose Burnside, who was so intrigued that he took it to George Meade. Meade was never a man to accept anyone's plan at face value, and he tossed the idea back to Burnside as something more fantastic than strategic. But Meade's objections were mostly bluster, so Colonel Pleasants was allowed to put his plan into motion.

Pleasants began to put his miners to work, burrowing a tunnel into the hillside, pushing a horizontal mine discreetly toward the rebel position. They worked for nearly a month, Pleasants himself overcoming the astonishing engineering challenges of a tunnel that eventually exceeded five hundred feet in length, some twenty feet beneath the Confederate position. The Confederates had suspicions about a mine and had employed listening posts deep in the ground, manned by soldiers who spent their shifts simply listening to telltale thumps from the earth below them. But Pleasants was not only a skilled engineer, he was also lucky, and although the rebels continued to feel certain that some activity was happening beneath their feet, they never discovered exactly what Pleasants and his coal miners had accomplished.

The mine consisted of a shaft that stood nearly five feet high, roughly four feet wide at the base, tapering to less than two feet wide at the top. At its terminating point, Pleasants had created a T, each side extending out some forty feet. By the end of July, eight thousand pounds of gunpowder in thirty-eight wooden barrels had been placed in the T, and the tunnel had been partially collapsed there to seal in the blast. The barrels of powder were connected to a ropelike fuse that led partway back to the shaft's opening. All Pleasants required now was the order from Burnside to light the fuse.

Immediately after Burnside approved Pleasants's plan, he had ordered a fresh division to train for the presumed breakthrough that the mine explosion would create. For weeks, the men were carefully instructed not to hesitate, to push quickly past whatever crater might result, to ignore the smoke and debris, to create a breakthrough in the rebel line that could be held long enough for Burnside to send forward more divisions. If successful, the breakthrough could become a hard blue wedge that could split Lee's entire defense along this portion of the Petersburg line and give Grant the opportunity to rout Lee's army completely out of the city. That was the theory.

As Pleasants was completing his final preparations, Burnside was confronted by an order from Meade that changed the entire scenario. The fresh troops, drilled so carefully on how best to take advantage of this operation, belonged to the U. S. colored troops, Burnside's all Negro division. At the last moment, Burnside received instructions that the black troops were to be replaced by white troops, that should this plan work, it would be "politically unwise" to place black troops in such a prominent position. Burnside was furious, but Meade's orders, agreed to by Grant, left no room for maneuver. Annoyed and grossly disappointed, Burnside responded to the change of plans by allowing his other three division commanders to *draw straws from a hat* to determine which division would be the shock troops assigned to make the breakthrough. The honor fell to Brigadier General James Ledlie, whose primary reputation among his men was for drunkenness during battle.

On July 30, some four thousand untrained troops waited in the predawn darkness, huddled behind the parapets and barriers of their own trenches. The men had no real idea what they were supposed to do and no idea what was about to happen to their enemy across the way. Their commander, Ledlie, was huddled deep in a bombproof shelter and many assumed he was accompanied by a whiskey bottle. At 3:00 a.m., Colonel Pleasants lit the fuse. To the searing dismay of his own engineers, who knew precisely what to expect, nothing happened. After waiting for more than an hour, two of Pleasants's men (possibly the two bravest men on the battlefield that morning) ventured into the mine to see why the powder had not ignited. They discovered that the fuse had malfunctioned at a splice, so, deep in the tunnel, they lit it again. At 4:44 a.m., as the men scurried back to safety, the fuse worked. The resulting blast threw an enormous mass of dirt and fire high into the air, shocking the Union soldiers who saw it. In front of them, 280 Confederate soldiers were blasted into the air. The explosion opened up a crater 170 feet long, more than 60 feet wide, and 30 feet deep. What was now supposed to be a rapid rush of carefully trained Federal troops turned into a clumsy sightseeing expedition. Ledlie's leaderless troops stumbled forward, rushed toward the crater, and began to stop, marveling at the chaotic scene. As more men filed out behind them, the jumbled confusion was complete.

On the Confederate side of the line, the shock was overcome far more quickly, and officers on all sides of the crater began to gather men and drive them toward the breach. Very soon, rebel artillery and musket fire was directed toward the crater, and the Federal troops began to seek shelter in the most obvious place they could find: the crater itself. In minutes, the still smoking hole in the ground became packed with Federal troops. Almost as quickly, Confederate soldiers drew up close to the earthen embankments on the far side of the crater and began firing directly into the massed targets below them. Though some Federal troops managed to push up and out of the deadly depression, most were simply trapped there. As men scrambled desperately to retreat, more Federal troops were ordered forward, creating more chaos in the no-man's-land between the lines. In a final irony for what was rapidly dissolving into a Federal disaster, the last division sent out from the Federal position was Burnside's U. S. colored troops, the men who had been so well trained to make the original assault. Now, they had nowhere to go and were immediately forced into

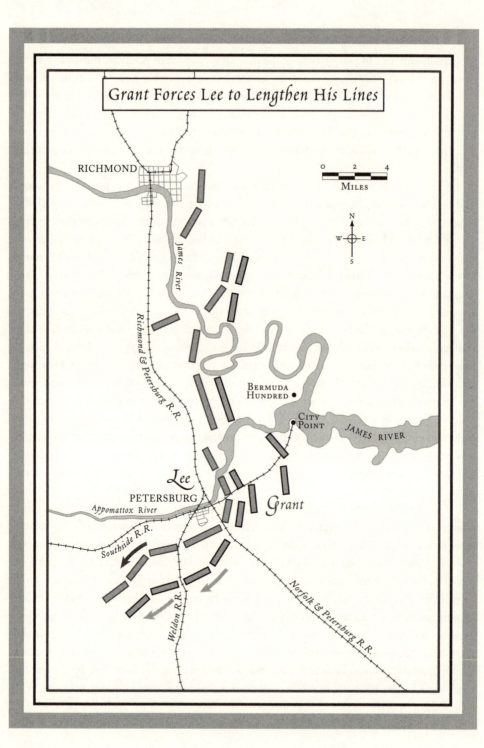

Grant Forces Lee to Lengthen His Lines

RICHMOND

James River

Richmond & Petersburg R.R.

0   2   4
MILES

N
W — E
S

BERMUDA
HUNDRED

CITY
POINT

JAMES RIVER

Lee

PETERSBURG

Appomattox River

Grant

Southside R.R.

Weldon R.R.

Norfolk & Petersburg R.R.

The crater, shortly after the battle, Petersburg, Virginia
PHOTO COURTESY OF THE LIBRARY OF CONGRESS

the carnage of the crater. The sight of black troops was an unfortunate inspiration to some of the Confederates who faced them, and in one of the most enormously regrettable episodes of the war, calls rang out from a number of rebel troops that no black prisoner would be taken.

By midday, the all-consuming horror was brought to a close. Despite Pleasants's ingeniousness and the accomplishment of his engineers, the fight that resulted had accomplished absolutely nothing except the loss of nearly five thousand of Burnside's men.

Grant was horrified by the results of the Battle of the Crater and responded by removing Burnside from command, an act that many felt was long overdue. Ledlie was removed as well after a board of inquiry determined that he had never left the protection of his shelter during his division's catastrophic attack.

With the disasters of Cold Harbor and the Battle of the Crater fresh in his mind, Grant put all his energy into conducting the siege, as well as focusing on the most effective ways to draw Lee's army into ever thinning lines. His most immediate goal became the railroads that fed Lee's army, and in mid-August, the Federal troops pushed westward, south of the city, toward the vital lifelines that Lee had to defend. On August 21, the fourth of the five rail lines, the Weldon Railroad, was captured and secured. Besides the plum of the railway itself, the move allowed Grant to extend his lines even farther west, and once more Lee was forced to do the same.

Though Lee was in no position to launch any kind of sustained assault at the Union position, raids were frequent, both sides parrying and thrusting at the other, particularly along the flanks. In mid-September, Confederate cavalry led by Wade Hampton made a wide foray around the Federal left flank and surprised Federal commissary officers deep in the Union rear by suddenly swooping in and nabbing a herd of cattle. Before the Federals could react effectively, Hampton and his men had led the captured beef back to Confederate lines, a blessed event for Lee's men, who had become used to rancid bacon and moldy bread. But Hampton's feat of cattle rustling was a lone bright spot for Lee's army in the war of attrition that Grant was now waging, a war that was grinding down the bodies and spirit of the men who somehow kept to their muskets.

Like the soldiers in Lee's command, the citizens of Petersburg had begun to feel the effects of the siege almost immediately. Even during the initial assaults, the city had not escaped the effects of the battle. Artillery shells fell into homes and buildings on the city's edge, destroying targets both military and civilian. As the months passed, the attacks continued, the shelling demoralizing the helpless civilians. Many left the city, as so many had done at Fredericksburg, refugees filling the roads and country lanes, carrying their most precious belongings, abandoning homes they might never see again. But, surprisingly, many stayed behind in a show of spirit that surprised even Lee. They went about their daily business, accepting the harsh routine of fire control and the occasional rescue of those who might have been caught in the collapse of a home. But when the shelling stopped, the more peaceful routines returned. The civilians supported their army, did all that was required of them, providing food and hospital space. But as the siege took hold, the suffering and sacrifice grew worse for both soldier and civilian. For the first time, Lee was encumbered by the reality that he no longer had the advantage, could no longer make the sharp, unexpected blow or lightning escape. His men continued to dig, and like their enemy across the way, they constructed and fortified an elaborate city within a city. Shovels replaced muskets as the tools of choice, and soon both sides had fashioned a complex network of connecting trenches and bombproof shelters.

For months, the Federal troops were supplied by an unending flow of steamships and sailing vessels that disgorged their guns and food and hardware onto the newly created wharves near Grant's headquarters at City Point. The Confederates could rely only on their dwindling rail traffic from the south, and they desperately protected the thin lifeline from the constant threat of disruption from Grant's cavalry. With the Weldon Railroad in

Confederate trenches, 1864–65, Petersburg, Virginia   PHOTO COURTESY OF THE LIBRARY OF CONGRESS

Union hands, goods from the Carolinas could travel up the rails only so far and then had to be transferred to wagons, another lifeline that Lee knew was far too fragile to survive for long. Faced with such a powerful enemy, whose resources seemed virtually unlimited, Lee had to plan carefully, hope for some opportunity, some mistake, some way to break Grant's iron grip on his army. But hope began to fade, especially as the news reached Petersburg from other theaters of the war.

The news came first from Atlanta. Sherman's task had been simple: Drive south from Chattanooga and capture the South's largest remaining city. With Bragg removed from command, the Confederates relied on Joe Johnston to hold Sherman back. But Johnston recognized the reality of his situation. Sherman had him outgunned and far outmanned, and Johnston could survive only by maneuvering his army away from Sherman's powerful grasp, much as Lee had done after the Wilderness. Unlike Lee, though, Johnston could never truly inflict major damage to Sherman's Federals. As Johnston's army backed closer to Atlanta, a chorus of southern politicians and newspapermen loudly condemned Johnston as being too timid to fight. Jefferson Davis needed little excuse to replace Johnston, whom he had always despised. In his place, Davis elevated one of Lee's most trusted subordinates, John Bell Hood. Hood would indeed fight, but he was no strategist, and on September 1, 1864, after several enormously costly battles, Hood was forced to abandon Atlanta. Instead of retreating eastward, to protect the Carolinas (and Lee's vulnerable southern flank), Hood took his remaining forces west and north, looping through Alabama, with the goal of returning to Tennessee. Hood hoped to destroy Sherman's supply lines, which would draw Sherman back out of Georgia, or, if Sherman stayed in Atlanta, Hood might recapture Nashville. If Hood had been successful, the entire western theater of the war would have become a tumultuous Union quagmire. Instead, Hood drove his army into a costly fight at Franklin, Tennessee, and then, in mid-December, Hood's army was utterly crushed by George Thomas, who commanded the Federals in Nashville.

Sherman, meanwhile, was now staring at the fertile open lands of Georgia with virtually no opposition. Thus did Sherman begin his "March to the Sea." By Christmas 1864, Sherman's army had carved a wide swath of destruction across the state of Georgia that concluded with the capture of Savannah on the Atlantic coast. The South had been divided yet again, another deep slice that severed southern Georgia and Florida from any meaningful involvement in the war.

While Sherman was thundering through the farms and small towns of Georgia, another event gave Grant final assurance that his control of the Union war effort would remain unencumbered. In November, Abraham Lincoln was reelected president by a substantial margin over his rival, the "peace" candidate George McClellan. Despite the horrifying toll the war had already claimed, the northern people (and the troops, who had been allowed to vote in the field for the first time) had given Lincoln a mandate to pursue the war. And Lincoln had passed that mandate along to Ulysses Grant.

With military catastrophe becoming too commonplace in the South, a desperate Jefferson Davis had once more called upon Joe Johnston to take command of the only viable army that could still directly assist Lee in preventing the total collapse of the eastern theater of the war. Johnston's command was still called the Army of Tennessee, but the name now had a hollow irony. Tennessee was in fact a Federal fortress. Johnston had in his command barely twenty thousand effective troops, who were now anchored in South Carolina. Outnumbered better than three to one by Sherman, Johnston could only watch and wait for the Federals to make their next move. Sherman's theories of war mirrored Grant's exactly. Cities made fine prizes, but wars were decided by the destruction of the enemy's fighting strength. Though Sherman knew that marching northward would eventually force Johnston into the open, before Sherman could make a decisive move toward John-ston, he had to remove the last remaining threat to his own flank. One more domino had to fall, the only effective southern seaport remaining in Confederate control.

Wilmington, North Carolina, was protected by Fort Fisher at the mouth of the Cape Fear River. Despite the Federal sea blockade, blockade runners had continued to make considerable use of the port, which provided vital supplies to Lee's army and now John-ston's as well. Clumsy attempts had been made to capture the fort previously, particularly by Benjamin Butler. But Grant renewed the effort, and the end came on January 15, 1865. Sherman was now free to march northward into the Carolinas, with no threat to his army from any Confederate stronghold on the coast. On February 17, 1865, Sherman's army marched into Columbia, South Carolina. There was nothing Johnston's army could do about it. The city was then consumed by fire, for which Sherman was blamed. But far more likely, the fires were spread from bales of cotton ignited by retreating Confederate soldiers.

The news of disaster after disaster churned a sickening despair inside of Lee and his embattled forces. As hope for some word of victory was drained away, the winter months in Petersburg caused more suffering in Lee's army than even the most resilient veterans could endure. The cold and the sharpshooters kept the men deep inside their protective shelters, which had become pits of mud and disease. The civilians in the town were over-whelmed by the desperate needs of their army, hospitals overflowing with more sick than wounded, sickness that passed to the civilians as well.

Lee's attentions now began to turn south, to Johnston, in the hope that by combin-ing the two Confederate armies, they might strike a sharp blow that would cripple or even destroy Sherman. The combined force, inspired by such a victory, could then turn north-ward to face Grant. To the Confederate commander, who often rode out among his suf-fering soldiers, it was a faint ray of hope. But the hope came from Lee's men as well, the ragged, sickly men who peered out to greet him, who still placed their faith in this gray-haired old man.

With the warmer weather, the mud began to harden, and both armies began to stir, knowing that someone's plan was in the works, one side or the other drawing lines on maps, some grand design that might break the backs of the men who huddled across the desolation of no-man's-land. Grant's plan had taken longer than he had imagined, but it was working; word of despair and collapse in Lee's army came from the mouths of the hundred or more deserters who passed into Federal lines every day. Grant had forced Lee to stretch his lines nearly thirty-five miles from flank to flank, and with the roads improv-ing, that strategy would begin again: more trenches and fewer troops to man them.

On March 21, 1865, word came of a fight at Bentonville, North Carolina. One wing of Sherman's Federals under Henry Slocum had been marching northward and had advanced right into the kind of confrontation Joe Johnston had hoped for. The Confederate commander believed he had been given an opportunity to crush a sizable piece of Sherman's divided army, but the fight had been inconclusive, and very soon Sherman had responded by bringing the rest of his army toward the field. Johnston had no choice but to retreat and hope to find another opportunity. News of Bentonville convinced Lee even further that the only hope for the Confederacy lay in uniting his army with Johnston. The priority would be to find the means to escape Grant's hold. The plan came to Lee from John B. Gordon.

On the east side of Petersburg, near Lee's far left flank, the Federals had a stronghold known as Fort Stedman. Behind that position, Gordon knew that the Federals had three additional forts, which contained artillery pieces that when captured could be turned to fire on the Federal supply depots and possibly even Grant's headquarters at City Point. If successful, the breakthrough could compel Grant to draw in his lines, to protect his base of supply. Such a move might provide Lee with exactly the opportunity he needed to drive his army up and out of their trenches, punching through a weakened gap in the Union lines. If Gordon's plan worked, the Confederates could make good their escape from Petersburg.

Gordon had planned his attack with great care, exercising utmost secrecy in the preparation of the details that had to be executed with precise timing. Fort Stedman was protected by rows of sharpened tree limbs, a miserable obstacle for infantry to push through. Gordon arranged for fifty men to advance in darkness with axes only. Once the Federal pickets in front of the fort were quietly eliminated, these axmen would quickly cut pathways through the obstructions. Close behind would come the infantry, and with Confederate troops pouring into the fort, the defenders there would be quickly overwhelmed. With the Federal cannon there in hand, the artillery could be turned around to hold back any counterattack from other Federal positions. Once the fort was secure, while it was still dark, three hundred handpicked men would file out toward the three additional Federal forts, with the same mission. Once the breakthrough was opened, Confederate cavalry could surge through, followed by more infantry, a combined force of nearly twenty thousand troops. As the gap widened, the Confederates would capture adjacent forts and artillery batteries, putting that entire section of the Federal line in serious jeopardy. It was an inspiring plan. On paper.

On March 25, 1865, in predawn darkness, Gordon's plan rolled into action. For a few agonizing minutes, the plan seemed to work, the Federal pickets quickly silenced, the men with axes cutting their way quickly through the obstructions. Gordon's troops rolled up into Fort Stedman in a shock wave that subdued the Union position without difficulty. Then the three columns of handpicked men started on their journey to find the Federal forts to the rear of Stedman. It was here that Gordon's plan began to fall apart. To the

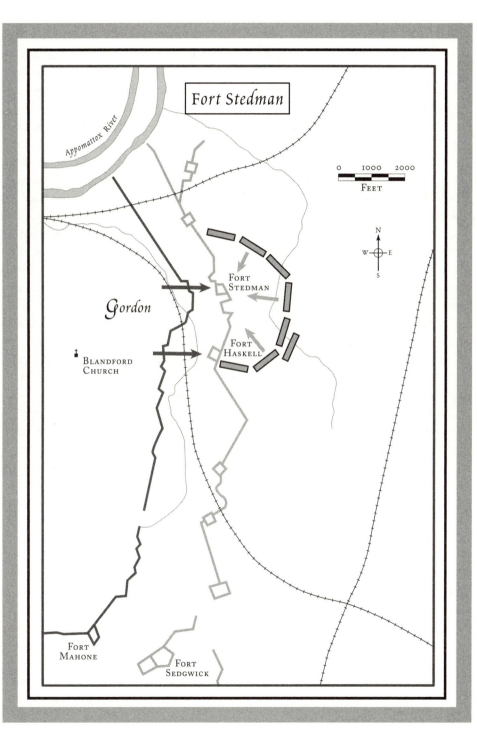

Fort Stedman

Appomattox River

1000   2000

FEET

N
W   E
S

Fort
Stedman

Gordon

Fort
Haskell

Blandford
Church

Fort
Mahone

Fort
Sedgwick

enormous despair of the three hundred anxious rebels, in the darkness, they could not locate the three Federal forts. The men were very quickly lost, far into Federal lines, and
could only stumble their way back toward Stedman, to pass the dismal news back to Gordon himself. But while the rebels were trying to make their way back, the sun came up,
and the Federal troops around them were coming to life. The response to the capture of
Fort Stedman was immediate and deadly. What was to have been a breakthrough instead
became a hotly compact battle, with Gordon's men fighting off waves of Federal troops
while they absorbed a hard pounding from nearby Federal artillery batteries. With Gordon and his men penned up in Fort Stedman and nearby positions, there was no place for
the waiting reinforcements to go, and once daylight had come, Gordon understood the
hopelessness of his position, as did Robert E. Lee. Lee soon ordered the Confederates to
withdraw, and while absorbing terrific fire, the Confederates pulled back to where they
had begun the morning. What Lee believed to be his greatest opportunity to break
Grant's siege had instead been a dismal failure and had resulted in four thousand casualties.

Though Grant's lines were already too formidable for Lee to force a breakthrough,
in late March, Grant was strengthened even more. After Phil Sheridan's stunning success
in routing Jubal Early's Confederates out of the Shenandoah Valley, the Federal cavalry
had returned. Now Grant had a powerful mobile force to enhance his already overwhelming advantage. Lee's chances for survival were diminishing day by day.

With the horsemen now at his disposal, Grant did not delay. Sheridan was sent westward, out beyond the Federal left flank. Grant was well aware that Lee's last escape route
was the South Side Railroad, the last rail link that connected Petersburg to points south
and west. Sheridan's mission was to lead his cavalry and the infantry of Warren's 5th Corps
toward the rail line. On March 31, both Warren and Sheridan confronted rebel forces, but
the Federal troops were surprisingly manhandled by the Confederates, under the command of George Pickett. As the two sides assessed their positions, Pickett was ordered by
Lee to hold his army around the key intersection known as Five Forks. On April 1,
the combined Federal troops attacked Pickett again. Though the Confederates had dug
themselves into a strong defensive position, something the Federals had learned to avoid in
a frontal assault, Sheridan pressed the attack forward anyway. On the Federal right flank, a
large body of Warren's infantry completely overshot their mark and passed right by the
Confederate left flank. Sheridan, who was the senior commander on the field, responded
to the error by relieving Warren of his command. Despite Warren's mistake, his men made
the best of their predicament and rallied to swing about and crush the Confederate left.
Within a short time, the battle became a distinctly lopsided affair, the Confederates swept
from the field by Sheridan's cavalry and Warren's infantry (now under the command of
Charles Griffin). The disaster for Pickett was compounded by his absence from the field.

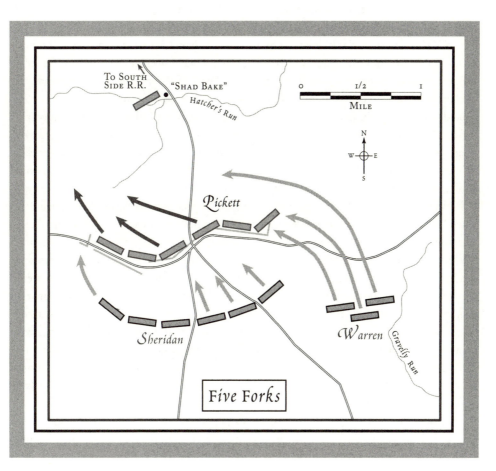

To South
Side R.R. "Shad Bake"

Hatcher's Run

0   1/2   1
MILE

N
W   E
S

Pickett

Sheridan

Warren

Gravelly Run

Five Forks

While Sheridan's attack pressed itself upon Pickett's lines, Pickett was miles behind his men, enjoying a "shad bake" (what we would call a fish fry) with some of his senior commanders. Though Pickett's presence would likely have made little difference in the outcome of the battle, it is one more illustration of the frustration that plagued Robert E. Lee, forced to rely on commanders who weren't up to the task.

With Lee's right flank denuded by the loss of Pickett's men, Grant saw the opportunity he had been waiting for. On April 2, the Federal commander ordered a full-scale assault against the entire Confederate position. West of Petersburg's main trenches, the Union 6th Corps forced a complete and massive breakthrough of the rebel divisions commanded by A. P. Hill. Lee responded to the crisis by sending Hill forward to that section of the line. One of Lee's last remaining veteran corps commanders was charged with learning just how bad the breakthrough was, and if possible, Hill was to attempt to rally his troops to hold the line. For Lee, the worst-case scenario now occurred. Not only could Hill not stem the tide, in the effort, Hill himself was killed.

With his entire position around Petersburg facing utter collapse, Lee ordered his men to withdraw into whatever defensive position they could create. To slow the Federals from consuming Petersburg itself, Lee's men kept a foothold in two small forts, named Whitworth and Gregg. For the rest of the day on April 2, rebel troops held the two forts and prevented the Federal troops from engulfing Lee's entire position. By the day's end, the two forts and the men who held them were in Federal hands. But their determination had given the rest of the men in the Petersburg defenses enough time to withdraw to defensive positions along the old Dimmock line. By nightfall, those embattled troops were relieved to see reinforcements, but their arrival was little cause for cheer. The fresh Confederates had come from Richmond, and their presence at Petersburg was a dismal hint of things to come. That night, April 2, Lee sent word to Jefferson Davis that all available troops were being ordered to join with Lee's forces. Richmond was to be abandoned.

Throughout the night, troops and civilians fled the capital, and farther south, Lee's army fled the remnants of their defensive lines at Petersburg. Lee watched as his men crossed the Appomattox River, hoping they could avoid any major engagement from Grant until they could rally at Amelia Court House, some twenty-five miles to the west.

The following morning, April 3, 1865, Grant was accompanied by a visiting Abraham Lincoln, and the two men rode with cautious triumph into Petersburg. But Grant did not rest on his laurels. Immediately, the Federal troops were put on the roads on two courses, one in direct pursuit of Lee's army, one parallel to it, keeping south of the Appomattox River. Lee's head start was thus only a matter of hours. Lee still had hope that he could reach Johnston's army in North Carolina, but first he had to drive his exhausted troops without pause on a grueling march. Like a weakening wounded animal, Lee's army was now pursued by two powerful hounds. Once more, Lee was in a race for survival.

Lee clearly understood that his army could not continue its march unless it was fed, and Amelia Court House lay on the rail line that ran south of Richmond. It was the same rail line that had carried Jefferson Davis and what remained of the Confederate government out of Richmond toward their new base in Danville, Virginia. Lee had sent urgent word to the commissary officers in Richmond that whatever railcars could be provided be sent to Amelia with what remained of the food rations, presumed to fill many warehouses in the capital city. As Lee's army struggled to reach Amelia Court House, they gathered up remnants of Pickett's troops and the troops under Ewell and Longstreet who had anchored the defenses at Richmond. On April 4, Lee's men marched into Amelia, desperately eyeing the line of railcars that was waiting for them. Their enthusiasm was short-lived. Instead of food rations, the cars contained gunpowder, shot, and shell, all the

The desolation at Petersburg, Virginia, 1865 PHOTO COURTESY OF THE LIBRARY OF CONGRESS

supplies for waging war. Lee's army still had nothing to eat. Worse, the hounds were closing in. Lee had no choice but to pull his troops back to their feet and continue the desperate march.

Close behind Lee, Sheridan's cavalry and Meade's infantry followed the rebel march,
while below Grant, Ord's Army of the James drove westward, intent on cutting off Lee's
escape route. All the while, Union cavalry darted in and out against Lee's flanks, hard
sharp bites into the side of the bleeding animal. But Sheridan was not content merely to
harass the Confederates with horsemen. He was followed closely by rapidly marching
Federal infantry, and Sheridan urged them in the strongest terms to press forward, keeping close to his cavalry. The Federal troops directly trailing Lee pushed harder as well, and
on April 6, disaster struck Lee's beleaguered force.

The fight took place around a winding stream that ran through low dips in the open
farmland. It was called Sailor's (or Sayler's) Creek. As Lee's army had become strung out
on the roads, gaps had opened, separating masses of men from the main body. At Sailor's
Creek, the troops under John B. Gordon, Dick Ewell, and Richard Anderson were suddenly cut off and surrounded by a mass of Federal cavalry and infantry. The fight was one-
sided at best, as some eight thousand Confederates were shot down or captured. Ewell
himself was captured, and Lee's army had suddenly shrunk by nearly a fourth.

Lee's men continued to stagger westward, some driven by instinct, some by their
dedication to Lee himself. Many simply fell out, collapsing by the road from exhaustion
and hunger. The Federals who pursued their quarry could not help but marvel at the debris of the Confederate army that spread along the roadway, muskets and blankets, canteens, equipment of all kinds. And in every patch of trees, at every farmhouse, men lay
alone or in groups, soldiers who were soldiers no more.

Lee had one remaining hope, that his survivors could reach the railway at Appomattox Station, where supplies were said to be waiting. The railway itself could provide escape
to Campbell Cout House, where the rail junction there could send them southward toward Danville. Whether his men were driven by dedication to their cause or dedication to
their commander, Lee himself was driven by faith that there was still the chance to reach
Joe Johnston, faith that the war was not yet lost.

Grant had faith of his own. On April 7, he wrote the first note to Lee that would result in an exchange of correspondence over the next two days. From both generals, the
words have a jousting quality to them, the notes passing back and forth between two commanders who saw the campaign through very different eyes. But Lee could not hide from
the reality that fell upon his army the night of April 8. The railcars were indeed waiting at
Appomattox Station, but Federal cavalry was waiting as well. For nearly a year, Lee's careful maneuvering had frustrated Grant's efforts at bagging the prey. Lee had won every
race, thwarted every Federal advance. But this time, the race belonged to the strongest

foe. Sheridan's cavalry had reached Appomattox Station first. Once again, Lee could not feed what remained of his army.

That night, Lee stared into a black horizon flecked with bits of firelight. It was the campfires of the Union army, and the fires wrapped around to the west, severing Lee from any open route toward Campbell Court House. After meeting with his senior commanders, Lee ordered that they make one final attempt to break through the Federal grasp. In the early morning of April 9, Lee's remaining cavalry, under his nephew Fitzhugh Lee, would drive westward, supported by John B. Gordon's infantry. Lee assumed that the campfires he had seen belonged to Federal cavalry, a force small enough that his men could drive through. With an opening secured, the rest of Lee's troops could seek the safety of the rolling countryside beyond and might find some way to reach the railway to the west.

The attack began as Lee had planned it, but Lee's wishful thinking was swept away by the reality. The campfires had belonged not just to Federal horsemen, but to infantry as well, and it was a force that was continuing to grow. Lee's army was cut off from any escape. The chase was over.

What remained of Lee's army now totaled some twenty-eight thousand men. Despite Sheridan's insistence that Lee's army be attacked with the full power of the troops in his command, Grant interceded and informed his officers that a truce had been called, that Grant was to meet Lee in the small town of Appomattox Court House. The meeting place had been carefully chosen, a private residence belonging to a man named Wilmer McLean. Between one-thirty and two in the afternoon, Grant climbed the steps of McLean's porch and moved to the front door of the house. Inside, Lee, with his lone aide, Charles Marshall, and several quietly nervous Federal officers, was waiting for him.

Grant and Lee meet at the McLean House, April 9, 1865, Appomattox, Virginia PHOTO COURTESY OF THE LIBRARY OF CONGRESS

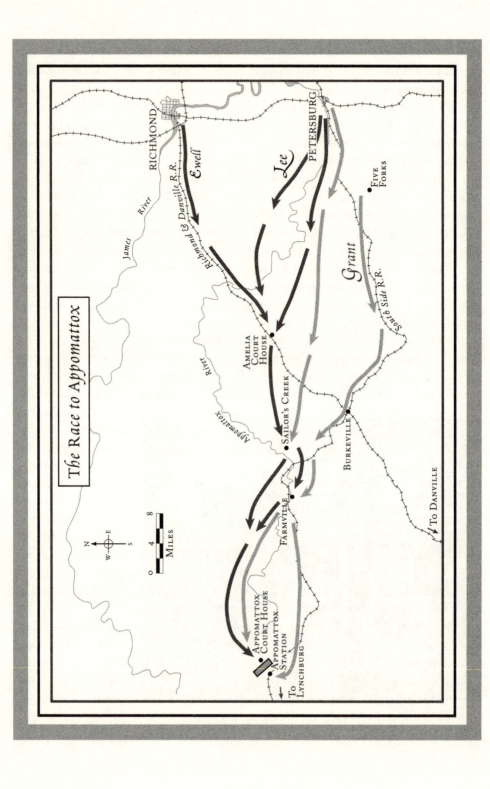

The Race to Appomattox

RICHMOND

James River

Richmond & Danville R.R.

Ewell

Lee

PETERSBURG

Five Forks

Grant

South Side R.R.

Appomattox River

AMELIA COURT HOUSE

SAILOR'S CREEK

BURKEVILLE

FARMVILLE

APPOMATTOX COURT HOUSE

APPOMATTOX STATION

To LYNCHBURG

To DANVILLE

N
W—E
S

MILES
0   4   8

Over the next two hours, there transpired one of the most dramatic conversations in American history. To the observers, Lee and Grant appeared as polar opposites, Lee attired in a pristine dress uniform complete with gold sash and ceremonial sword, Grant wearing the dust and grime of a hard day in the saddle. The meeting was cordial and dignified and somber, and when it was over, Lee had signed the documents that agreed to Grant's terms for the surrender of Lee's army.

At Lee's request, Grant authorized that rations be provided for Lee's desperate men, and as Lee rode away from the McLean House, Federal artillerymen began firing their cannon in celebration. Grant immediately ordered the guns into silence. Lee absorbed both gestures and recognized, as did Grant, that despite their differences, they were both soldiers, and both men had done their duty.

WHY IS THIS BATTLE IMPORTANT?

Though the war is not yet officially over, the end of Lee's army means the end of hope for the Confederacy. The Confederates still field three armies: E. Kirby Smith's Army of the Trans-Mississippi west of that river; Richard Taylor's Department of East Louisiana, Mississippi, and Alabama; and Joe Johnston's Army of Tennessee in North Carolina. But no one expects any further military conflict to yield substantive fruit. Joe Johnston begins talks with Sherman, and on April 26, 1865, Johnston's army formally surrenders. Taylor follows on May 4, and Smith officially ends the war with his surrender in Galveston, Texas, on June 2, 1865.

Though Grant continues to be criticized for what his enemies describe as a wanton disregard for the lives of his soldiers, his understanding of war puts him far ahead of his time. For centuries, war has been a gentleman's game, where chivalry and high-handed manners disguise the ugliness of man's most brutal instinct. Grant simply throws off the cloak. The stark reality is brought home by the descriptions of the men who endure it, the graphic wounds they carry, and the photography that forces the civilian public to digest the horrifying truth. Regardless of the attacks on Grant's methods, Abraham Lincoln knows, and eventually the American people will accept, that Ulysses Grant is responsible for the victory.

Though Grant might be condemned for besieging a large city, and thus causing needless suffering to a large civilian population, the fact is quickly revealed that throughout the ten months at Petersburg, barely half a dozen civilians are killed. At the very least, Grant's reputation benefits from enormous good luck.

Lee's hope of uniting his army with Joe Johnston's is likely a fantasy that would have brought few successes. On the march out of Petersburg, Lee, who began the campaign there with roughly fifty-five thousand troops (estimates vary radically), reaches Appomattox with half that many men, a large number of whom no longer carry their muskets, and men who are in no condition to fight. Had they succeeded in adding their meager strength to Johnston's Army of Tennessee, Johnston's total effective force would still have been enormously outnumbered by Sherman, who was itching for a chance to finish the job.

To some in the South, the war is decided for the North by the abandonment of Richmond on April 2. What remains of the government of the Confederacy moves by rail southward to Danville, Virginia, and then southward again to Charlotte. Jefferson Davis becomes little more than a fugitive, and he is captured on May 10, 1865, at Irwinsville, Georgia.

As has happened at every major battle, heroes and buffoons emerge. With the conclusion of the war, Grant no longer has to concern himself with political generals, Benjamin Butler in particular. The utter ineptness of both Butler and William "Baldy" Smith is largely responsible for the siege of Petersburg ever having to be carried out. The siege, as it turns out, lengthens the war for ten months longer than if, in June 1864, Grant had been able to smash effectively into Beauregard at Petersburg or Lee closer to Richmond.

Winfield Hancock does little to live up to his former reputation as a fiery field commander, yet the fault lies not with the man, but with the miserable festering wounds he had received at Gettysburg. In November 1864, after months of painful suffering, Hancock steps down as 2nd Corps commander and thus is not on the field at Appomattox.

Gouverneur K. Warren vigorously protests his dismissal by Phil Sheridan, but despite his sterling performance at Gettysburg, Warren has been plagued by a multitude of battlefield sins that combine to drain away his reputation. Sheridan's dismissal of the man is not reversed until fourteen years later, when a court of inquiry clears Warren of misdeeds at Five Forks.

Well before Appomattox, Sheridan's reputation as a master cavalryman had been cemented by his performance in the Shenandoah Valley, giving rise to a near mythical reputation for gallantry ("Sheridan's Ride") that Sheridan embraces completely. Though Grant, and especially Meade, find the man to be disagreeable at best, no fault can be found with Sheridan's performance in corralling Lee's army in April 1865. However, in a minor footnote of history, Sheridan's reputation could have been greatly altered at Appomattox. Grant arrives for his meeting with Lee just as Sheridan is preparing to order an all-out assault against Lee's crippled force. Had Sheridan's attack gone forward, the result would have been a slaughter that would have cemented an entirely different reputation for Phil Sheridan.

There are many more examples of men whose reputations rise during and after the Petersburg siege. Lieutenant Colonel Henry Pleasants, the Pennsylvania miner whose brilliant engineering resulted in the Battle of the Crater, receives his due and is promoted to brigadier general. Joshua Lawrence Chamberlain is promoted to the same rank and is severely wounded at Petersburg (twice). After recovering, Chamberlain returns to the army to command a brigade at Appomattox, where he is promoted to brevet major general. He is then singled out by Ulysses Grant to command the surrender ceremony on April 12, 1865, during which Chamberlain orders his division to salute their counterparts, led by Confederate general John B. Gordon. Many of the men on both sides of the line record that moment as the true end of the war, the moment when the healing begins.

For the Confederates, the collapse of Lee's army comes in some part from the inability of many of his generals to rise to the occasion. Neither Dick Ewell nor Richard Anderson nor George Pickett performs when the need is greatest. Though Longstreet returns to Lee's army shortly before the end, he is never in a position to do any more than organize the escape from Petersburg. Throughout much of the siege, A. P. Hill rises to the occasion by holding back nearly every Union assault he faces, until the day of his death on April 2. John B. Gordon and William "Billy" Mahone shine brightest in the final days, Mahone's men being most responsible for crushing the Federal breakthrough at the crater as well as handling a portion of Lee's troops on the final march. Both E. Porter Alexander and Lee's nephew Fitzhugh Lee, are reined in by their commander, preventing the young men from embarking on what they believe to be the South's best hope: a guerrilla war, waged from mountain hideaways against the northern occupation of southern cities. Robert E. Lee rejects the idea completely and forcefully, rightfully suggesting that such a tactic would destroy any hope of rebuilding the economy of the South and cancel out any hope of healing the nation.

Like Grant, Lee has his critics, though it is hard to imagine any other Confederate commander maneuvering his army as effectively during his remarkable chess game with Grant. Only when Lee is forced into the trenches at Petersburg is the end for his army assured. Modern revisionists have questioned the morality of Lee's actions, suggesting that once Lee recognized the hopelessness of his army's situation, he should have accepted the inevitable. The question has been posed: How could a man faced with the inevitability of defeat, who maintains such a devout adherence to the principles of his religion, continue to order his men to fight? That might be a question best debated by philosophers. There is certainly speculation, as is suggested at Gettysburg, that Lee deludes himself into believing that God will provide for his army, that victory is an eventual certainty.

I believe that passing such judgment on Lee is a useless exercise in hindsight, a shortcut to understanding both the man and his time. Lee most certainly understands that, like Richmond, he is a symbol, and like Stonewall Jackson, he is a source of intense inspiration for desperate men. The evidence greets him everywhere he goes, on every inspection of his troops, on every foray along the disease-infested trenches of Petersburg.

The *power* of that experience, the *weight* of that responsibility in Lee's mind, cannot be measured in modern terms. Lee fought on because his men expected him to. His men fought on because he expected it of them.

Traveling around the country, I've occasionally been confronted by hostility toward Lee by those who define him as a traitor to his country and to his oath as an officer in the United States Army. This attitude can be found as well during the Civil War, and his death in 1870 does not silence the condemnation. His American citizenship is not restored until the mid-1970s (the results of a lobbying campaign aimed at Congress in which my father, who was *not* a southerner, played some role). Despite those who would have seen him hanged (and I've spoken to many who feel that way), the fact remains that a century and a half later, he is still revered as the South's most beloved and respected hero. The fact that Lee is regarded as both hero and traitor is one indication why, to some, the war is still being fought.

The final lesson learned from Petersburg is that war will never be fought the same way again. For the first three years of the Civil War, the tactics are guided by the ways of Napoleon. Generals on both sides have been taught by French textbooks that the proper way to wage war is to march in straight massed lines, directly into the faces of the enemy. But Napoleon did not have the rifled musket or the rifled artillery piece, and with such improvements in the technology of war, those tactics are disastrously outdated. By 1865, few soldiers in either army will blindly accept the order to make another Pickett's Charge or the June 3 attack at Cold Harbor. On both sides, the importance of the musket is equaled by the importance of the shovel. What had once been considered "unmanly," hiding in a trench, is now the accepted way to fight a battle. But Petersburg provides a contradiction as well, one that Lee in particular recognizes too well. If an army loses its mobility, then combat becomes simple attrition. (The lesson is painfully ignored by all sides in 1914, at the start of World War I, when Napoleonic tactics are still employed. When the slaughter drives the men underground, they remain stagnant and thus absorb an astonishing mortality rate for three full years. It is only when an American, John "Black Jack" Pershing, brings American troops to the field of France that the principle of combining good cover with rapid mobility is put into use. The result, in 1918, is victory.)

Beyond the obvious significance of Lee's surrender, there is a poignancy to what occurs at Appomattox that transcends the horror of the previous four years. Grant's surrender terms, which Lee accepts, are not intended to punish the South. That simple gesture enables the nation to begin its difficult process of healing. Unfortunately, Grant's good intentions are virtually wiped away by the assassination of Abraham Lincoln, which occurs only days after the surrender documents are signed. Lincoln's second inaugural address had expressed the same conciliatory sentiments, "with malice toward none; with charity for all. . . ." But those sentiments are erased by the pistol fire from John Wilkes Booth.

Old Blandford Church and Cemetery

ONE OF THE MOST HISTORICALLY SIGNIFICANT SITES IN VIRGINIA rests on the crest of a broad hill just west of the Petersburg National Battlefield. Not nearly as well-known as places like Monticello, Williamsburg, Mount Vernon, or the state's various battlefields, the church in particular is a gem that deserves far more recognition than it receives.

The church was founded in 1735 by Peter Jefferson (Thomas's father) and was a focal point for the young community that became modern Petersburg. However, the church was used only until 1806, when it was replaced by the construction of a new facility. The abandoned church thus fell into disrepair. The church was deeded to a private owner in 1818 and within a few years became the property of the city of Petersburg. The structure served as a hospital during the siege, but nothing was done to preserve the building itself until 1882. In the interim, the windows had become ivy-encrusted holes, the doorways were wide open, and the wood floor had rotted away. In 1901, the Ladies Memorial Association of Petersburg converted the church into a Confederate memorial and embarked on an extraordinary quest to create a unique tribute to the Confederacy. They contracted with Louis Comfort Tiffany, the renowned stained-glass manufacturer in New York, to construct windows for the church, and the results are simply amazing.

At a cost of roughly $350 each, Tiffany designed, manufactured, and installed a total of fifteen stained-glass windows. Tiffany's intentions were to design a memorial to each state whose soldiers were presumed to be buried in the Blandford Cemetery, and his design combines certain of each state's characteristics with a religious theme, most notably the figures of eleven Christian apostles or sainted evangelicals. Each window is a unique piece of artwork, and taken in total, they can be overwhelming. At the time, individual state legislatures and other fund-raising groups were asked to provide the money to pay for their own state's window, and thirteen states complied (including the nonsecessionist states of Missouri and Maryland; the one nonsecessionist state that could not provide funds was Kentucky, whose economy was in such a state of chaos that the legislature there felt such an expense could not be spared). The windows were installed from 1904 through 1912 and remain today one of the most astounding exhibits of Tiffany artwork available to the public eye.

Throughout the church itself are amazingly substantial wooden pews, which were constructed at a cost of $7 each. Note the seat boards. Each one is a single plank some sixteen inches wide. The ceiling timbers date to 1882 and have undergone necessary repairs over the years. The design is distinctly nautical, as though you're standing inside an inverted ship, the beams above your head forming a distinctive "hull."

Though this is no longer a consecrated church, numerous services are performed here, and amazingly, the church can be booked for weddings at a bargain price of $500 (which may change).

There is one marked grave actually within the church itself: one of the church's founders, Theophilus Feild (yes, that is the correct spelling).

As you tour the cemetery, note the geography of the land here. As was typical in many towns, the cemetery was placed on the highest point in the area, presumably to be "closer to heaven."

I recommend asking the staff who maintains the Reception Center for a tour of the grounds. They can save you a great deal of time searching for grave sites and notable headstones, on which, in some cases, the details have been nearly obliterated by the elements. One of the first characteristics you notice of this cemetery is the variety of iron railings that surround many of the plots. No two of these railings are alike.

The oldest grave here dates to 1702, well before the cemetery was founded, and belongs to Richard Yarbrough (the spelling of his name varies in the records, which often contradict the spelling on the gravestone itself). There are likely several graves here that are older still, most located close to the church itself, but the headstones have been erased by time. Two headstones were impacted by cannonballs during the siege, and they can be pointed out to you by a guide. One interesting bit of lore is the grave of Nora Davidson, who is said to have originated our national observance of Memorial Day. One of the first Memorial Day services was held here and might have inspired the movement to create the national holiday. Other states and locales have disputed this, however.

In terms of relevance to the Civil War, the Blandford Cemetery answers that nagging question once more: Where are all the Confederates buried? Approximately *thirty thousand* of them are here, including General William "Billy" Mahone, who secured the Confederate victory at the Battle of the Crater. As is typically the case, less than 10 percent of the Confederate remains here are identified.

Grant's wharves at City Point, Virginia, 1864   PHOTO COURTESY OF THE LIBRARY OF CONGRESS

Grant's Headquarters at City Point

A SHORT (AND SOMEWHAT CONFUSING) DRIVE NORTHEAST OF PE-
tersburg will take you to what is today Hopewell, Virginia. This point of land is
formed by the confluence of the Appomattox and James Rivers. Prior to Grant's
arrival here in 1864, this area was a fairly peaceful waterside community. In mere
weeks, once the bulk of Grant's army had crossed the James River, the small town
became one of the busiest seaports in the entire world.

The National Park Service now controls the property that encompasses
Grant's headquarters. The land was established as a plantation in 1635, and the
original owners, the Eppes family, controlled the land for more than three centuries. Their main house, which is currently under restoration by the Park Ser-

vice, is called Appomattox Plantation, which of course causes serious confusion to those visitors who aren't familiar with the location of the surrender site, which is some eighty miles away.

Note the single small cabin. This is a reconstruction of Grant's actual headquarters (and living quarters) during the siege of Petersburg. The original cabin

Ulysses Grant, son Jessie, and wife Julia at City Point, Virginia

PHOTO COURTESY OF THE LIBRARY OF CONGRESS

was carted off to Philadelphia, which had it for more than a century. The cabin was reassembled close to its exact foundation in 1981 and today includes roughly 5 percent of the materials from the original cabin itself. There is a plaque in front of the cabin showing how the place appeared in 1864, when it was one of several such structures that housed Grant's staff and administrative offices. Today, there is a huge hulking sycamore tree in front of the headquarters cabin, and you can see the same tree (much smaller) in the photograph from 1864. Consider that on this ground, in that one small cabin, Grant was visited by his wife, Julia, and their son Fred, met twice with President Lincoln, and had meetings with every major figure in the Union command, including William T. Sherman. Until Lee's lines gave way in April 1865, nearly every major decision of the Union campaign was made on that spot.

I suggest taking a short stroll to the land's edge. If you gaze out across the magnificent peacefulness of the wide rivers, note that the land across the way (northward) is the general location of some of the Seven Days' Battles. A prominent mound on the horizon is Malvern Hill.

The wide waterway in front of you offers no hints that in 1864–1865, this was a massively congested supply depot. Photographs are on display that show City Point to be jammed with ship and barge traffic, great wharves stocked high with supplies of all kinds. I have spent considerable time absorbing the magnificent panorama of this view (as did Grant), and I've often tried to imagine the sounds

Jeff at Grant's headquarters, City Point (Hopewell), Virginia (Note the "witness tree") PHOTO PATRICK FALCI

and sights that could be experienced there, what it was like for Grant to step among the tools of his army on his way to greet the president as Lincoln's boat drew up to the wharf. In today's world, it is typical that a military commander or even the CEO of a major corporation controls an enormous human machine, some kind of entity that is rarely seen or felt by the one in charge. But here, a short, unassuming man named Ulysses Grant controlled a war machine like no other that had existed in history. And here, at City Point, it flowed past right in front of him. To paraphrase an observation Grant made at the time, if Lee could have somehow seen this place, could have seen for himself the never-ending supply line that kept Grant's army fit and fueled, the Confederate general would certainly have realized the hopelessness of his army's situation and might have surrendered sooner.

Grant is elected president in 1868 and so will still have the opportunity to put Lincoln's healing words into national policy, but the damaging effects of Reconstruction prevent the great chasm between North and South from closing. Despite the fervent hopes expressed by both Lee and Grant at Appomattox, in various ways the wounds from the Civil War will remain open into the twenty-first century.

WHAT YOU SHOULD SEE

*A*s I have advised throughout, Petersburg is another park where a guide can provide the best tour experience. The battlefield totals twenty-seven hundred acres, though many important tour destinations lie beyond the park's borders. In the park itself are examples of the Petersburg trenches and bombproof shelters, and the primary road runs generally between the positions of the two armies. There are two sites in particular that I would emphasize.

On the main National Park Service road, signs will direct you to the site of Fort Stedman. I have heard a great many comments that the fort itself seems so small. But Stedman was simply one in a lengthy chain of fortifications that ran for a total of thirty-five miles. Stedman, like the strongholds on either side, held an artillery battery, and by combining their field of fire with adjacent batteries (Federal Battery #11 is clearly visible nearby), the artillery and musket fire could entirely blanket the open ground in front of these strongholds. On the Confederate (west) side of the field, note how the hillside falls away. This is how John B. Gordon was able to maintain secrecy as he brought his forces up close. The lay of the land muffled the sounds of his troops. The open ground that Gordon's troops crossed was at that time a cornfield. Currently, the park is restoring much of this ground by removing the undergrowth where appropriate.

Modern view of Confederate trenches, Petersburg, Virginia PHOTO PATRICK FALCI

Along the main park road, between Battery #12 and Fort Haskell, the ground is being cleared as well in order to show exactly what the two sides faced during Gordon's desperate fight.

Farther along the Park Service road, you will come to the second site I strongly recommend. It is probably the most visited spot on the battlefield, and for good reason. This is the site of the Battle of the Crater. When you leave your car, walk out into the field by bearing to the right. (Footpaths lead you in various directions.) You are moving into the position of the Union lines. Note the woods to the far right, the overgrowth that clogs a deep ravine. This was an old railroad cut and obviously provided good cover for the mass of Union soldiers positioned there. (The brush wasn't there at the time.) The Park Service has done an exceptional job of preserving the tunnel entrance, adding a bit of sandbag modernization resembling the original tunnel opening on the sloping hillside, which was lined with timbers for support. For reasons obvious to any lawyer, the entrance to the mine, though visible, is barricaded (to keep those people who have no brains whatsoever from trying to go inside). This area was the position of the Union picket line, not their main line, which is behind you, farther down the slope. Thus, at the time the mine was ignited, the Federal troops had to advance a good ways up the slope before reaching the blast site. This didn't help their mortality rate, especially when they were attempting to retreat.

Entrance to the Union mine that resulted in the Battle of the Crater, Petersburg, Virginia
PHOTO PATRICK FALCI

As you walk parallel to the route of the mine itself, you can see depressions in the ground. These represent the inevitable cave-ins over the years. The ground is still danger-ous, and collapses continue to occur, particularly during and after heavy rains. In other words, keep off. At the crater itself, keep to the near (Union) side first. Though I've heard some people express disappointment in the size of the crater, time has of course eroded the great maw that was blasted here. Just to the left of the Park Service plaque, you can see two main depressions. This is the exact spot where the powder magazines exploded. With a little imagination, try to feel what it was like for fifteen thousand Federal troops to swarm this ground, many packed right into the depression itself. Note the tall embank-ments on the far (Confederate) side. From those earthen walls, hundreds of Confederates fired with virtual impunity into the mass of humanity below them, some simply tossing bayonetted rifles as spears.

Follow the path around to the far side of the crater, and note the steep embank-ments that served the Confederate soldiers so effectively. Out on either end of the crater are two small concrete markers. These indicate the farthest advance of the 2nd Pennsyl-vania Heavy Artillery, who, fighting as infantry, advanced barely thirty yards past the crater itself. As you move back toward the parking lot, note the long rows of depressions in the grass. These are the actual locations of the opposing picket lines. Target practice indeed.

Outside the park boundary, you can visit numerous battery positions as well as Poplar Grove Cemetery, which holds the remains of more than six thousand Union dead.

Farther west, on the Boydton Plank Road (which is U.S. 1 at this location), you will spot the marker indicating the place where Confederate general A. P. Hill was killed. It's a short walk into thin woods, a location that has only recently been secured. If you drive farther west, passing beneath Interstate 85, turn right on White Oak Road (Route 613). This will take you to the Five Forks battlefield. Though the Park Service is working to restore the lands to their 1865 appearance, much of what you see is simply woods and fields. The intersection itself provides the obvious answer to why the place is called Five Forks.

The routes that will eventually take you to Appomattox are somewhat circuitous, but the Park Service has done an admirable job of marking the way. If you make that drive, the one site worth diverting to is the Sailor's Creek battlefield. This is now a state park and is dramatic in that you can see the entire field of battle as it was viewed by both armies. The creek itself winds through a narrow stretch of woods, and signs indicate the bridges that cross at precisely the same place where Gordon marched his army and where Anderson, Gordon, and Ewell made their stands.

Appomattox is a place every American should visit. The reasons are mostly symbolic, though historical artifacts and exhibits are a must-see. The courthouse itself is a reconstruction of the original, which burned in 1892. The McLean House is a reconstruction as well, but for strangely different reasons. In 1893, the entire house was dismantled to be

The crater today, Petersburg, Virginia   PHOTO PATRICK FALCI

hauled to Washington, D.C. as an exhibit (though the materials were never actually moved). For decades afterward, no one seemed to care if there was any commemoration on the spot where this monumental event actually took place. It wasn't until 1935 that Congress voted to acquire land for the park itself, and the park wasn't officially designated a National Historical Park until 1954. The buildings in place now exist mostly on the sites of the originals, though there is a bit of "Colonial Williamsburg" here, in the sense that the park is a little too pristine. But don't be deterred. The exhibits housed in the courthouse (now the Visitor Center), the excellent bookstore, and the McLean House do much to convey the extraordinary importance of what happened here. Note the small Confederate Cemetery, a tiny parcel of private land that holds the remains of nineteen soldiers who died here.

Follow the signs to the "Surrender Triangle," the exact spot where Joshua Chamberlain's men saluted Gordon's Confederates. There are few pieces of ground on this continent that hold the memories of that small bit of country lane.

Contact Information

SHILOH NATIONAL MILITARY PARK
Shiloh, Tennessee
Website: www.nps.gov/shil
Visitor Information: (731) 689-5696

ANTIETAM NATIONAL BATTLEFIELD
Sharpsburg, Maryland
Website: www.nps.gov/anti
Visitor Information: (301) 432-5124

FREDERICKSBURG AND SPOTSYLVANIA NATIONAL
MILITARY PARK
Fredericksburg, Virginia
Website: www.nps.gov/frsp
Visitor Information: (540) 373-6122

GETTYSBURG NATIONAL MILITARY PARK
Gettysburg, Pennsylvania
Website: www.nps.gov/gett
Visitor Information: (717) 334-1124

VICKSBURG NATIONAL MILITARY PARK
Vicksburg, Mississippi
Website: www.nps.gov/vick
Visitor Information: (601) 636-0583

CHICKAMAUGA AND CHATTANOOGA NATIONAL
MILITARY PARK
Fort Oglethorpe, Georgia
Website: www.nps.gov/chch
Visitor Information: (706) 866-9241

NEW MARKET BATTLEFIELD STATE HISTORICAL PARK
New Market, Virginia
Website: www4.vmi.edu/museum (Link to New Market Battlefield)
Visitor Information: (866) 515-1864

RICHMOND NATIONAL BATTLEFIELD PARK
Richmond, Virginia
Website: www.nps.gov/rich
Visitor Information: (804) 226-1981

PETERSBURG NATIONAL BATTLEFIELD
Petersburg, Virginia
Website: www.nps.gov/pete
Visitor Information: (804) 732-3531

Acknowledgments

FIRST AND FOREMOST, THIS BOOK COULD NOT HAVE BEEN COMPLETED without the tireless efforts of Patrick Falci. Patrick was my right-hand man throughout the entire process of assembling materials, researching, traveling, and walking the ground. His dedication and passion for the understanding of the Civil War through historical preservation and interpretation is unequaled. As well, Patrick is a first-person spokesman for the legacy of those who gave so much to this period in our history. Through his vivid portrayal of Confederate general A. P. Hill, not only in the film *Gettysburg*, but at venues all over the country, Patrick does as much as anyone I know to keep the history of this era alive.

The following have contributed much time and effort toward my understanding of both the history of the events described here and the ground on which those events occurred. I am enormously thankful to all.

Ted Alexander	Historian, Antietam National Battlefield
Mike Andrus	Supervisory Park Ranger, Richmond National Battlefield Park
Betty Angell	Guide, Old Blandford Church and Cemetery
Martha Mann Atkinson	Site Coordinator, Old Blandford Church and Cemetery
Matt Atkinson	Park Ranger and Guide, Vicksburg National Military Park
Gabor Boritt	Director, Civil War Institute, Gettysburg College
Chris Calkins	Chief of Interpretation, Petersburg National Battlefield

Alan Doyle	Guide, Shiloh National Battlefield
Judith Drury	Administrator, New Market Battlefield State Historical Park
Colonel Keith Gibson	Director, Museum Programs, Virginia Military Institute
Scott Harris	Director, New Market Battlefield State Historical Park
John Hennessey	Chief Historian, Fredericksburg and Spotsylvania National Military Park
Gary Kross	Licensed Battlefield Guide, Gettysburg National Military Park
Jim Lewis	Park Ranger, Stones River National Battlefield
Michael Anne Lynn	Director, the Stonewall Jackson House
Lee Millar	Guide, Shiloh National Battlefield
James Ogden	Chief Historian, Chickamauga and Chattanooga National Military Park
Don Pfanz	Historian and Guide, Fredericksburg and Spotsylvania National Military Park
S. Waite Rawls	Executive Director, the Museum of the Confederacy
Jim Schroeder	Guide, Stones River National Battlefield
Linda Wandres	Executive Director, Central Virginia Battlefields Trust
Terrence Winschel	Chief Historian, Vicksburg National Military Park